CONCRETE REVERIES

Also by Mark Kingwell

*Nearest Thing to Heaven: The Empire State Building
and the American Dream*

*Nothing for Granted: Tales of War, Philosophy, and
Why the Right Was Mostly Wrong*

Classic Cocktails: A Modern Shake

Catch & Release: Trout Fishing and the Meaning of Life

Practical Judgments: Essays in Culture, Politics, and Interpretation

The World We Want: Virtue, Vice, and the Good Citizen

Marginalia: A Cultural Reader

Canada: Our Century (with Christopher Moore)

Better Living: In Pursuit of Happiness from Plato to Prozac

Dreams of Millennium: Report from a Culture on the Brink

A Civil Tongue: Justice, Dialogue, and the Politics of Pluralism

MARK KINGWELL
CONCRETE REVERIES
CONSCIOUSNESS
AND THE CITY

VIKING

VIKING
Published by the Penguin Group
Penguin Group (USA) Inc., 375 Hudson Street,
New York, New York 10014, U.S.A.
Penguin Group (Canada), 90 Eglinton Avenue East, Suite 700,
Toronto, Ontario, Canada M4P 2Y3
(a division of Pearson Penguin Canada Inc.)
Penguin Books Ltd, 80 Strand, London WC2R 0RL, England
Penguin Ireland, 25 St. Stephen's Green, Dublin 2, Ireland
(a division of Penguin Books Ltd)
Penguin Books Australia Ltd, 250 Camberwell Road, Camberwell,
Victoria 3124, Australia
(a division of Pearson Australia Group Pty Ltd)
Penguin Books India Pvt Ltd, 11 Community Centre, Panchsheel Park,
New Delhi – 110 017, India
Penguin Group (NZ), 67 Apollo Drive, Rosedale, North Shore 0632,
New Zealand (a division of Pearson New Zealand Ltd)
Penguin Books (South Africa) (Pty) Ltd, 24 Sturdee Avenue,
Rosebank, Johannesburg 2196, South Africa

Penguin Books Ltd, Registered Offices:
80 Strand, London WC2R 0RL, England

First American edition
Published in 2008 by Viking Penguin,
a member of Penguin Group (USA) Inc.

1 3 5 7 9 10 8 6 4 2

Some of the selections in this book have been previously published; citations appear on page 237.
Pages 270–73 constitute an extension of this copyright page.

Library of Congress Cataloging-in-Publication Data

Kingwell, Mark, 1963–
Concrete reveries : consciousness and the city / Mark Kingwell.
p. cm.
Includes bibliographical references and index.
ISBN 978-0-670-03780-3
1. Sociology, Urban—New York (State)—New York. 2. Sociology, Urban—China—Shanghai. 3. City and
town life—New York (State)—New York. 4. City and town life—China—Shanghai. I. Title.
HN80.N5K56 2008
307.7609747′1—dc22
2007042796

Printed in the United States of America
Set in Minion

for Molly

Contents

The situation of consciousness as patterned and checkered by sleep and waking need only be transferred from the individual to the collective ... Architecture, fashion—yes, even the weather—are, in the interior of the collective, what the sensoria of organs, the feeling of sickness or health, are inside the individual. And so long as they preserve this unconscious, amorphous dream configuration, they are as much natural processes as digestion, breathing, and the like. They stand in the cycle of the eternally selfsame, until the collective seizes upon them in politics and history emerges.

—Walter Benjamin

1.
Hard and Soft

i. Beautiful Concrete

The next time it rains, go out and touch some.

Find a wall or a bench or just a stanchion, and run your hands along the spongy, almost-smooth surface.

Feel the tough, wet muscularity of it. Skim your fingers over a few of the thousand small holes—bubbles really—that notch the outside. Pebbles and other tiny bits are lodged in the surface, looking like you might just pry them out. You will not.

Trace the little runnels that cut between the slabs, or the little circles of the snap ties. Imagine the iron rebar skeleton inside, the bones for this rugged flesh.

But before you do any of that, just look at it. Look at the chiaroscuro patterns the rain is painting on the micro-pitted planes, the way the wall seems to be weeping its way from light to dark, in running streaks, like mascara. We call it gray, as if that were one simple color, but concrete is dozens of shades at once, from various off-whites through to charcoal. It has swirls and patterns, little islands and continents stained on the extended map of its face. Concrete is beautiful, never more so than in the rain.

Yet it is a material people love to hate, for reasons lodged often in conventional disregard and a prejudice for more "natural" materials such as wood or finished stone. Mostly, though, it is because we have not been given the opportunity to see concrete properly. There are many spectacularly egregious examples of its abuse: squat Soviet-style blocks full of bureaucrats, and those windswept, boxy warehouses for intellectuals we call modern universities. Surely much of the hostility we feel toward concrete is owing to the brutalist annexation of its loveliness, the way it was taken over and made into those thick, tough slabs that block out the sky. Any material becomes the sum of its treatments, and concrete has been made to look leaden, solid, heavy. The standard view is summed up by the words of one architectural critic who noted that concrete "has figured heavily in numerous architectural monstrosities, not least because the cheap, durable substance oozes despair and seems to suck up light."

Concrete is the basic material of the urban moment, and not just on the outside of big institutional edifices or office towers, the concrete jungle of the alienated metropolitan imagination. Witness Esther Greenwood on page one of Sylvia Plath's *The Bell Jar,* describing one summer in New York: "Mirage-grey at the bottom of their granite canyons, the hot streets wavered in the sun, the car tops sizzled and glittered, and the dry, cindery dust blew into my eyes and down my throat." The streets themselves, particulated, rise up and cling to your skin, the windowsill, pieces of paper left undisturbed too long. A fine soot envelops every surface and recess. We begin to feel not merely dirty but as if the city is attempting, all unnaturally, to render us into its own material form.

Concrete is cheap to produce and easy to use. When in doubt, pave or pour. Perhaps too cheap and too easy. Thus the urban death maze of concrete canyons, harsh and impenetrable; the toxic city, with invisible death rays emanating from the materials palette itself, crumbling blocks of disease; the barrier or fence, blocking movement or imprisoning ethnicity. Concrete may even be implicated in a species of architectural war crime as urban planners are co-opted by the total mobilization war machine to create insurgent cities, or to destroy invaded ones more effectively: concrete as strategic intervention.

This understanding of the material is not wrong, exactly, just one-sided. In the right setting, brutalism has its own peculiar appeal, and sometimes bunker-style institutions or looming office buildings are just what we want in a hard-bitten urban landscape. Stock denunciations of concrete cloud the issue: There are lots of ugly brick and wood buildings too. More to the point, concrete is not inherently cold, inhuman or brutal. Like many good things, it can be bent to bad purposes, but we should not blame the material. Try this instead: If you treat concrete well, it will reveal new layers of possibility, new aspects of beauty.

Concrete is also expressive and rewarding, a human material for all its toughness. It is capable of making a complex statement, exciting a nuanced reaction. Concrete now decorates the interiors of downtown offices, setting off traditional high-end polished wood and frosted glass with its appealing density and strength of purpose. It provides a different, firmer kind of grace note in otherwise lush parks and public squares.

You can have it inside your home. There is concrete-patterned wallpaper, realistic right down to the gravelly details. Some adventurous designers have installed concrete counters, floors, even dining-room tables. Set off with a patch of grass, a concrete table is a study in liminality, the textures of outside brought into the heart of the cozy domestic interior.

Changes to the materials palette make other forms of liminality possible. In 2004 the young Hungarian architect Áron Losonczi invented a material he called Litracon (light-transmitting concrete), made by adding glass and plastic fibers to the usual mix of sand, gravel, cement and water. A wall fashioned of Litracon is not transparent but is translucent enough to allow a play of light and shadow between inside and outside, like the thin marble panels that clad the Beinecke Library at Yale University (Skidmore, Owings & Merrill, 1960–63): stone refashioned as almost glass.

Not surprisingly, the cost of producing Litracon, because of the glass and plastic fibers, makes it unsuitable for widespread use in everyday construction. "The most sensible commercial use," one writer noted, "might be see-through barriers of the sort that shield the halls of government from car bombs. Since 9/11, the United States may have a bunker mentality, but that doesn't mean our bunkers need be drab."

ii. Freedom in a Frame

It is easy to forget that concrete was lauded in the same revolutionary terms, and by the same visionaries, as the modernist material of choice, glass. Glass walls, Bruno Taut enthused, make a house "a vessel for the divine … a salutation of the stars." Oskar Schlemmer, writing in 1929, said, "I have seen the future," and it is a dream of "a perfected glass culture." Walter Benjamin, a year later, went farther, or from transcendent to practical-political, anyway: "To live in a glass house," he said, "is a revolutionary virtue par excellence." Both were surely influenced by Paul Scheerbart's 1914 treatise on the use of glass in architecture, which dismissed the retrograde baselines of "brick architecture and wooden furniture," and the stuffiness of closed rooms.

Glass, newly reliable and cheap, the not-true-solid of molten sand made into sugar, delighted the seers of modernism's first moments. It was transparent and light, freedom in a frame. It allowed, for the first time, practical efforts to realize Walter Gropius's maxim of modern architecture—that it should fashion the void, not the mass. Just as music arises from, and subsides into, silence, sustained along its temporal course by the nothingness between the notes, so buildings should sculpt the spaces of life, the insides and outsides and in-betweens, by way of negative gestures, removals and obliquities: Architecture should disappear itself, in effect, in the achievement of success.

Within this invisibility, seeing becomes possible for the first time. Schoenberg on Alfred Loos, at his death, noted that his interiors treated space three-dimensionally, seeing every object "from all sides simultaneously … as though it were made of glass." Le Corbusier's much-quoted dictum that a house is a machine for living in may be offset by a less familiar one: that a house, if generously opened up by glass, is a body X-rayed by the sun. Skeleton and muscles and tubes all show themselves in their beautiful functionality. More explicit utopian architectural projects went farther, seeing a host of changes all lined up

The citizens of Oslo imagine the city of the future, in white LEGO blocks.

as part of the glorious emancipated, thrilling and, above all, speed-geeked future to come. Antonio Sant'Elia's futurist urban vision, for example, was structured by comprehensive changes in materials, offering "surrogates for wood, stone and brick" in the up-to-date forms of "reinforced concrete, iron, glass, cardboard, fibre." (The laborers who hauled the Empire State Building into being were more practical: At the base of the world's then tallest building, they installed medallions celebrating elevators, machines, decoration—and concrete.)

Glass has lost much of this philosophical traction for reasons similar to but less obvious than those afflicting concrete. Philip Johnson's Glass House in New Canaan, Connecticut, probably marks the end of that optimistic era, the prophet of the International Style himself a casualty of the banalities to come. Glass falls victim to its own success, rising often in prosaic condominium towers along ocean- and lakefronts everywhere, the same floor-by-floor deployment that drains glass of its revolutionary potential even as it floods the spaces with light. Glass is thus annexed to the unreflective reproduction of spaces, in office towers, high-rise apartment blocks and shopping malls that are "modular, unitary, and sanitized," in the words of Rem Koolhaas. Here the use of "brick, tile, plastic, stainless steel, composition board hung from suspended ceilings, and unpainted concrete" allow a practical desire—to lower costs and build quickly—to disguise an ideological desire, namely to erode through bland efficiency all traces of human inhabitation or particularity. The resulting constructions are nonspaces, an escape from the possibility of meaning.

iii. Concrete Visions

Instead of making concrete more transparent, let us try, instead, to see concrete more clearly.

The word itself has a good sound, and rich connotations: definiteness, the tough-minded opposite to woolly abstraction. Concrete is what we desire concepts and thinking to be, perhaps even in philosophy. Even, or especially. "Thought is surrounded by a halo," Wittgenstein remarks in *Philosophical Investigations,* probing this trope of hardness in thought:

> Its essence, logic, presents an order, in fact the a priori order of the world … It is *prior* to all experience, must run through all experience; no empirical cloudiness or uncertainty can be allowed to affect it—It must rather be of the purest crystal. But this crystal does not appear as an abstraction; but as something concrete, indeed, as the most concrete, as it were the *hardest* thing there is.

Wittgenstein's concrete-crystal play, not to mention the doubling of *hard* as both difficult and resilient, suggests a lurking irony. Philosophy's pursuit of the hardest ideas, which are also the most perspicuous, tangles itself in confusion, trying to find a *super*-order between *super*-concepts—a sort of *superhardness* of thought, indeed, as the presumed result of conceptual analysis. Whereas, as Wittgenstein goes on to say, if words such as *language, world* and *experience* have any use at all, "it must be as humble a one" as belongs to words such as *table, lamp* and *door.*

We might just perform the same kind of meaning-is-use reversal on the humble material before us. Familiar as an adjective—applied to courtroom evidence, music composed entirely of street sounds, and poetry based on the vagaries of typography—concrete is, at the same time, a material of infinite pliability. Could we all perhaps learn to love its versatility and fungibility—its willingness? Could we come to appreciate the way it takes on form, its doughy elastic principles? Concrete does not need to be ripped, like wood, or forged, like metal, or cut, like stone. Instead, it is mixed and poured, like batter into a pan. You make concrete by combining cement and gravel and water, creating the cold lava of pure potential in those big mixing trucks that thump down your street on their way to a building site.

Frank Lloyd Wright reminds us that concrete is "a plastic material," essence seeking form. More so even than kiln-fired bricks, concrete is elemental alchemy, the stuff of the earth gathered up and mixed. Concrete, the basic stuff of the built environment, illustrates a basic tenet of Aristotelian metaphysics. The next time you are tempted to disdain a slab of lovely gray-white concrete in your building or parking lot, consider this: Concrete is the necessary conjunction of pure form and primary matter. In building, as in life, you cannot know the dancer from the dance. In the world of our experience, there is no such thing as form without matter, nor matter without form.

All material things show this lesson, but concrete teaches it better than any other material. It is as close to elemental, available earth as we are likely to see, almost—if never quite—matter-as-such. Concrete is momentarily unformed matter seeking its natural completion, filling in the last corners of its allowed space, finding a form. It is possibility rendered material, hope in an industrial-strength mixer.

Concrete Reveries

"The truly utopian act is to manifest current conditions and dialects. Practice description. Description is mystical." (Lisa Robertson)

When the mixture sets, the form is fixed; but the available forms are limited only by the human imagination. Why do we make concrete so often into slabs when it could also be made into mounds? Look at it. Nothing in concrete wants to be a flat wall all the time, as if it were hemmed in at some fundamental level, like the hard edges of bricks or those Erector set–like cubes fashioned from I-beam steel and sheet glass. Concrete wants to be, as well, an eye-filling groundswell, an organic, emergent property of the landscape. It wants to be a rock, a stone, a hump of matter pressing up out of the ground.

Concrete is a material capable of cambers and blobs more primeval, more deeply rooted, than the angles and boxes we will make later. Straight lines, the powerful limbs of the spatial grid and perspectival precision, are pleasing to us in the way order or scheme always is, laid over a rough world; but sometimes roughness and curves are better for accommodating the soft architecture of the city, the psychic constructions of memory and desire, the palimpsest of dwelling, with the layerings of emotion and yearning that sustain and breathe life into the merely built forms.

Concrete gives us both. Its brutalism tamed, concrete opens up a profound connection to the earth. Concrete is the stuff of dreams. It is the world itself coming into being. And the city fashioned of it, those hard streets and unsmooth precincts, is the site where our dreams can take up their concrete contours.

iv. The Implications of Grue

The transnational-global city is the most significant machine our species has ever produced. Each massive conurbation, from Shanghai to Seattle, Toronto to Tokyo, is a testament to the human "desire to master nature," that general drive for order, cleanliness and beauty, which Freud puts at the center of the civilizing project. At the dawn of the twenty-first century, it is only a small exaggeration to say that cities are us, and we are cities. And yet, we fail, again and again, to understand them correctly. Almost all of our models or metaphors for thinking about cities are inadequate—not excepting the idea of "machine" used just a moment ago. Jane Jacobs labeled cities "problems in organized complexity," an accurate tag that nevertheless stands out as an example of defining without definition.

Cities are not biological entities, though they exhibit certain organic features, such as growth, disease and decline; they are not battlefields, though they are often riven by violence; they are not markets, though goods and services (also, to be sure, bodily fluids and air and excrement) are exchanged in massive volume through their various conduits, physical and otherwise. Nor are they architecture, despite being in large part accumulations of buildings. The urbanist Kevin Lynch identifies five attempts at a unifying model for the city: an organism, an economic engine, a communications network, a system of linked decisions and an arena of conflict. But these labels or models serve only to extend the problem they mean to solve. Each of these five models is both accurate and limited. While they may be rivals in terms of attention or resources, the models are neither exclusive nor exhaustive. The truth of one does not entail the falsity of another, and so multiple models may apply at once; and no single model explains or covers all the phenomena of a given city, so one model will not do. They are like incomplete transparent overlays on a flip chart: Each model (with its associated explanatory power and ideological assumptions) can be added or subtracted at will; but no amount of manipulation of the overlays will explain the city as such.

One reason for this is that all such models are diachronic: They use given time-slice analysis to try to predict, and so plan, future events. But prediction in cities, as in life, is a confidence game. Even good predictions now are likely to generate bad ones in future if the model remains static as the city changes. The philosopher Frank Cunningham, taking a page from analytic epistemology, argues usefully that, so far from being inductively predictable, cities are *grue-like*.

"Grue" is a term of art coined by the philosopher Nelson Goodman for an imaginary color that is now green but at some unknown future point will be blue. Two things at time T are both apparently green, but one is actually grue, meaning that at time $T + n$ it will be blue. (There is a complementary color called "bleen" with the reverse properties:

blue, then green.) We might wish to argue, by induction, the proposition that *all emeralds are green* because all emeralds so far discovered have been green. Thus the corollary predictive proposition that *emeralds will be green in the future*. But if $T + n$ has not yet passed, all emeralds so far discovered are also grue. So how can we say, based on present experience of their being green, that emeralds will be green in the future?

Grue captures the general problem with inductive reasoning: namely, predicting future events based on our experience of present ones is ensnared in a contradiction. Grue, says Cunningham, "exposes a limit to the reliability of expectations based on experience: observations supporting a belief that something is green equally support its being grue." According to David Hume's well-known proto-grue argument against induction, we cannot prove that the sun will rise tomorrow based on our experience of past sunrises because reliability of experience cannot be employed as a premise in a proof attempting to establish reliability of experience. Cities make concrete an issue that, with the example of grue, is merely a thought experiment. We cannot rely on our past and present experience of cities to predict future events in them; and yet, our past and present experience of cities, including their being subject sometimes to rapid unpredictable change, is all we have to go on.

The practical implications of grue (rather than green) cities is that models must be employed with skepticism. Likewise, predictions and plans must submit to a basic provisionality when it comes to what is being predicted or planned. A simpler way of expressing this caution is to say that cities are not systems or markets or arenas but, rather, *collisions*: of natural conditions, material forces and human desire. Like automobile and aircraft crashes or other literal collisions, they may obey certain general laws (or law-like generalities), but, beneath these, they are a tangle of vectors and imponderables. We can search through the wreckage with a fine-toothed comb and still not determine precisely what happened to get us here; and, even could we know that, it would not prevent every possible future crash, only possibly minimize the risk of some.

Lest that metaphor seem too morbid, consider that cities are also, on this anti-inductive view, like persons. That is, they are forms of *embodied consciousness*—neither minds nor bodies conceived separately from the other but conjunctions of both. Just as a person is not a mind using a body, or a body invaded by mind, a city is reducible to neither its citizens nor its material base, its built structure. Nor, for that matter, is it susceptible to any simple ordering of priority between the two. A neutron-bombed city is not a city but a ruin; a city without the structures to match its citizens' aspirations and dreams is perhaps still a city in name but an incomplete and devastated one—another kind of ruin.

All of this is really to say that cities are *places*. That may sound obvious (or merely deranged); but the ostensible obviousness of the concept belies a depth of challenge. What, after all, is a place? We say: It is an area of significance, a physical staging ground. But it is more than that. It is somewhere that matters, where we find or lose ourselves, where understanding good and bad is forced upon us. Places are environments, sites of action, horizons of concern. They are infused with our aspirations and beliefs, reflecting and shaping them both. *Finding your way* means moving from place to place—even if, most of the time, we do not think consciously about it, lost in the reveries of our own projects and aims.

The great movement of global urbanization that began in the Late Middle Ages continues, inexorably, to gather up Earth's population to itself, massing us together more and more densely in sprawling nodes. Given its affinity, almost unity, with the very idea of civilization, this massive, centuries-long process of urban migration is arguably the most significant thing we have done to our planet, and ourselves. It cannot be stopped or reversed, but it can be interrogated. The process has sometimes been violent and spasmodic, a kind of prolonged cancerous episode whose most obvious symptoms are growth and innovation, especially in the field of environmental mastery,

combined with widespread poverty, disease and violence. The realities of large-scale and often forced massing, frequently noted if rarely understood, can create surprising local conditions. There are expected outcomes, such as the "feral city" phenomenon, where civic order, especially law enforcement, breaks down entirely and is replaced by gangland territorialism. In a 2004 *World Policy Journal* article, security experts James Miskel and Peter Liotta argue that the failed state models popular during the 1990s should give way to a failed city analysis. The shift signifies more than simply a matter of adapting war-waging strategies that focus on cities rather than countries; it also acknowledges that service provision and taxation at a national level are far less important to most people than that found at the civic level. Cities are clearly far more susceptible than nations to gang-directed criminality, in part because of density and opportunity. Such criminal activity typically occurs in a form of downward spiral: The more

Edge City, or chaotic order, in Mumbai, India.

that gangs gain a foothold in a city, the harder it is to police any part of the civic territory, thereby offering new criminal opportunities. Hence, the problem of feral and near-feral cities, especially in the heavily populated areas of South America, Asia and Africa.

As urbanist Ken Stier notes, when public service deteriorates, "residents are forced to hire private security or pay criminals for protection. The police in Brazil have fallen back on a containment policy against gangs ruling the *favelas,* while the rich try to stay above the fray, fueling the busiest civilian helicopter traffic in the world (there are 240 helipads in Sao Paulo; there are 10 in New York City)." Other cities are likewise dangerous: Johannesburg, where much of the city center has been tacitly ceded to squatters and drug gangs; Mexico City, which is witnessing soaring crime despite an army of almost a hundred thousand police officers; Karachi, where 40 percent of the population lives in slums that are breeding grounds of Islamic extremism and violence. The last makes clear the larger security problem. The larger world powers, having felt the internal threat posed by such extremism, now see they have a stake in extending order not just to nations but also to cities. Richard J. Norton, writing in the *Naval War College Review* in 2003, notes that "traditionally, problems of urban decay and associated issues, such as crime, have been seen as domestic issues best dealt with by internal security or police forces." Under emerging conditions, "that will no longer be an option."

And yet, not all the news is bad, even in the urban environments that count as most anarchic. Norton himself suggests that with the possible exception of Mogadishu, there are no examples of a truly feral city. Meanwhile, one in six people on the planet lives in an uncontrolled city environment, an urban squat or an ex-urban shantytown. This includes homeless people in wealthy North American and European cities, vast populations skirting the megacities of North Africa and South America, and countless miniature communities of ramshackle city life all over South Asia, East Asia and Southeast Asia: the vast jumbles of people scattered around and through Mumbai or Shanghai or Manila. This 16 percent of the world's humans lives without government services or infrastructure: no police, no plumbing, no public transit. No rent, and no taxes. And yet, we do not find here the violent chaos that might be expected. Crime rates in these unregulated cities are often lower than in propertied areas, where comfort and envy levels are higher. Cooperative solutions are frequently forced by circumstance.

It would be bizarre to posit this self-organizing survivalism as a model for structured living, but it does attest to the human ability to make places out of the least promising natural and material conditions—a kind of workaday utopianism neither fanciful nor totalizing. Or we should rather say, after Foucault, a *heterotopianism*: not the no-space of the discredited utopian imagination but the very real spaces of difference within the otherwise smooth exchanges of the "official" city.

v. The Decline of Public Space

There are many books about cities and architecture, and in a sense this is one of them. But only in a sense, because my focus here is one neglected in most writing about public space, architecture and urban planning. My main concern is to put into question *the idea of threshold* and explore the movement created by boundaries and limits, the over-

Utopian plan: the classical lines of a Fourierist phalanstery (1808?), home to 1620 persons living in harmony.

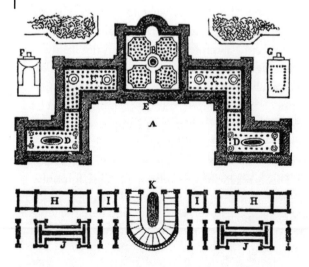

flowing edges of real places. Since human civilization began, *inside* has meant order, warmth, security and sanity; outside is chaos, cold, fear, disorder, danger and madness. But what makes for the line between, and what forces, mischievous and benign, are at work in drawing it?

The pages that follow are rooted in the discussion of public space begun in a previous work, *The World We Want*. There, Walter Benjamin's disputatious correspondence with Theodor Adorno, as well as the sprawling genius of *The Arcades Project*, was used to motivate arguments about the virtues of citizenship. The main points of the critical position are by now familiar, if not a little worn. Public spaces, so often colonized and banalized by commercial hawking and relentless visual and aural clutter, have ceased to be sites of political discourse. Because the materiality of public spaces is crucial to their function, and because that materiality is the result of minority design—two obvious facts often neglected in talk of public space—the main concern was the twinned duties of architects and "ordinary" citizens to realize norms of justice in the actual built environments of their cities and towns.

Even as the high priests of contemporary architecture set themselves up as visionary artists or seers in a throbbing celebrity economy, architecture frequently ignores or underestimates its civic influence. Architects certainly deserve admiration for what they, alone among us, can do: create new monuments of the built environment. When Howard Roark, the architect hero of Ayn Rand's *The Fountainhead*, points to a building and says, "I don't care what anyone says about me; I built *that*," one cannot but admire the material certainty of his pride. But one toxic result of recent "starchitecture" culture is the steady stream of theoretical bafflegab that pours from architectural schools and journals. This is usually the result of what we might call "philo-sophical backformation": finding some plausible-sounding theoretical cladding to hang on an already conceived, even completed, structural project. Self-respecting architects would not allow useless aesthetic decorations to mar their designs, yet they perpetrate intellectual design crimes by the week. This is forgivable pretension, perhaps, but only if architectural discourse allows itself to be penetrated from the outside—if it allows its boundaries to be crossed.

An overtly political conception of space is inadequate to the realities of building. In particular, any blithe abstract argument in favor of public space is susceptible to penetrating insights, from both phenomenology and aesthetic theory, about the neglected epistemological differences between the concepts of space and place. My earlier discussion was not only too brief but, perhaps answering a desire of my own, too sanguine. It failed to take into account the violence and energy throbbing in the public/private threshold, the economies of dirt and blood that run beneath the smooth surfaces of cities. As a result, the argument fell prey to the fiction of a spectral public sphere, a too-rational idea of public space. In that sort of public space, to put it bluntly, nobody ever spits or defecates; nobody dies or is buried.

Contrary to common belief, cities exist in time rather than space: This is part of what makes them places. Or rather, we ought to say that cities *make space timely,* and so change our own relation to time. (Architecture, Vincent Scully said, is a conversation between generations.) We make a mistake—a rather traditional and by no means unhelpful mistake, of one-sidedness—if we try to understand the politics of cities in terms of public space. Abstract reflection on the politics of public space rapidly reveals its insufficiency and distortion, not least because abstraction here can blind us to the fact that the politics of public space are also always matters of metaphysics and epistemology. I mean that the politics of public space raises questions of knowledge and reality that politics alone cannot address, but without which politics must remain stunted and incomplete.

The task is to turn around and reenter the heart of places—to be somewhere in particular, as an embodied consciousness. As so often in philosophy, we need to go back before we can think of going forward. The pages that follow are only a beginning in what must be a long philosophical investigation of the built environment, especially the late-model form of cities. It takes inspiration from political, architectural and philosophical sources, in particular the branch of philosophy known as phenomenology, which investigates the conditions of conscious experience. The experience at issue here is the one of being in place, with place understood in this instance to be an urban location. I do not investigate, except by incidental contrast, the important experience of "natural" places—although I would argue that nothing is natural until we make it so, and that nature is a concept that always exists by contrast with something else (artificial, awkward, human, urban). The result is not anything like a complete phenomenology of places, something probably no single person is capable of producing, certainly not in one volume; nor is it a theory of architecture.

Instead, thoughts and experiences of real cities are interleaved with more overtly philosophical arguments about publicness, consciousness and threshold. Architectural practice is queried for its political possibilities without seeking a flat-footed account of civic accountability. The hope is that, taken together, these soft and hard, concrete and abstract reflections will cast light on the way we occupy places, how that happens, what it means and why place is so important to whom we think we are.

vi. Speaking of You

Finally, a word about point of view, or *person*.

This book, like all books, is a kind of machine. A machine of illusion, creating of necessity the expectation of linear investigation. Of necessity because, although it seems to present itself all at once, a book is a time-based medium. The sentence is the line, indeed the vector, pointing in one direction. The paragraph and the page in turn create, as I will argue later, an orthogonal grid of sense-making. Sections are divided and named. Chapters are mapped. The spine gathers the pages between covers, ordering them and separating the whole of the book from everything that is not the book.

We may say, following the standard insight of deconstruction, that *there is nothing outside the text*—meaning that all texts imply, respond to and anticipate all other ones. But it is equally true, as Gilles Deleuze and Félix Guattari write, that "a book only exists by means of an outside, a beyond." Books point beyond themselves, at least to the reader, and possibly to what we like to call the world. Normally, this is a matter of power: language as representation, and representation as control.

Well, are you or aren't you?

YOU ARE HERE

But if their machine qualities are subverted or destabilized, books open up multiple *lines of flight*, to use the familiar deleuzoguattarian phrase. They become a jumble of insides and outsides, Möbius strips rather than gridded pages of sentences ending in declarative full stops …

You will notice that some of what follows, including this sentence, is written in the second person. That is, the text will speak of *you* and that pronoun's various cases. This form of address runs the risk of generating an unhelpful, even crippling, alienation effect. As some hostile reviewers said of Jay McInerney's 1984 novel *Bright Lights, Big City*—a rare recent work written entirely in the second person about drug-fueled Manhattan nightlife—the undeniable temptation when one reads "And then you went into the bathroom at Arena and did two lines of Bolivian marching powder," is to say, *No, I didn't.* By the same token, however, the advantage of the second person, when it works, is the strange, stretching intimacy it creates between writer and reader—an acknowledgment in the prose that the act of writing is a stilted and time-lapsed attempt at communication, one consciousness trying to penetrate another.

The second-person point of view acknowledges the important limitations on writing's authority. The subjective first person, deceptively chummy and confessional, and the stern third person, laying down the law, are both fictions. Also fictional is the notion that there is no choice other than these; rock-solid objectivity ("Now, this is how it is!") or presumptively weak subjectivity ("Well, this is how I feel!") somehow exhausting the available options when it comes to writing, thinking or the truth. There is an alternative superior to either, though it requires us to discard this soothing false dichotomy. Finding our way in a text, just like finding a way in the world, is not a matter either of attaining transcendental conviction or of receiving flattened-down personal opinion. It is, rather, an exercise in engagement with the other, accepting the risk of being unsettled by the importance of what matters to us.

The second-person point of view involves a deliberate and revealing destabilization of the limiting subjective-objective dyad. Like the middle voice praised by Martin Heidegger for allowing ontological insight—*the dishes dry,* we say, indicating an action without an actor, a state of being that is neither movement nor stasis—the second person can serve to unsettle the assumptions of thought. There is very little of it to be found in the pages of canonical philosophy. There is some use of the first person in the tradition, notably in Plato and Descartes and certain passages of Hume and Kant, and there are the dramatic dialogic experiments of Plato, Hume and others. What we mostly find, unsurprisingly, is a surfeit of third-person assertion, the voice of intellectual authority.

We should always ask of the voice of philosophy, as Jean Hippolyte does, "Who or what is speaking? The answer is neither 'one' [or 'das Man'] nor 'it' [or 'the id'], nor quite 'the I' or 'the we.' This name dialectic which Hegel has revived and interpreted and which designates a dialectic of things themselves, not an instrument of knowledge, is itself at the heart of this problem." Or, to put it in more vivid terms still, recall the inimitable voice of Nietzsche: "Gradually it has become clear to me what every philosophy so far has been: namely, the personal confession of its author and a kind of involuntary and unconscious memoir." Consciously or otherwise, that dialectic of *the one* and *the I* is enacted in all philosophical writing, indeed, is what invests philosophy with a rich strain of irony. The kind of writing worthy of our attention—by which, of course, I mean *your* attention—attends to but cannot resolve that tension. For the irony is structural: It can be ignored, but it cannot be avoided. Even the most revealing and honest self-portrait is a spectacular ruin: a failure, realized in the mirror or *speculum,* to convey my consciousness to you, the concrete other. Among the many reasons for this failure is the central fact that my consciousness *is* you.

The starting point of what follows, a point to which I return more than once, is Descartes's founding move in the *Meditations on First Philosophy*: the establishment of the isolated "I" as the subject *and object* of philosophical reflection. This occurs in a philosophical treatise that is disguised as a memoir, making the uncovering of the unconscious that much more difficult. As the subject who speaks, in the first person, Descartes is considered a *foundationalist* philosopher in that he seeks to find firm ground for belief, to lay a foundation for knowledge, after entertaining spectacular versions of skeptical doubt. The success or failure of his project, his resulting edifice of belief, has preoccupied philosophers ever since, and his ideas about consciousness are therefore the traditional prologue to any discussion of consciousness. That holds true for me, even as the mind–body distinction asserted by Descartes is everywhere challenged.

In addition, though, this work is concerned with the other Descartes, the mathematician who gave the world the powerful x–y grid of biaxial space. These two thinkers are in fact one, of course, and so the unconscious motivation behind the conscious memoir form of the *Meditations* is, I suggest, a devotion to the supremacy of abstract space. Descartes rends the person asunder, splitting us into disembodied nonspatial minds and mindless spatial bodies, because of his prior devotion to the abstract grid. Epistemology (theory of knowledge), philosophy of mind (theory of consciousness), and physics (theory of reality) are inextricable in Descartes. This is well known. More important still, and so far neglected, is the fact that epistemology and philosophy of mind are further linked to the real grids and spaces that we conscious entities occupy, the streets and places of actual cities. Epistemology is architecture, and architecture epistemology, because both concern our experience of the world *as space*. And because architecture in turn concerns public spaces, we find ourselves in the realm of politics—which really we have never left.

Threshold leverages this cluster of ideas, and the book works its way from the outside in, from architecture to consciousness, trying to get closer and closer to the heart of threshold. Putting consciousness back into place means asking about lines and boundaries, where they are and what they mean. The result of these reflections is twofold: a renewed appreciation for the complexity of our conscious lives, our being in place, and, more practically, a sense of urgency for our engagements in the creation of new democratic cities. Every city is, in a sense, a city of the imagination, an unrealized project. Together, as citizens, we try to create our own city in the form, or forms, we think best. This book is not a blueprint for an ideal city or a utopian primer; it is not any kind of blueprint. It is, rather, a series of incomplete sketches for thinking, and arguing, about what places mean to us. Sense of place emerges as the necessary political antidote to the displacement and placelessness characteristic of the mediated world.

Although I have tried to make them as accessible as possible, these remain somewhat difficult ideas for those without an extensive background in philosophy. The concrete examples of New York and Shanghai—cities as much symbolic as real—anchor the first half of the book. Numerous examples and illustrations supplement the theoretical discussion throughout. In addition, I refer to the work of a number of writers and philosophers, not all of whom will be familiar to all readers. This is inevitable in a field of thought as rich as this one. Nevertheless, it should be possible to follow the train of thought without becoming distracted by the names or necessarily undertaking a study of each thinker's work. Readers interested in the philosophical context for various arguments, as well as specific citations, are directed to the Bibliographic Essay.

And so we step across the threshold together …

2.
New York, Capital of the Twentieth Century

i. Approach to LaGuardia

Your A320 skims into LaGuardia from across the Hudson
River Valley, past West Point and the swimming-pool and
football-field suburbs north of the city and, wheeling, snips
a corner of that prime real estate, exotic and remote, where

yacht clubs and tiny islands and massive houses carve up the visual field like a big slab of surreal computer-generated images. The approach is over bay water and, looking down, the plane's shadow surfs its way up to meet the lowered gear, interrupted at the last minute by the apron of runway concrete sliding into place like a cartoon plate, flash-extended to prevent food from hitting the floor. Off to the right—your view if you are lucky enough to be sitting on the right—floats the undulating steel and stone mesa of Manhattan.

Walter Benjamin labeled Paris the capital of the nineteenth century in his monumental work of cultural excavation, *The Arcades Project,* that dense, unparalleled, unfinished flotsam-and-jetsam chronicle of revolutionary history, literary struggle and sexual ambition in the West's most beautiful and most sedimentary city, the birthplace of modernity. New York's essence will not surrender the same kind of archaeological depth, though there are some exceptions (uncovered pre-Columbian cemeteries on Staten Island, revealed abandoned subway trails beneath Wall Street sidewalks), because it tends to erase and rebuild rather than layer; it has always been more tabula rasa than palimpsest. New York became the world's most populous city in 1950, finally surpassing London, but held this dubious (and often misleading) honor for just three decades or so before Tokyo outgrew it in the 1980s. Of course, mere size says nothing about the wealth or poverty, the interests or achievements, of a city. It is no measure of genuine importance. In the twenty-first century, of the estimated twenty-two cities whose populations will exceed ten million, none is in Europe and just two are in the United States, while seventeen are in poor countries of Asia, Africa, and Latin America. Already some of these developing-world cities have reached populations higher than twenty million, soon quickly to approach thirty.

But setting aside the issue of size, New York, like Paris, occupies the world-historic position relative to its century, maybe an even greater one than the French capital, and it demands an equally nuanced connoisseur's gaze. All the more so because New York's reign, like Paris's when Benjamin came to construct his elaborate intellectual billet-doux during the 1930s, is now over. In a sense still hard to realize, even now wispy and unresolved, it is no longer simply or without further ado

Climb along the wing, and touch the city ...

what its tourism department banners proclaim: the capital of the world. If the City of Light's centrality shifted with a fatal gunshot in Sarajevo, New York's shifted even more obviously, and monstrously, at the moment—still so weirdly hard to reconcile, to accept as real—when two symbols of twentieth-century technological and capital success met in a long imagined, long implied confrontation. "Before the fire, before the ash, before the bodies tumbling through space, one thin skin of metal and glass met another," Adam Goodheart wrote of this terrifying conjoining of icons. "Miles apart only moments before, then feet, and then, in an almost inconceivable instant, only a fraction of an inch. Try to imagine them there, suspended: two man-made behemoths joined in a fatal kiss."

That New York was the crossroads of these two journeys—skyscraper rising from the ground, airplane arrowing through the air—as it has been for so many others in both real and virtual space, seems wickedly fitting. It offered a fiery working-out of what, once demonstrated, appears inevitably contained in the separate terms, like a logical proof set forth. Of course New York. Of course the Twin Towers of the World Trade Center, whose name itself proclaimed an intersection, marked a cross on the global-influence map. And of course the jetliner—not least because the previous terrorist attack on the Twin Towers, the attempted bombing from the underground parking garage, comical and insectoid in retrospect, exposed the fatal lack of lethality in anything deployed at ground level. Like the constructive aspirations of the grid-measured city itself, birthplace of the elevator and the steel-spined building, the material realizations of the panoptic desire to rise above the street, to see and measure the city from above, attaining the transcendence of the bird's-eye (or god's-eye) view, the purveyors of destruction *looked up*.

New Yorkers, famously, do not. At street level, your attention has to be focused on walking, moving through the grid. The surface logic of the grid says: You will always know where you are; there will always be a call-out of coordinates, offered to cab-driver or cell-phone interlocutor, that will place you without error on the shared mental map. You are in one place; you are on your way someplace else: This much is given. The route is probably obvious, or anyway there is an obvious array of permutations of uptown-and-crosstown (say) that are, in grid terms, functional equivalents. Even the major airports, so irritatingly inaccessible by public transportation, offer just a few versions of bridge-or-tunnel, FDR or BQE choices. Occasionally, if your destination from LaGuardia is somewhere midtown, say the Theater District, your driver will adopt a novel route: through Central Park at dusk, costless romance just as efficient as a straighter route. But these gems of discovery are rare.

"The city looks its best from the air," the critic Kenneth Tynan says, "or by night, or when you are drunk; in any circumstances, in fact, except

Map of Manhattan after the 1811 plan: Urban jumble at the foot of the island resolves into orthogonal order as you move uptown.

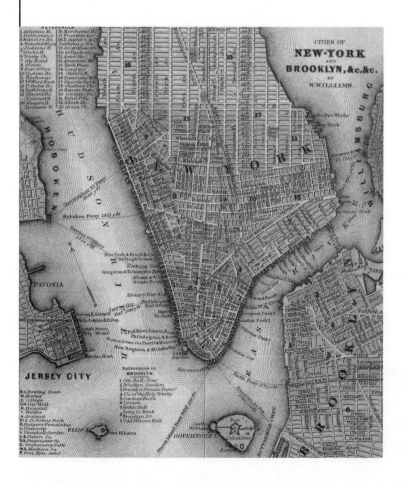

those of stone-cold sobriety, by day, at street level. Abnormal itself, it demands an abnormal approach." But that flight is a flight of fancy, for sooner or later you must walk, and then you must devote your attention to getting where you're going as quickly as possible. The basic rule of walking in New York is: at all costs, don't break stride. (The sub-rules, as defined by a helpful *New York Times* writer, include keep right, no sudden stopping, get off the phone, and no mall-walking—i.e., at a bovine pace four abreast.) "Don't break stride" might even serve as a motto, appropriately imperative and workaday, for the city as a whole, for the country, for the culture. For the century; indeed, for the whole millennial odyssey so starkly ended in the fall of 2001.

That is a cliché, of course, and therefore suspect. Yet, like all clichés, it has its roots in truth. And to turn the gaze on such a mythologized place as New York, a genuine world-historic capital, is always and necessarily to sift through overdetermined materials, to find yourself saying again what has been said before. The meaning of New York, as with the meaning of baseball or childhood or death, is always a little shop-

View from the street: You can see the Chrysler Building in the distance.

Hybrid skyscraper: a souvenir postcard of the Woolworth Building (Cass Gilbert, 1913), fifty-five stories high.

LITTIG & CO.

570 odd feet
55th story   Was up this
last winter.

WOOLWORTH BUILDING, NEW YORK.

worn and premature, a little tinged by the obvious. But this problem cannot be avoided if we are to say anything at all. We might think to circumvent the difficulty by cultivating greater and greater degrees of insouciance—the longtime inhabitant's refusal to take any particular interest in, let alone be impressed by, anything objectively interesting or impressive—but that is not so much avoidance as a different kind of cliché, a new form of not looking up. And so it merely adds, now in the form of attitude, a new, second-order cliché, an overarching inevitability of the ever-said, another thing we always already know about New York.

There is, finally, no escape from these escalating levels of self-consciousness, the layers of New York's meaning laid over each other like the levels of the city itself, all those enfolding maps and grids, from subterranean arteries and muscle tissue through the concrete skin of the streets, to the raised edifice-limbs and even airplanes thrown beyond. The problem cannot be evaded any more than gravity, and the mundane egg of the world, can be conquered entirely. So not only will I risk saying here what has been said before, I will do so in tones of romantic melancholy that belong, I know, to the first blush of a deeper but still temporary acquaintance, that space somewhere between tourism and residency when you feel the emotions of a love affair you know must end. This is what the critic Jed Perl has called "the adolescent city," that shimmering land of half-fantasy, at once true and false, that presents itself to artists and writers when they first come to write about a place such as New York or Paris or London—the sense of slightly awed but boldly sanctioned arrival, of Gatsbyesque ambition about to succeed (or not), dreams about to be realized (or dashed). I mean the way we all feel when, well dressed and fresh-faced at least in imagination, we step off the train for the first time at Grand Central or Gare du Nord or King's Cross.

But New York, says Perl, "maybe more than London or Paris or Rome, appears in art and literature as pure metaphor—as the sign or symbol of triumph, of loneliness, of romance." And "if one thing is certain, it is that there is no getting to the bottom of New York." It also has the effect of sweeping everything else off the table of your imagination. "We saw the mystic city of the new world appear far away, rising up from Manhattan," the arrogant young Le Corbusier reported of his

1935 arrival in New York on the ocean liner *Normandie,* there to teach the tower-masters about the City of Tomorrow. "It passed us at close range: a spectacle of brutality and savagery. In contrast to our hopes the skyscrapers were not made of glass, but of tiara-crowned masses of stone. They carry up a thousand feet in the sky, a completely new and prodigious architectural event; with one stroke Europe is thrust aside."

You feel his desire there, beneath the confidence and intensity. You feel the magnetism of the high-built beautiful city, beckoning and ruinous, coy and fatal. Not the City of Glass, yet, but certainly more than the City of Light. Le Corbusier called it the City of Incredible Towers, but let us rather call it the City of Towering Dreams, the dreams that are not quelled even by your own, however many years of accumulated realism, savvy and wisdom: dreams to make you young again.

Of course, not everyone feels the same tug, or feels it the same way. "New York makes even a rich man feel his unimportance," Henry Miller writes in *Tropic of Cancer.*

> New York is cold, glittering, malign. The buildings dominate. There is a sort of atomic frenzy to the activity going on; the more furious the pace, the more diminished the spirit. A constant ferment, but it might just as well be going on in a test tube. Nobody knows what it's all about. Nobody directs the energy. Stupendous. Bizarre. Baffling. A tremendous reactive urge, but absolutely uncoordinated.

> When I think of this city where I was born and raised, this Manhattan that Whitman sang of, a blind, white rage licks my guts. New York! The white prisons, the sidewalks swarming with maggots, the breadlines, the opium joints that are built like palaces, the kikes that are there, the lepers, the thugs, and above all, the *ennui,* the monotony of aces, streets, legs, houses, skyscrapers, meals, posters, jobs, crimes, loves … A whole city erected over a hollow pit of nothingness. Meaningless. Absolutely meaningless.

ii. The Gaits of the City

> And in the dark tunnel, in the haste, heat, and darkness
> which disfigure and make freaks and fragments of nose and
> eyes and teeth, all of a sudden, unsought, a general love
> for all these imperfect and lurid-looking people burst out in
> Wilhelm's breast. He loved them. One and all, he passion-
> ately loved them. They were his brothers and sisters.
>
> —Saul Bellow, *Seize the Day*

The two of you approach the subway tunnel, one of the small rat-like ones for the 1 and 9 at 23rd and Sixth, except the 9 no longer runs because of the construction downtown, and the smell of hot air ema- nating from the entrance, the burp of subterranean gas squeezed out from the innards of the city, the miles of tunnel-intestines and steel- girder bones, is both familiar and comforting. It does not exactly stink, though there are animals and piles of garbage and human effluents down there. It smells homey and warm and alive, like the taste of breath from your lover's morning kiss, or your mother leaning over you in the evening with the Vicks VapoRub ready to apply to your cold-wracked chest. It mingles, the belched-up air, with the other smells of this corner, all corners: the flaming meat and warming rolls of the hot-dog cart; the sickly near-gag rising from sugar-coated pecans; the always- autumn tang, the global odor of cities, from roasting chestnuts.

And this is where you will kiss and say goodbye for who knows how long; and she says, poised on the edge of the downward steps, prepar- ing to enter one of those *cuts* in the skin of the urban body, the gashes leading down and underground, "This damn city restores my faith in humanity."

Wryly, but yes, it does—despite everything, including the sentimentality of even thinking so. Because consider how unlikely, how fantastic and multifarious, the lines of cooperation and negotiation that daily make the city possible. New York, like all cities, is a collective experiment in barely averted chaos, a play of vast possibility within the mapped order of the grid. It flows, and that is amazing, because it should not;

its congestion, the final gridlock where all the movement suddenly overcomes itself, snapping into the crystalline rigidity forever implied but always avoided, is right there: the culture of congestion, a petri dish of transactions and aspirations and discourses. It allows so much to happen even while not forcing any specific part of itself upon you. It allows you not to attend, as E.B. White put it, and so makes all events optional. Thus does it bestow the "queer prizes" of loneliness and privacy, the great freedom to move or be crushed.

That is why those Randian hymns to the towering individual architect, the underground hero of Grand Central, are so comically off the mark. Expansive individualism, sure; but *for everyone*. The genius of the city, of all cities, is its layered, fluid, always shifting contracts between sovereign individuals, each dependent on all the others for their sovereignty. Indeed, the sovereign individual is revealed by the city as a myth, a legal or political abstraction unrooted in real experience of the urban lifeworld. There is no heroism here, except the collective and ordinary kind acted out by all of us who are right here, right now, making our own kinds of future, one move—one place and one occasion—at a time. That is one reason why *movement* is everything: The future is always somewhere else, it has to be pursued. The movement of people

The view from the platform: speed and stasis meet under the skin of the city.

is just one layer or map, one trace of the flow, just as the grid is just one way to scan the four-dimensional psycho-geography of the city. Rise above, or go below, and the movement continues. The street is just the ground, merely grade one. Or, better, it is what homegrown New Yorkers call whatever lies beneath their feet, even in the depths of an Adirondack forest or Nantucket beach: It is *the floor*.

Stand above the Grand Concourse of Grand Central at rush hour and watch the way the people move across the floor. The nearly anarchic yet still somehow functional mass of undulating vectors—all those people all moving in subtly different directions, around and in front and behind their fellow citizens, sliding and dodging and negotiating the blocks and reverses and interference coming toward them at video-game speed. The pressure of movement is valved by small releases, little quick-step rushes and raised-eyebrow warnings, so that the number of actual collisions falls to an implausible minimum. Standing up above it, looking down from street level, reveals something of a cross between a massive group dance number and a human acting-out of some mad scientist's chemical experiment, molecules rolling over, combining, repelling, ricocheting off one another.

"I grew up in the South," Roy Blount Jr. notes, beginning a memorable essay on how to walk in New York.

> I can do the traipse, I can do the gallivant,
> I can do the lollygag, and I can do the slow
> lope. I can hotfoot it, I can waltz right in
> and waltz right out, or I can just be poking
> or dragging or plowing along. As a young-
> ster I skedaddled. I believe that if called
> upon, for the sake of some all-in-good-fun
> theatrical, I could sashay. But I know that
> these gaits have their places, and on the
> other hand there is New York walking. You
> think you know how to walk in New York?
> No you don't, unless you *know* you know
> how to walk in New York. Otherwise you
> just impede the flow.

Indeed. You must enter all intersections at a full clip, even if the light is against you. Even, or especially. You must keep your eyes saccading left and right, scanning for openings and possible trouble spots ahead: the young mother with her baby carriage; the clutch of slow-moving teenagers with lit cigarettes in their waving hands, like the spikes on an old-fashioned armored vehicle; tourists with maps gazing up or ambling along with ruminant placidity. There is always somebody moving at the wrong speed. Another frustrated *New York Times* writer, observing the crush of out-of-towners during summer, suggested that natives be allowed to carry foam batons, harmless but useful for gently pushing dawdlers off to the side, as if slow-moving trucks on a freeway incline.

Auden: The art of living in New York City lies in *crossing against the light.*

Dance floor: Grand Central Terminal concourse.

All cultures develop distinctive ways of walking, variations on our shared upright posture. Daily movement, not just dance or ritual, conveys meaning, at a minimum inness and outness, as surely as clothing or haircut. Maybe more so: They say one can always recognize a friend by his walk, even if all else about him has changed. Ways of walking are exclusive, unforgiving and utilitarian, not to mention economic. The ghetto-born pimp roll, as Tom Wolfe called it, signaled an urban defiance of convention with its characteristic hitch of the hip—a move later so widely copied, by black and white alike, that it lost its niche. Even the words of walking draw an implied boundary of class or subculture: the difference between truckin' and strolling, for example. A character in P.G. Wodehouse may ooze, oil, filter, trickle or pour. He may foot it or leg it or ankle it. He may breeze, stream or sidle. These are not pedestrian modes for everyone. In Wodehouse, the game is always afoot, with thefts and assignations and multiple reversals of fortune, and the range of available gaits is a direct function thereof: silence, secrecy, startled speed—these are the modes of drawing-room comedy. In this airtight world, characters always float or flee.

Wodehouse was no stranger to the adolescent city, as it happens. Moving to New York at the age of twenty-two, he found a natural habitat in the transatlantic expanse between the two major English-speaking cultures, successfully subjecting each to gentle satire for the amusement of the other. "To say that New York came up to its advance billing," he wrote of his adopted home, "would be the baldest of understatements. Being there was like being in heaven, without going to all the bother and expense of dying."

I grew up on the Prairies, and so I can't really do the gallivant or the sashay. If you ask my father, he will tell you that I did some pretty accomplished lollygagging, but that was all indoors and stationary. I can, however, do the trudge and the stagger because that is what snow-bound streets and stiff winds demand. I don't see myself trickling, ever, but with the right soundtrack I can probably strut a little. I can do the peculiar wide-legged flop that comes with wearing snowshoes. I can do the skate, that socks-on-hardwood slide which carries you (and the imaginary puck) from the TV room into the kitchen for dinner. I can, less willingly, do the top-of-snow scamper, the twinkle-toed small-step scurry, and various other improvised gaits that keep you from falling through even if you don't have any snowshoes. Nobody walks like that down in Georgia, I bet, where Blount was reared, because nobody had to. As that thoughtful walker Aristotle knew, when it comes to *peripatesis,* necessity is the mother of mode.

In New York, Blount and I and everyone must learn to deal with a more demanding set of perambulation vectors, a unique cluster of challenges. "To be a New York walker," Blount writes, "you have to be *big city* enough to cut through three nuns, two dogs being intimate against their walkers' wills, a four-vehicle fender-bender, and a multi-lingual fistfight without missing a beat or making *any* kind of contact with *any*body and then to take an intersection of Broadway and a major cross street in stride—diagonally against both lights—while someone is coming from the other direction pursued by transit police and a bus is turning left in your face."

Yes, and there's more still to consider. "You can't intimidate a bus," Blount adds, a little unnecessarily.

> You can't fake a bus. But you can time your cut around the bus in such a way that you're using the bus as interference. Against most cabs, you can stick pretty much to your route.... But you can't be bluffing. You've got to be clearly prepared to take the hit. And to be fair you've got to give the cab a way to avoid you without losing momentum. If you don't do that, the whole system breaks down. New York walking is like broken-field running, only it's a whole field of running backs all trying to *just barely* avoid being stopped without actually running.

Yes. Because (a) running is always a sign of failure. It is the primary, only seemingly antithetical, corollary to the don't-break-stride imperative. Running means you have mistimed something, or incorrectly calculated the extent of an obstacle and now are behind the changing light or ongoing traffic. No, no, no, no! And notice, too, the importance of the fact that (b) the system is in peril at every moment you participate in it. The cab can't break stride either, because that is the imperative of motorized traffic, especially cabs, as much as of the pedestrian kind. The process is a symbiotic form of near chaos, an ongoing half-formed critique of the city's movement-based utilitarian imperatives. Pedestrians are judging their routes based on cabs that neither slow down nor swerve beyond certain predictable limits. Drivers from out of town who start slowing down, even pausing for walkers, are a menace to everybody. It's like breaking the timing switch on a fine-tuned engine. First some pinging, then a noticeable loss of efficiency, maybe a stall, and the next thing you know, you've got plugs misfiring and pistons coming through the manifold.

These days, that particular form of human-based gridlock, the always-implicit embodied disruption of the smooth flow of traffic, happens about 11,000 times a year in New York, when a pedestrian is struck by a car or truck in this ongoing ballet-battle between walkers and drivers, the essential movement-drama of the daily streets. Naturally, when it comes right down to it, pedestrians tend to lose the battles if not always the war. Vehicle-on-walker fatalities are steady at about 200 a year, but that is still a lot even in a city where death is never far away. (Things used to be worse: In 1965, 14,846 pedestrians were injured by cars or trucks, and 438 were killed. Who says there's no progress?) Every now and then, as happened just a few months ago in midtown Manhattan, a mad driver will go on a pedestrian-bopping rampage, a personal version of *Death Race 2000*.

In its high-impact way, this is urban visionary Jane Jacobs versus the city's autocratic master-planner Robert Moses all over again, walkways against expressways, with routine jaywalking at once the urban-renewal crowd's (sometimes foolhardy) assertion of pedestrian supremacy and the everyday New Yorker's habitual expression of city sophistication. Successive mayors have tried to cut down on jaywalking with stiffer fines and public relations campaigns, but their efforts confess their own futility: These leaders know their citizens too well to think the efforts will actually work. "There's city pride associated with jaywalking," one New Yorker told a *Times* reporter not long ago. "We view people who don't do it as rubes."

But it's more than mere sophistication; it is a form of faith. That necessary full-confidence float into the busy intersection, first demonstrated to me two decades ago by a buddy from Brooklyn, is based on an iron-clad (and yet so often unfounded) belief that a path will clear, a channel open: We are, each one of us, that other Moses. As always, walking

"The city is like poetry: it encompasses all life, all races and breeds, into a small island and adds music and the accompaniment of internal engines." (E.B. White)

expresses the complicated, contrary soul of New York: it's not the languorous, aimless stroll of the *flâneur* but a walk with a more transcendental sexiness, a dream state extending well past the mundane utility and work-related speed that started you off. The *flâneur* is, after all, a kind of fugitive from implacement. Even if his pace is slow, his task is relentless and hungry; he does not want to stay still. His utopianism is one of lack, an always not-yet, that keeps him pressing for the next corner, the next stolen glimpse. As with the structure of desire itself, satisfaction is impossible, is indeed categorically ruled out. We do not see the speed-fetish of the futurists, but there is nevertheless the same feeling of discontent and predation. The *flâneur* is a hunter, and presumptively male; female walkers are coded otherwise, as streetwalkers or potential victims or, too often, both. The *flâneur* will not be hunted or importuned; he both annihilates and inhabits his lack. His gaze is constantly renewing itself, deferring its pleasure, enclosing him.

Paris is the city of the *flâneur,* and its dream-logic accommodates him in ways that New York's generalized desire does not. The rhythm of walking and jaywalking in this twentieth-century city is addictive in a different—and you want to say more liberating—way. The sense of possibility beckons constantly, but the hunting that results, the quick-pace restlessness, opens rather than encloses desire. Beneath the *flâneur*'s slowness there is a frenzy of disappointment and repression; beneath the jaywalker's press of speed there is rapture, moments of thinking about thinking. You feel you could go on forever, lost in a reverie of movement, finally lifted beyond concentration or destination, hitting cross streets and dodging dawdlers all the way into infinity (or the Bronx). This outward demonstration of big-city brashness reveals, deep within itself, a thoroughgoing spirituality—it is utopian hope in miniature, and rescued from self-defeat. Speed melts to an inner slowness, and you seem to rise up off the pavement, dancing and sliding and slashing along.

Michel de Certeau, philosopher of everyday life, did not possess Roy Blount's New York savvy, but he got the essence of city walking right. "To be lifted to the summit of the World Trade Center is to be lifted out of the city's grasp," de Certeau writes, in what is now recognizable as the high modern year of 1982. "When one goes up there, he leaves behind the mass that carries off and mixes up in itself any identity of authors and spectators. An Icarus flying above these waters, he can ignore the devices of Daedelus in mobile and endless labyrinths far below. His elevation transfigures him into a voyeur." Now the grid of the city emerges in a broad, transparent triangle flowing northward, all out in front of the 1370-foot-high gaze. And yet, from this totalizing, voyeuristic position the viewer has no choice, ultimately, but to return to ground level and walk, to create the diagrams of everyday life, Aristotle's thoughtful ramble about what it means to flourish as a human.

"The ordinary practitioners of the city live 'down below,' below the thresholds at which visibility begins," de Certeau says. "They walk— an elementary form of this experience of the city; they are walkers, *Wandermanner,* whose bodies follow the thicks and thins of an urban 'text' they write without being able to read it. These practitioners make use of spaces that cannot be seen; their knowledge of them is as blind as that of lovers in each other's arms."

They no longer see. But they walk, as they must, carving the city's narrative arcs across concrete surfaces, negotiating the urban scene's fluid but essential boundaries between public and private, anonymity and identity, possibility and limit. "The act of walking is to the urban system what the speech act is to language or to the statements uttered," de Certeau says, illuminatingly. Walking appropriates space, acts it out, establishes relations within it:

> Walking, which alternately follows a path and has followers, creates a mobile organicity in the environment, a sequence of phatic topoi.... And if it is true that the phatic function, which is an effort to ensure communication, is already characteristic of the language of talking birds, just as it constitutes the "first verbal function acquired by children," it is not surprising that it also gambols, goes on all fours, dances and walks about, with a light or heavy step, like a series of "hellos" in an echoing labyrinth, anterior or parallel to informative speech.

Walking is thus a series of yo's and so-longs, engagements and disengagements, in the often sexy conversation of the city. Think of those slight eye-lock glances at attractive strangers on the street, maybe a dozen of them in the course of a good day, that provide a few electrifying nanoseconds of romance, little flickers of interest never to be pursued. Indeed, this is not so much walking as dancing, and just as full of potential; "not a simple-minded precision dance with everyone kicking up at the same time, twirling in unison and bowing off en masse," Jane Jacobs writes, "but an intricate ballet in which the individual dancers and ensembles all have distinctive parts which miraculously reinforce each other and compose an orderly whole. The ballet of the good city sidewalk never repeats itself from place to place, and in any one place is always replete with new improvisations."

A walk, a conversation, a dance. Or perhaps, better still, the ongoing *film* that is the street scene. "New York walking isn't exercise," Blount says, "it's a continually showing make-your-own movie." Here you will see "every kind of hat, every kind of eyes, a man with *psst* tattooed on his arm." Or, in the maybe less vivid but no less true words of Herbert Muschamp, here we observe "the integrity of that most democratic, social, informational, commercial, accessible, hard-working and efficient piece of infrastructure yet devised by humankind—the New York City street." And that is why we stroll and gather where we do, in parks and on corners, lounging on stoops or indulging the mobile pleasures of this twentieth-century alteration of *flânerie,* to at once watch and create the movie of urban life, the unfolding collective grid–structured story of our being here, of life itself.

Solvitur ambulando, medieval monks liked to say: It is solved by walking.

iii. Don't Look Up

> Skyscrapers, as we all recognize, also express an aspiration towards freedom, a rising above. They may be filled with abominable enterprises, but they do transmit an idea of transcendence. Perhaps they mislead us or betray our hopes by an unsound analogy.
>
> —Saul Bellow, *More Die of Heartbreak*

There are exceptions to the don't-look-up rule, all of them notable. Just the other day walking down Fifth Avenue, I noticed people looking up at the sky behind me, in defiance of the unwritten rule. Groups were gathered on corners, waiting for lights to change, and instead of scanning oncoming traffic for left-turners or slow-starters or other instances of automotive halt, lame and lost that make for street-sized breaks in traffic, they were unabashedly gazing up at the Empire State Building. Others, walking north, were committing the unthinkable crime of looking while walking, the pedestrian equivalent of driving with your hands over your eyes. I was walking south and so should have ignored it all, but could not.

Order and proportion: the Palladian ideal at every scale.

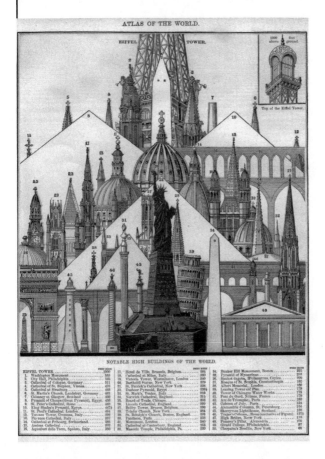

I didn't actually stop and look—places to go, people to see—but I waited for open spaces of sidewalk, stretches like an empty country road where I posed less of a danger to myself and others, and quickly craned my neck to see what had mesmerized the notoriously unimpressed, had melted the on-principle sangfroid of the Manhattanite. In quick stolen glances I saw the awesome central shaft of the Empire State, that blocky heavy-shouldered slab—so masculine and tough, almost brutal, compared with the slim spaceship grace and gorgeous Art Deco silver of the Chrysler Building—burnished gold in a bath of late-afternoon, early March sunshine. It was 5:30 and the base of the building was covered in slanting shadows thrown by the surrounding buildings, and out of the dark pedestal the high tower soared and floated in a way I have never seen before, the never-used dirigible mooring at the summit sparkling and sharply limned, seeming almost punched out physically—sharply etched—against the cold blue sky. The sun on the stone was like plasma, nearly alive, and I thought of the way the same evening glow used to cloak the neo-Gothic buildings of my university town, felt the same mix of comfort and awe.

I thought, too, that this same sight, mere months ago, might not have provoked such a devoted, unaffected reaction in the pedestrians. There is a new and sincere love-affair with the skyscraper here. There is a sense of mourning mixed into our aesthetic appreciation. To be sure, almost nobody mourns the aesthetics of Minoru Yamasaki's Twin Towers, which were banal and undistinguished, an overdone essay in bigness. Yamasaki was notoriously afraid of heights, and so it is tempting to see the towers as an elaborate exercise in revenge, or displacement. Yamasaki seemed to say: "I'm going to build the tallest building in Manhattan; it will be ugly and serviceable and starkly utilitarian. It will have no redeeming aesthetic virtues. Then, just to be certain you get my point, I'm going to do it again." But this new round of appreciation is unrelated to those arguments about scale, unrelated too to the debates about what will arise, if anything, on the site of destruction. The other day there was news of a plan to drop a nuclear bomb on Manhattan. The threats, whatever they are, have not been eliminated. We mostly forget this, because we have to: I'm walking here, I'm on my way, no time to think morbid thoughts. But looking up at the Empire State, we think: *Maybe it's you next.* And that, in its own strained way, is a look of love.

Love, as Freud said, always involves a delusional overappreciation of the love-object, a distortion of reality that papers over defects and softens the lens of judgment so that blemishes and wrinkles do not show. Inside the shafts of the fated buildings, a fury of getting and spending, an orgy of gouging and usury, of the money-world. Which is to say, The World; the center of the world. Not so much transcendent as joyfully base. Or rather, a celebration of the base and material so exhaustive and constant, so sincere and extended, that it becomes its own kind of transcendence—that, indeed, squeezes out all other kinds of transcendence. This conjoining was glimpsed early even in the now revered Rockefeller Center complex, which Lewis Mumford used as the launching pad for a well-judged stream of complaint in limpid *New Yorker* sentences, announcing himself as the city's smart, no-nonsense critic.

"Of all possible forms of the office building, the tower is the most wasteful of elevator space in proportion to floor coverage," Mumford said in 1931, indicting what Rem Koolhaas would later condemn as the culture of congestion.

> The architects who have put forth vertical transportation as a remedy for street congestion—which in turn is caused by this very overcrowding of the land—are only having their little joke. In other words, the tall skyscraper is the businessman's toy, his plaything, his gewgaw; in an expansive mood, he calls it alternatively a temple or a cathedral, and he looks upon the romantic altitudinous disorder of a modern city with the same blissful feeling that the Victorian industrialist had for his factory chimneys, belching forth soot and foul gases.

Which is to say what is obvious but often unspoken, namely that the logic of elevation as the solution to congestion is mired in self-defeat: It is an iatrogenic illness, creating the problem even as it claims to solve it. In still other, residential guises, moreover, the skyscraper has traced a depressing declension from the Radiant Cities imagined by Le Corbusier, in which (as he said) "the entire city is a Park," to the bleak, hostile reality of public-housing projects in the Bronx and Toronto's Jane-Finch corridor and Brixton and Southside Chicago, where clusters of towers throw long shadows on unused patches of grass and pedestrian-free streets, practically inviting crime and decay and hopelessness.

Above all, though, do not be fooled by the language of God that is everywhere invoked in the wake of destruction. As the man said when he asked to put the sign enjoining God's blessing on America in a Home Depot window, this is not really about God. When every pizza box carries the very same injunction, when every schoolroom in Michigan and Virginia and Utah proclaims the trust we have in God, do not be fooled that this is religion as religious people understand it. How could it be? This is, rather, the official state religion that the United States Constitution actually forbids, but diluted and made palatable in the red, white and blue tones that are now beyond question. This is patriotism by other means, acceptable theocracy, civic virtue made metaphysical. It is not a coincidence that, although the deity is not mentioned in the text of the constitution, his trust is invoked on every coin and bill of the sanctioned currency.

And so with the beautiful buildings striving skyward, folding the world of our existence into meaningful contours—the earth touches the sky and makes its height real, the long shaft connects us mortals to the divine within us. Outside, a material expression of freedom and the possible beyond. Inside, commerce and greed. Logical contradiction? False analogy? Or just the basic tensions of the world as we know it? The Empire State is, each night now, colored with red, white and blue lights. It is powerful and impossible to ignore, but many people still prefer the otherworldly sight of the Chrysler, with its sleek glow and curves of illuminated chevrons, like a perfected image of urban life: Gotham realized. In a light rain, against the never-quite-dark sky, it is graphic, gothic, iconic. Who cares what evil lurks in the hearts of its daytime inhabitants?

Don't look up!

iv. Escape from the Grid

"There's nobody else here."

—Travis Bickle in *Taxi Driver*

New York, or more specifically Manhattan, is the expired century's most appropriate emblem not least because it embodies the gridded map of late modernity's aspiration, both good and bad. The city was founded in 1623 but didn't really find itself until the 1811 Commissioners' Plan gave optimistic, if not fantastic, structure to the undeveloped land lying to the north (the city's population was then less than fifty thousand). The plan, adopted with changes and natural-setting variations in many other New World cities, including Chicago, San Francisco, Toronto and Montreal, was itself merely a localized extension of the Land Ordinance adopted by the Continental Congress in 1785, which divided all unsettled land in the United States into a massive grid of regular townships six miles square, with lines and concessions to match. Not even a continent is bigger than geometry's rule of reason.

The city soon becomes a function of its site, an upthrust mass of forced congestion and constrained aspiration, like unset concrete pressed through crisscrossed rebar, or dough squeezed through a patterned nozzle. "The overwhelming mass of its architecture, in which time crossed and mixed, did not ask for attention shyly, like Paris or Copenhagen, but demanded it like a centurion barking orders," the narrator of Mark Helprin's *Winter's Tale* says of yet another young man's arrival in the city. "Great plumes of steam a hundred stories tall, river traffic that ran a race to silver bays, and countless thousands of intersecting streets that sometimes would break off from the grid and soar over the rivers on the flight path of a high bridge, were merely the external signs of something deeper that was straining hard to be." And what is that "something deeper"? Chaos, or a higher order? Order *within* the chaos? Ambition? Transcendence, perhaps. The essence of life itself.

In any event, the grid, so apparently regular and dominating, the complete totalizing system of command and control where one is always *localizable,* a crossroads-node on a foursquare map, actually unfolds itself here into pleats of infinite possibility. The streetscape itself allows us to escape, without the aid of more explicit antisurveillance tactics offered by such pro-privacy groups as the Institute for Applied Autonomy: maps that show walkers the path of least surveillance between any two points in Manhattan, or instructions for how to disable inappropriate cameras.

"The Grid's two-dimensional discipline creates undreamt-of freedom for three-dimensional anarchy," says Koolhaas in *Delirious New York,* his sometimes cranky, sometimes loving "retrospective manifesto" for the city and its culture of congestion. Koolhaas, like Mumford and de Certeau before him, sees the grid as, at once, the realized urban panopticon, a form of imposed rationality in which you are always *somewhere in particular,* and a scene of endless contingency, whose meaning is that which cannot be controlled. It is a structure that opens and closes simultaneously. "The Grid defines a new balance between control and de-control in which the city can be at the same time

Manhattan skyline: Where are you standing right now?

ordered and fluid, a metropolis of rigid chaos," Koolhaas writes. "With its imposition, Manhattan is forever immunized against any (further) totalitarian intervention.... Manhattan is an accumulation of possible disasters that never happen."

Contrast this liberating duality with the counterargument offered by nongridded suburbs of post-1950s exurban sprawl, the achievement of late-model city planning. "The city," says Yi-Fu Tuan, "is time made visible," and the word *architecture* itself—the *archi-techton*—alludes to our originary task, our construction of the origin or overarch. But look how time gets compressed and obliterated in the vast majority of buildings from recent decades, the nostalgic enclaves of our banal postindustrial comfort. A suburb, says Lewis Mumford, at the moment of its inception, is "an asylum for the preservation of illusion." The insight is prescient. The suburb is a space of forgetting, where domesticity flourishes precisely because it succumbs to its own infantile logic: expensive comfort from which all signs of exploitation have been removed. The garage, the swimming pool, the barbecue—suburbs exist in winter too, but their images are all of summer. Patio lanterns. Tall cool drinks. A late-model convertible under the breezeway.

No wonder we love them. In the confusing can-of-worms streetscapes, where only residents—if even them—can find their way, we reverse modernity's urban dialectic. Not the freedom-within-control of the inner-city grid but a pervasive dullness within apparent freedom. Banal dreams of the future are entertained (maybe realized!) in architecture dominated by the past: pitched roofs and gable windows, manse houses set shoulder to shoulder on tiny lots, turning their backs on the street, each other, the world. This is "not merely a child-centre environment," Mumford concludes, but one "based on a childish view of the world." Suburbs sprawl the way kids do, heedless, comfortable, indulgent. Don't worry. Relax. Play. It's not yet time to grow up. Life on holiday!

The grid, for its own grown-up part, made all future planning and profit simpler than ever. The 155 parallel streets, each two hundred feet apart, and the dozen one-hundred-foot-wide north-side avenues soon carved the city into salable lots, each twenty-five by one hundred feet. "As an aid to speculation the commissioners' plan was perhaps unequaled," John W. Reps says in his study *The Making of Urban*

America, "but only on this ground can it be justifiably called a great achievement."

Everyone knows Manhattan is a cocktail. Literally, it is a mix of rye and sweet vermouth, garnished with a cherry, with its golden-brown glow and submerged bar-fruit sunset. Figuratively, it is the shaken-not-stirred mix of its people, occupations, desires and commodities: the constant movement and interchange, the ceaseless transactions of discourse, flesh, food, ideas and bodily fluids. The iconography of New York is heavily weighted toward Manhattan: the black-and-white mythopoeic images of the Chrysler, the Empire State, the Woolworth, the sun-shafted expanse of Grand Central. With some notable gritty or kitschy "downtown" exceptions (*Taxi Driver, Desperately Seeking Susan, Slaves of New York*), New York films seem always divided into one of the two large categories of black-and-white glamour and Technicolor glitter. Superficial difference aside, this is a binary function motivated by an identical and insistent mythologizing urge. Woody Allen's *Manhattan,* for instance, that black-and-white love letter to the city incidentally posing as a romantic comedy, is inconceivable in ordinary color.

Thus, in the movies, New York is apparently always in bleak mid-winter or bathed in golden autumn, but always aglow in one way or the other. In the movies, Manhattan weather is much more evident and important than it is in real life. Pedestrians are more welcome and more comfortable. All of this is at odds with circumstance. The famous 1969 urban planner's guide for Manhattan renewal fingered the essential problem in terms clearly borrowed from the alarmist Lewis Mumford, who described midtown Manhattan as "solidified chaos" and dedicated his life to making it more grassy and garden-like—a utopian mission composed of equal parts inspiration, nonsense, futility and charm. "There are few places to escape from the crowd or to relax in an open space," the planners lamented, in terms now all too familiar. "It is difficult to be visually aware of the changing seasons since there are few places to see leaves changing color, for snow to remain white. Finally, the basic elements of sunlight, natural light and fresh air are unnecessarily denied the millions who must circulate both above and below ground."

For these critics of the city's emergent late-century properties, and its tendency to grow a world of inhuman Borg-like slabs and noxious antihuman automobiles, the problem was deep-seated and philosophical mistrust of technology's power over the spirit. It is no coincidence, for example, that their words were published in the same year as Stanley Kubrick's *2001: A Space Odyssey* was released. Listen to the worry in their voices:

> The new slab city pattern is epitomized on Third Avenue. Its rows of interminable reflecting surfaces have replaced the rich texture and weather-beaten variety of its former buildings; and even Park Avenue's new-era elegance becomes tedious when every building has a plaza and every lobby is transparent. The anonymous, cool surfaces of the emerging environment seem more expressive of the new machines than of the humans who control them and whose needs for human contact remain.

The machines are taking over! The grid is bigger than all of us! This, it is worth noting, was some eight years after the cold shower delivered by Jane Jacobs, then living on Hudson Street, in *The Death and Life of Great American Cities*. Density itself, she argues, is never the enemy of urban vitality; on the contrary, if the density is mixed-use, pedestrian-friendly and entertaining, it animates the city. Jacobs's focus on success rather than failure was out of step with the ideologically minded mandarins of what is not for nothing called urban planning—as if a genuinely world-historic city could ever be *planned*. And yet, her anti-utopianism often rises to incoherent hectoring, a new kind of antinormative normativity, alive with contradiction and special pleading. "Orthodox planning is much imbued with puritanical and Utopian conceptions of how people should spend their free time, and in planning, these moralisms on people's private lives are deeply confused with concepts about the workings of cities," she writes. "The preference of Utopians, and of other compulsive managers of other people's leisure, for one kind of legal enterprise over other is worse than irrelevant for cities. It is harmful." Indeed, she rejects the very idea of architectural planning, though more with metaphor than argument: "To approach a city, or even a city neighborhood, as if it were a larger architectural problem, capable of being given order by converting it into a disciplined work of art, is to make the mistake of attempting to substitute art for life. The results of such profound confusion between art and life are neither life nor art. They are taxidermy."

Despite the grandiosity of Le Corbusier's plans—and the banal disaster they turn out to be in practice—this is not so. Planned quarters thrive in some cities, especially if they are deliberately kept at the scale Jacobs approves, namely pedestrian-friendly and low-rise, perhaps with some high-rise landmark or monument buildings for orientation and what Kevin Lynch calls "imageability." The premise here, presumably, is that people know exactly how to use their liberty, if just left alone by the "wishful frivolity" of Le Corbusier and other purveyors of "Radiant Garden City Beautiful." At the same time, Jacobs is prescriptive and withering on the American fondness for the automobile, the very thing she and the other West Villagers opposed in the Fifth Avenue extension and the West Side Highway elevation. "There is a silver lining to every-thing," she notes wryly about the car-domination threatening to domi-nate all of urban America. "In that case we Americans will hardly need to ponder a mystery that has troubled men for millennia: What is the purpose of life? For us, the answer will be clear, established and for all practical purposes indisputable: The purpose of life is to produce and consume automobiles."

The lacuna is obvious. Without planning, people's desires quickly succumb to the spirals that create exurban sprawl and automobile-dominated cities, results far more heinous than anything to be found in the utopian imagination. Jacobs wants people to be free, but only if their idea of freedom is the same as hers. At what point do eyes on the street become a new form of surveillance society, neighborhood community a kind of panopticon?

In midtown Manhattan it is indeed possible to forget that this is an island, a place, anywhere at all. Massive rectilinear Central Park, 840 acres carved out of the potentially pricey real estate by extraordi-nary acts of civic will and vision in 1858, is still bound and confined by the strictures of street and avenue, overshadowed by gothic towers and glimpses of impossibly expensive penthouse gardens or famous resi-dential hotels. Even in the very middle of the park, with its bosky undulations and curving wooded drives, it is impossible to lose sight of the fact that you are in the middle of a concrete achievement that houses eight million other people. Whereas it is all too easy to forget, standing at the corner of 42nd Street and Fifth Avenue, say, when you can see neither river nor, except in patches, sky, where the earth is all concrete, that this place was once uninhabited, the center of a humid, overgrown island.

Here and there the original sub-uniform shape reasserts itself, reminding us that the regularity of the grid is an artful imposition, an ordering (and, of course, profit-based) scheme laid over what was and still, somehow, remains a natural site. Indeed, the grid comes to be in part out of a recognition of those natural limits, the edges of the island and the water that surrounds us, most often invisibly, crowding possibilities and demanding that planners go Cartesian and then go up, up, up to achieve the densities necessary for true wealth to be created—if not distributed.

The grid goes wonky in places such as Chinatown and the West Village, down in the corners of the island, where it is still possible to get lost. The pattern of its regularity, struggling out of the still wayward mass of the city's oldest neighborhoods, doesn't really come clear until 14th Street, except on the east side around Tompkins Square Park and the East Village. It's as if the city wandered around for a while, loitered and strolled and messed about, before finding its stride and taking off northward, into the uncharted expanse of the island, with a regular gait. Once you are on the grid, walking north can feel like climbing a ladder, taking you onward and upward, first to the riches of midtown and then to the comforts of the Upper West Side, all the way to an attic of poverty in the city's northerly corners.

The regularity collapses, as if from the weight of building and wealth and aspiration carrying on above it. Here you may get lost even in the city in which you live—something Benjamin regarded with a special kind of awe, writing of his native Berlin. Getting lost in London or Venice is no great challenge; getting lost in New York feels like an achievement, a gift. In the West Village, where I used to live, the streets are tangled and sometimes even curved—they refuse the logic of uniformity. Most of them have proper names (Bedford, Morton, Barrow, Bleecker), but some retain, as if for a joke, the system's names while evading the system's plan. West 4th, for instance, my street, slides across Manhattan in a roughly westward line and then cuts northeast at a sharp angle, such that, just feet in either direction from my front door, it crosses both West 10th and West 11th streets, which are themselves cutting down toward the Hudson in an antic southwesterly manner. A whole wide slab of the map on the West Side here is cut loose from the rough north–south orientation of the rest of Manhattan, instead lining itself up parallel to the river. And at the edges of this capricious chunk of

Le Corbusier's *Ville Contemporain* (1922), or City for Three Million Inhabitants: sixty-story cruciform skyscrapers with glass-curtain walls and steel frames, set in vast parkland, reached via a central transportation hub.

land, the join is herky-jerky and weird, as if two pieces of otherwise square cabinetry had been haphazardly glued together at forty-eight or so degrees.

When I first moved here and was learning my way, I had a series of predictable mishaps: walking too far south before cutting over, having to backtrack, choosing maximally inefficient routes from my big, shabby, luxuriously quiet apartment in the West Village to the office up near Gramercy Park or a nearby bar on Barrow Street or Eighth Avenue. At the same time, like all residents of New York, however short term, I prided myself on my mastery of the city's geography. It goes without saying that I never asked for directions or carried a map, always walking with a determined and purposeful stride even when I wasn't entirely sure of myself. As a result, I was asked for directions often. I answered the requests with a cheerful certainty that was often out of step with accuracy, and I would walk away from these encounters—almost immediately realizing I had just sent the hapless pedestrian on a path in defiance of the laws of physics, successful completion of which would involve either deployment of teleportation devices or permeable bricks and brownstone—with a sense of profound satisfaction. I always had a feeling that it was just a second too late to turn back and correct myself, my inept Virgil's version of *l'esprit d'escalier*. I built gates where no gates could be found—an urban libertarian's dream. We all wish to do this, to walk through walls, to make everything solid melt in air. Sometimes just to get where we are going more quickly, more efficiently; but also, and maybe more profoundly, to get where we can only imagine we might find ourselves.

Jane Jacobs says it is one of the signs of a functional, civil public space that people will offer directions to the obviously lost without being asked. And she is right—but only if the directions help. In later days I tried to resist the temptation to offer directions to people, even when I had come to know the neighborhood well. *If they don't ask,* I said to myself while passing clearly perplexed map-scrutinizers emerging from the subway at Christopher Street, *I won't tell.* But it was hard.

v. Pity New York

Cities are, by definition, full of strangers.

—Jane Jacobs, *The Death and Life of Great American Cities*

In a long-ago philosophy paper, a colleague argued vividly against the thesis of total indeterminacy in human affairs, and for the necessary presence of the shared lifeworld, by means of a Manhattan example. Against all evidence of chaos and diversity in belief, he argued that there are certain things we share even without knowing that we do or what they are.

Suppose you were lost in the city, without money or means of communication, and had to meet the one person who could help you. With no way of contacting this person—your brother, your accountant, your social worker—how would you do it? It's a vast city, after all, and there are so many ways to lose yourself even in the logical grid: to lose your way, your money, your marbles. Where do you go? How do you effect the hookup?

There is a right answer to this question, as a survey of people discovered. You go to Grand Central Terminal, at noon, and wait by the famous clock-capped information kiosk in the middle of the Grand Concourse. Of course you do. Your party will be there, too, because she also knows that this is *the right answer*. This is not so because of some configuration of the universe but, rather, because within the logic established by the city, the many superimposed grids of urban sense-making, this is what counts as the correct answer. It is conventional, not metaphysical; but it is not contingent because it could not be otherwise.

And that, finally, is New York's great gift to us: a shining manifestation, a joyful and apparently inevitable working-out, of the passing century's possibilities. It was, in every sense, the right answer. And the destructive events of the millennial year make that more obvious, not less.

The T-shirts and commercials now everywhere to be seen read (with the famous heart symbol signing love for NY), "I love New York more

The right answer.

than ever," as though to emphasize the love that is undiminished by fear or anxiety, by the body blow to the city's self-regard. The heart carries a little bruise, a shadow of hurt, on one side near the tip. But notice how the sentiment betrays its own weakness even as it insists on this "more." In the old days, "I love New York" was an expression of defiant regard, a claim about one's insider status. New York was widely reviled, a symbol alternatively of urban decay, gross corruption or cultural arrogance, and so to love it was to proclaim one's sophistication, or willingness anyway to accept the grit and hatred-from-beyond as reasonable cost for living here. It was the genteel equivalent of an actually far more common New York claim (or injunction)—"Fuck you!"

To say you love something *more than ever* is to admit that it might not be worth your love any more, that you might be *expected* to love it less—love it despite its weaknesses, say, or by overcoming presumed, perhaps unvoiced, objections. Why should we love New York more than ever, after all, now that one end of its famous skyline has been brought low? Well, because it has been attacked and brutalized, and we are standing by it. But that is sympathetic love, compassionate love, the love of reassurance (for ourselves and for the city). There was a time when the sentiment would have been out of place, would have made no sense. Now, it is a sign on the surface of a new form of defiance even as, underneath, it lets out a whisper of sadness.

Sympathy is even, as *The New York Times* reported not long ago, the city's new tourism hook: "The destruction of the World Trade Center has emerged as a powerful selling point for New York City," the story begins, "invoked again and again to make the case that big events like the Super Bowl, the Grammy Awards ceremony and a proposed joint meeting of Congress all belong in New York." Not to mention the World Economic Forum and maybe the next Summer Olympics. And it is working, at Ground Zero and in midtown and in the newly Shanghaied, or Hong Konged, version of Times Square. Once seedy, now awash in great slabs of neon and twenty-four-hour-a-day pixilated news, sports and advertising, Times Square hosts the sympathetic tourists—herds of nearly identical girls with long straight hair, big shoes and little skirts, off to the theater; gangs of slow-moving, ball-capped Southerners recording all the moving pictures on their Sony digicams, liquid crystal displays soaking up all that ambient light. It is garish, beautiful and, finally, prosaic.

Sympathy marketing is savvy, to be sure, but also sad. *Now more than ever.* Once upon a time in the West, it was enough just to proclaim your love for New York: It was aggressive and loyal and a little bit cool. That time is gone, and New York love has changed along the way. "New Yorkers surrender to empathy," Koolhaas writes.

> The tragedy of 9/11 inspires a mood of collective tenderness that is almost exhilarating, almost a relief: hype's spell is broken and the city can recover its own reality principle, emerge with new thinking about the unthinkable. But politics interfere [and] the transnational metropolis is enlisted in a national crusade. New York becomes a city (re)captured by Washington. Through the alchemy of 9/11, the authoritarian morphs imperceptibly into the totalitarian.

The time of unquestioned, unquestioning urban supremacy is over; New York, no longer an incubator of dreams, becomes a spectral colony, an imperial theme park. A century ends. The capital shifts.

Still true?

I ♥ NY
MORE
THAN
EVER

3.
Public Spaces, Public Places

i. The Triumph of Postmodernism

It is a truism, but a worthwhile one to note, that the concept of postmodernism was adumbrated in architecture before appearing elsewhere. Postmodernism concerned language and style before it was a condition or a form of knowledge suitable to, or demanding of, report: the difference between postmodernism as an aesthetic and postmodernity as a state of affairs. The specifically architectural use of the adjective is distinct from, and narrower than, both the familiar literary applications and the "incredulity towards metanarratives" analyzed by Jean-François Lyotard. In architecture, the postmodern is a natural extension, usually critical, of the modern orthodoxy; it refers, often indeterminately, to a cluster or trend of building designs that sought release from the rigid sleekness of normative architectural modernism by mixing and quoting various styles and through liberal use of materials. Frank Lloyd Wright's organicism, for example, is transitional in a wide historical sweep that moves from the utopian aspirations of Le Corbusier and the gestural ones of Mies van der Rohe to the contextualism and allusiveness characteristic of late-century building.

Such narratives are, of course, themselves worthy of suspicion, if not incredulity; they are, like the detective's solution, imposed after the fact as a form of libidinal release under the aegis of telling a coherent story, which is to say, *making sense.* And yet, despite differences of specificity in usage, the mixture of bricolagiste style with a perceived collapse of undiluted "rational" aspiration makes postmodern architecture not unlike postmodern thought more generally. As with the often remarked but never resolved slippage between modernism (in architecture, in poetry) and modernity (in politics, in society), the style is a fitting and dynamic relative, perhaps codeterminant, of the historical condition. Postmodern architecture is, at least in part, an intellectual reaction against the perceived failure of utopian social-revolutionary agendas associated with Le Corbusier and Mies (and, less accurately, Wright). "The new buildings of Le Corbusier and Wright did not finally change the world, nor even modify the junk space of late capitalism," the critic Fredric Jameson writes, "while the Mallarmean 'zero degree' of Mies's towers quite unexpectedly began to generate a whole overpopulation of the shoddiest glass boxes in all the major urban centers of the world."

This is what we may label "the standard view," with an aggressive and idealistic modernism burning itself out in an excess of postwar construction, such that critics soon saw that "its Utopian ambitions were unrealizable and its formal innovations exhausted." So the story goes.

Jean Nouvel's Opéra national de Lyon,
France (1993).

And according to this dominant narrative—a narrative which is at once contingent and necessary—architecture now progressed, or anyway moved on, from this adolescent utopian ambition and onto a different stylistic crisis. The leading figures were now united not on anything like a shared style, or even a theory, but in what might be called an *attitude*, in many cases meeting the conditions of displacement and disintegration characteristic of globalized development with a large-scale and stylistically novel form of building. Architectural theorists Marc Augé and Hans Ibelings, among others, have labeled it "supermodernism," citing the buildings of Jean Nouvel and Dominique Perrault. These constructions are often found as part of the centerless conurbation Charles Jencks dubbed the "heteropolis," the City-of-Tomorrow masses in Berlin's Potsdamer Platz and Shanghai's Pudong New City, often exhibiting what I have labeled "monumental-conceptual architecture"—signature buildings, many of them gestural, on a vast scale. This is, we might say, architecture of meganarrative, not metanarrative.

Shanghai's Pudong New City as seen from the Bund, in Puxi.

Consider some prominent recent examples. The Berlin-based architect Daniel Libeskind was briefly in the public eye for his World Trade Center reconstruction project and subsequent ouster by David Childs of Skidmore, Owings & Merrill, the long-standing skyscraper master-firm from Chicago, who gained control of that much-disputed project. Libeskind is also the muse behind a less spectacular project, the three-year, Can$150-million renovation—or "renaissance"—of the Royal Ontario Museum (ROM) in Toronto. In both designs Libeskind has shown himself a master of high-profile success in the current architectural market. The ROM project especially, a striking crystalline outline, is a good example of the sort of mutation a recent vogue for distinctive, high-profile architecture, often in museums, has created—though it was not included in a 2003 Berlin retrospective exhibition of Libeskind's designs, the crystal design represented instead by the similar Victoria and Albert Museum renovation, since abandoned.

Such architectural megaprojects, including Frank Gehry's Bilbao Guggenheim, Peter Eisenman's Wexner Center for the Arts at Ohio State University and the City of Culture of Galicia in Santiago de Compostela, and Libeskind's Jewish Museum in Berlin, exert an influence disproportionate to their number, becoming the focus of most recent nonacademic (and much academic) debate about architecture. With the possible exception of airports, a more obvious supermodern site, museums emerged as the central *Baustellung,* the dominant form of the new century. To be sure, far more building is in fact being done in more banal forms, notably the many dozens of high-rise residential and office towers rising everywhere, from London's Canary Wharf to Shanghai's far-flung suburbs to Toronto's waterfront; but this great volume of undistinguished square-footage, surely more indicative in its mediocre way of the dreary downside of supermodernism, does not acquire the status of a signature building—literally does not signify—and so fails to be noticed.

This cannot be surprising; the position of megaprojects astride major public spaces makes the projects highly visible, all the more so because they are supported usually by public money and municipal concessions. Like all urban architecture, they belong to everyone, including future generations. In many cases, they are driven by form rather than content. The Bilbao Guggenheim, for example, was not built to house

Destination architecture: Frank Gehry's Guggenheim Bilbao, Spain (1997).

or display an existing collection—there was none—but as a U.S.\$100-million, 256,000-square-foot end in itself. The Galician centre, with a projected cost of \$125 million and 810,000 square feet, also has no existing collection, selling itself instead on the 173-acre mountaintop site and Eisenman's thrusting stone walls that one commentator describes as looking "as if they were pushed right up through the earth." The irony in play is not precisely postmodern but is nevertheless striking. The public warehouse of artifacts, itself a modern invention dedicated to democratized cultural sophistication, offered a narrative of general diffusion and edification as private collections became public in well-marked public places. Now it is self-displaced by the museum as artifact, the so-called destination building visited more for its exterior than after anything within. Functionally, such museums might as well remain empty.

The philosopher and art critic Arthur Danto, prompted by the aggressive antimonumental façade of the Museum of Modern Art on West 53rd Street in Manhattan, half-foresaw this development. MoMA (the name itself a self-conscious familiarity, like a chummy romper-room tag) reduced a previously grandiose institution, the art museum, to just another midtown storefront, a signal of resistance. Danto proposed that a notional "museum of museums" would trace such lines of change from deliberately intimidating beaux arts neoclassicism, with long staircases and columns consonant with edifying Great Masters, to clean-limbed modernist skepticism, suitable to Pollock or Klee. What Danto did not, and could not, see was that the museums themselves would usurp the bulk of attention and dispense with the works entirely, outstripping them in a media-saturated aura economy.

All the mentioned projects, and others of even more recent vintage— Diller + Scofidio's Museum of Contemporary Art in Boston and, still more, their temporary Blur Building on Lake Neuchatel at Yverdon-les-Bains, Switzerland, a "structure" that existed only as a man-made fog mass suspended above a ramped bridge—share a penchant for the monumental-conceptual. Moreover, many of the now familiar architectural stars hard at work securing and realizing such large-scale public commissions were first celebrated in a 1988 show at the Museum of Modern Art in New York, assembled by Philip Johnson and guided by Eisenman, which marked a development of modernism from within its own radical wings. Gehry, Libeskind and Eisenman were joined in the show by Zaha Hadid, Rem Koolhaas, Bernard Tschumi and Wolf Prix of Coop Himmelb(l)au. (Many of these practitioners have, in recent years, been awarded architecture's most prestigious prize, the Pritzker: Koolhaas in 2002, and Hadid in 2003.) The personalities of such figures are indispensable to the cultural contradictions typical of supermodernism. Its uneasy but necessary celebration of a Great Man stereotype, a visionary hero, is often communicated synedochically by their preliminary sketches, which become tropes of genius sold on T-shirts, baseball caps and the like in the museum gift shop—the frozen gesture of genius, swiftly commodified.

This superstructure of aesthetic romanticism, updated via technology, rests atop a diversified but invisible base of labor and capital, usually an undisclosed mixture of public and private. Donors are landed by their desire to consort with genius, to ally themselves with a vision. Thus the institutional pressure from all sides to maintain and extend the Great Man myth, the meganarrative, is considerable. A second-order contradiction, indeed pathology, arises when a perceived outsider

Diller + Scofidio's Blur, Swiss Expo (2002).

Concrete Reveries

who attempts criticism of the works is personally attacked in return, or disallowed from the debate—a clear sign of subcutaneous unease about the "genius" of the designs and the hermetic circle around them. Sometimes these counterstrikes come in a form of accusations using the very categories the critic challenged: the benefits of an economy of celebrity, (lack of) visionary status, the importance of preliminary sketches, and so on. Such charges are, to say the least, confused.

ii. Monumental-Conceptual Architecture

Monumental-conceptual architecture is not to be confused with simple theoretical architecture. Waves of theory-driven architecture are hardly new, with ideas borrowed liberally from fashionable philosophical works emanating mainly from Paris, Bologna and Berlin—Eisenman's use of Chomsky, Derrida and Vattimo; Tschumi's debt to Debord and the situationists; Diller + Scofidio's Lacanian probes; everyone's use of Heidegger and Benjamin. From the admittedly judgmental perspective of professional philosophy, such "theory" architects and, especially, their lesser acolytes, often appear to be little more than intellectual magpies, distracted by anything shiny and new. In this they might be said merely to follow, perhaps to refine, a tendency already deeply inscribed in the collective practice of architect talk, what the critic Nathan Silver memorably describes as "a bit like advertising, with ideals and cultural pretensions added ... as if dug out from a kitchen midden of contemporary jargon, ideological polemic, historical reference, and some overcolored scenic description."

Architect talk, says Silver, "is not an orderly string of words but a field ... a landscape" in which any available marker, or sign, may be seconded to service. Its primary function is not thought itself but, rather, influence on the outcome of a complicated decision that will create something providing, at its best, the occasion for thought. Thus the relentless shifting of reference points, a restless sense of novelty, as theorists and, indeed, individual concept words fall in and out of fashion. Hannah Arendt was once the de rigeur theory touchstone and is no longer, having been shouldered aside by, as it might be, Deleuze and

Guattari or Castells—a fate that has also befallen her work in political-theory circles. In this sense, architect talk, and so *a fortiori* architect theory, is always already unmoored from the dock of sense, more a phatic performance, and exchange of blank tokens, than the communication and debate of ideas.

The theory-driven architects of the late postmodern exemplify this tendency in a manner and to a degree that Silver himself could not have fully anticipated writing in the late 1970s and not yet reckoning on voguish intellectual trends or, rather, the trendy versions of intellectual positions still to come. But at least the debts incurred by these architects were, in most cases, openly stated, and sometimes added to the complexity of the thoughts the buildings occasioned—surely as much as can reasonably be asked. If a Derridean building or Deleuzian blob-and-fold structure should prove to be less interesting in reality than in theory, well, so what? One could always simply note the theory, judge the building on its merits and move on. Nor was the theoretical cross-pollination all for show. Many of the most successful buildings of the past twenty years, especially Hadid's and (some of) Gehry's, are minor masterpieces of situation, transforming sites with mixed materials and arresting spaces in a manner unavailable to either modernist or postmodernist styles. Even here, however, a certain sameness emerges, especially in hotel and airport designs—paradigmatic supermodern locations. The ubiquity of "warm" millwork, stained wood slats, rounded armchairs and brushed-steel handrails reduces them to banal signifiers of "luxury" or "prestige," those Asian-minimalist inflections that project the glossy look of upmarket retail locations and frequent-flier hotel lobbies alike, unvarying from Zürich or London to Sydney or Hong Kong.

The newest large-scale works pose a somewhat different problem, one characteristic of the postmodern–supermodern shift. Though Johnson's MoMA show grouped Gehry, Koolhaas, Libeskind and the rest under the banner of deconstructionist literary theory, in fact the group is united only in its facility with ideas and subsequent success, especially in highly contested museum commissions. With open theory-debts now somewhat out of fashion, architects of the first order have taken to selling their game in terms of concepts rather than theories—a sketch or simulacrum of theory, a theory of theory, where ideas are often unmoored and scattered (and also, to be fair, sometimes brilliant and bold). The theory sketch and the literal sketch are related insofar as the latter becomes a signifier (albeit a false one) of possession of or mastery over the former, and hence its susceptibility to the very consumeristic reproduction that renders it null. Theory/concept is a fine distinction, yes, but we might say that is a matter of responsibility. Theory, whatever else it does, makes demands of a sort that still themselves signify, despite any antimodern efforts to the contrary. Theory demands coherence, consistency in application and defensibility. Concepts, as I shall use the term, and the monumental-conceptual

Self-conscious posing on one of Bernard Tschumi's follies in Parc de la Villette, Paris (1982–87): deconstructing meaning by disrupting line and order.

architecture they allow, are free-floating and undemanding, such that the mere play of ideas, the juggling of concepts, is seen as a sufficient justification, an end in itself. Postmodern architecture was not conceptual in this sense; it was, approve the adjective or not, theoretical.

The question then becomes: Are the monumental-conceptual works living up to the responsibility of public money and public attention, or are they large-scale con games feeding the self-indulgence of a new breed of installation artists, the architect as seer? To answer that question we must not only examine current architectural practice but also appreciate the breaches that have occurred in the notion of public space. Although much of the rhetoric of late-modern debate was and is condemnatory of current urban experience, it is far from obvious that calls for returns to public space, or enlarged versions thereof, are valid—or, anyway, are free of lingering vestiges of a utopianism we might regard as bogus or unsupported. Nor, for that matter, is it immediately clear that a more implaced or situated architecture is the answer to alleged losses in democratic accountability or individual connection to the built environment. Here, indeed, modernist narratives of emancipation and participation linger far past their dismantling in other quarters. Nevertheless, we must take seriously the calls for a vibrant public sphere and subject them to the close attention that neither architectural monumentalism—often self-congratulatory and self-indulgent—nor everyday denunciations of style—often shortsighted and driven by narrow grievance—allow.

The issue is considerably complicated by the dynamic between style and substance or, rather, by style, in architecture, being a substantive issue. While the very idea of style is regarded with dismay or even disdain by many architects anxious not to have theirs cramped by expectations arising from previous buildings, it is nevertheless employed by them to divide the field of building, past and present, as minutely (if not as precisely) as the language of construction orders the parts and tasks of building itself. In this latter case of precise language-use the imperatives are straightforward, indeed almost Wittgensteinian. We move from block, slab, pillar, beam and "I want you to bring me a slab"—the apparent beginnings of language in Wittgenstein's *Philosophical Investigations*—to finer grades of meaning-use realized by finials, cladding, aedicules, dentils, annulets, modillions and mutules.

Style-designators can be as narrow, but they are rarely as uncontroversial—or as useful. Charles Jencks, himself responsible for more than a few style-signs becoming widespread, among them "postmodern" itself, both parodies and celebrates the semiotics of architecture through fanciful gestures of naming in his entertaining book *Daydream Houses of Los Angeles*: "Spreadwing Cadillac," "Ronchamp Ski-jump with Mushroom Overtones," "Topiary Fascist." This might be considered the bright side of the very same "junk lingo" condemned by critics, with its "nouning" of verbs (a "merge," a "surround"), fashionable logico-philosophical inflections and agglutinative neologisms, often in German. These are—to use a building term already appropriated by biology, among other discourses—spandrels: features of an edifice that serve no obvious purpose.

There can be no simple diagram for how verbal language meets visual language here (or indeed elsewhere), and philosophical discourse is hardly free from the very same forms of necromantic obfuscation found in architectural discourse. There can, moreover, be no clear line between a necessary piece of technical language and a bit of jargon employed to elevate the speaker and intimidate the listener. The real

Topiary: part of the new organic materials palette?

issue must always be how, or how well, architecture serves the common good—a central concern at least since Vitruvius attempted to understand the meaning of architecture and thus created a language of architecture. ("If this ethical concern is difficult to recognize," Alberto Pérez-Gómez writes rather hopefully, "it is because it is internal to the practice of architecture rather than an external adjunct to some formalistic or technical activity.")

We should therefore pose two cardinal questions for any practical language or sign-system oriented to the politics of the built environment: (1) Does it make thought more or less likely, and (2) Does it exclude for the sake of exclusion? These questions, and these questions alone, can help us understand a public sphere that, though everywhere being materially constructed, remains spectral.

iii. Architecture and Politics

The political dimensions of the Cartesian legacy are hard to overestimate, though many do their level best to underestimate them—itself a political move on the order of other ideological erasures. Architecture poses special problems for political theory, for while it affects everyone, not everyone can affect it. Indeed, experience appears to show that it is a civic mistake to try. Witness, for example, the tangle of conflicting interests that clustered around the World Trade Center reconstruction, a series of squabbles and rejected shortlists that sadly resembled an academic committee meeting. Although it is always a collective practice—a meeting of creative mind and constructive body—architecture thrives on leaps of imagination, ruthless ambition and the unlikely conjunction of money, ideas and opportunity.

The sustaining myth of current monumental-conceptual architecture, overturning the "organizational anonymity" of the postwar period, is the cult of the celebrity-architect, understood to be one part rogue genius and one part savvy media manipulator: Howard Roark crossed with Andy Warhol. This phenomenon has shown all the dismal signs of a standard mass-culture feedback loop, such that, as in all phantom economies, even stories dissing the celeb architects become part of the system of celebrity. Architectural discourse disappears inside successive self-reflexive spirals, obscuring the real questions of community-creation and economic impact posed by large civic buildings: How is public space affected? How is the given city as a whole benefited? How is your experience, and mine, altered by this new place, this addition to our shared horizon of concern, the cityscape? Architects tend to view their work either as a matter of material manipulation, entirely devoid of ideational responsibility, or, fleeing to the opposite pole, as a kind of art form immune from outside challenge or evaluation. Neither attitude is helpful when we want to assess architecture in its real context, as the occasion for thought, the embodiment of political consciousness, the enabler of (or barrier to) vibrant citizenship.

Architectural beauty belongs to what Arthur Danto calls the "third realm" of beauty: the realm of application, where beauty is neither natural (sunsets and fields) nor purely artistic (the so-called fine arts). It is fair to say, given that this realm also includes fashion, advertising, design, cosmetics, interior decoration and much of everyday visual culture, that it is a far more significant feature of urban life than the other two combined—in volume, certainly, but also politically. There are political issues in fine art too, of course, but generally they concern the basic question of whether (or sometimes, less often, how) such art should be political. In the third realm, beauty is always political because it always addresses, in some manner, how to live. Third-realm beauty may be aspirational, admonitory or inspiring. It may, too, frequently, be merely consumeristic. It may be all of these at once. But it is in this realm that urbanites realize whatever remains of the old Platonic connection between beauty and justice, occupying their public spaces to negotiate the daily business of being citizens together, finding inspiration and provocation alike in their shared surroundings.

Architecture, more than the other aspects of the third realm, must grapple with these political implications. It is, after all, a form of aesthetic immortality, inflicting itself on future generations and shaping thought and action for decades, sometimes centuries. (An artwork need not appeal to anyone, Adolf Loos said, but a house is responsible to each and every one of us.) Architecture is insistent, inescapable, assertive. Few paintings, and even fewer books as time goes on, can hope to do as much. And the sad truth is that a bad or banal building can easily last as long as, and sometimes far longer than, a good one. Architecture exists not in the isolated context of autonomous art, where the universe of meaning inherent in a painting, say, is contextualized only by other paintings, but in a larger and more complex context where its boundaries with the street, the cityscape, the world of social meaning are permeable and fluid. You must walk around and through the building as well as gaze at it; your physical body is always implicated in its created spaces. But that body is also your socialized body, an intersubjective fact similarly involved in negotiating relations with others through their myriad postures: coworkers, visitors, consumers, lovers, citizens. The building stands firm, perhaps representing but also disclosing—creating, shaping—social relations over time.

That endurance, sometimes painful, possibly uplifting, is part of what Arendt means when she recognizes the city as a "worldly artifice" that

Palace of the Soviets, 1934: the triumph of superheroic scale.

А В О Р Е Ц   С О В Е Т О В   С. С. С. Р.

can provide the durable site for our "comings and goings" as mortal creatures. The durable world is "a non-mortal home for mortal beings"; like great art and literature, it extends "a premonition of immortality … something immortal achieved by mortal hands." Durability is essential to the city's ability to ground our projects, to give them life beyond an individual span. Sometimes, indeed, architecture itself becomes the trans-mortal project, as in the generation-occupying construction of medieval cathedrals: Meaning is achieved not by witnessing completion but by participation in the service of an imagined completion. Arendt calls this durability "reification," using the term positively for once, as against the more common notion of reification as the distortions typical of power, the rendering of a current arrangement into "how things are," the exposure of which is the usual job of critical theory. Architecture in its civic role is reification redeemed, public space created and so, finally, politics enabled. Just as democracy is the only reliable safeguard of architecture, architecture is the only reliable site of democracy.

Or it might be. Arendt herself does not pursue this lead, and so leaves her emphasis on politics as conducted in a "space of appearances," an apparently abstracted public space that, notwithstanding the claims of civic durability, seems to have no concrete, that is to say, architectural, rendering. (This despite the use of the phrase in Baird's title.) There is, she argues, a different and more important kind of immortality in the thoughts and deeds of mortal persons via the enacted narratives of life. This is the essence of politics: collective human action as a durable achievement, almost a form of art. But architecture remains, on this view, pre-political. It may enable thoughts and deeds but cannot create them. Public space is a central concept of Arendtian politics, but it is a space that does not advance us very far from the abstractions typical of more traditional political theory. Arendt does not, as it were, take public space seriously as a *real* place.

She is far from alone in this. Discussions of public space, when conducted by political theorists, tend to originate in ideas about the "public sphere," a notional space in which claims are made, objections raised, dialogue attempted. In one influential version of this idea, the public sphere is the place where all those affected by a decision are allowed to articulate their interests, this participation alone defining justice. The interests themselves are channeled and molded by the constraints of reason, understood both as rationality (consistency, fairness) and reasonableness (willingness to acknowledge the interests of the other). Jürgen Habermas and John Rawls, the two dominant political thinkers of the twentieth century's latter half, both defend versions of this public sphere, and, despite many important differences, share a Kantian debt in the idea of public reason. Political theorists have largely accepted the cogency of this idea; yet, objections are rife. Some are relatively minor and can be solved, or anyway managed, with extensions and refinements of the theory: Who speaks for those who cannot speak themselves because of handicap or delusion? What if there is no agreement on what counts as reason? What if the most powerful media of information are systematically distorted, twisting the facts and arguments available to citizens? But some objections are even more searching and throw the idea into larger doubt; Arendt's is one of these. The public sphere is, I have said, a notional space. That is not to say it is nonexistent, just that it is a space of discourse rather than of physical occupation. Where do we find it?

Speaker's Corner, Singapore: Nothing to say?

Well, in courtrooms and parliaments and constitutional discussions; also, perhaps, in voting booths and television talk shows and the op-ed pages of newspapers. Certainly in seminar rooms and lecture halls. But, having visited or occupied most of those spaces myself, I can tell you what you already know: The powerful ones are only rarely rational, and the rational ones still more rarely powerful. Moreover, access to many of these spaces is limited; they are not, with the exception of the polling booth, the presumptive province of each and every citizen.

Such an awareness of democratic limits might prompt another thought about extension: that the solution to the problem of the public sphere is to widen its scope, enlarge its horizon. But the thought quickly goes into tailspin, not least because the idea of full participation is, depending on your political proclivities, either utopian or dangerous (or both). Habermas speaks, in a familiar Kantian vein, of the regulative ideal of reason, the distant star by which we steer our practical ship. But even if we accept the cogency of the ideal, its regulative power is much diminished, if not obliterated, if most citizens lack access to its implementation. In any case, the regulative ideal of reason, although we might accept its theoretical connection to justice if given world enough and time in the seminar room, remains rather thin political soup. It stirs few hearts and builds no walls.

The public sphere, we are forced to conclude, is another disciplinary abstraction, an academic chimera. For notice that the "citizens" who are thought to occupy it are themselves attempted political versions of the isolated modern consciousness, and the imagined space itself is an ultimate x–y abstraction, not even a two-dimensional drawing but an omni-dimensional one. The public sphere in this conception is a non-spatial space populated with consistent, articulate and well-intentioned persons whose particular interests are sufficiently plastic as to be funneled through a grid of debate. In Rawls's early version of the theory, isolating intuitions about fairness, persons were asked to distance themselves from their own identities: choosing a basic social structure from a position of deracinated ignorance, where they don't know who, in particular, they are. The idea is that such limits on knowledge will generate just rules because nobody will want to find themselves at a disadvantage once the veil of ignorance is lifted. The procedure is fair, certainly; accurate, never. Subsequent revisions failed to solve the basic

problem of how such a process can have critical bite on an irrational and chaotic world. In the words of one critic, pursuing this abstract line of thought, political philosophy has "condemned itself to political nullity and intellectual senility."

iv. Post-Utopian Dreams

And so the Arendtian thought about public space arises as an apparent challenge to this pervasive rationality abstraction. It focuses on public spaces as lived realities. But the challenge does not go far enough. Lacking a concrete engagement with architecture, it allows the "space of appearances" to remain ultimately as unreal as the public sphere of reason.

Rather than reforming political debate, let us examine the real spaces where debate can happen. Architecture has endured its own share of utopian difficulties, of course, but it has the virtue—or we should perhaps say, the possible virtue, for nothing is guaranteed—of reality. Architectural thinking may be utopian in the pejorative sense, but architecture itself never is. For better or worse, it is right in front of us, a persistent fusion of useful and useless that "indicates a utopian perspective inherent in architecture," as the critical theorist Albrecht Wellmer suggests. Architecture always both asserts itself and points beyond itself; it at once creates the thresholds of space and asks for their supervention. It achieves utility—sheltering, producing, enabling leisure—without ever freeing itself, or us, from aesthetic provocation. Aesthetic imagination, says Wellmer, is in architecture "in the service of articulating, clarifying, and structuring and thereby transforming contexts of utility, with the aim of *making sense* of them"—as in making them both perceptible and intelligible.

Indeed, a given piece of architecture was often here before us and will likely be here when we are gone, so short is our individual stay. Unlike political participation, even on a positive (some would say romantic) view of able and dedicated democratic citizens, architecture is *not optional*. It influences us in countless ways both obvious and subtle. We cannot understand ourselves without it, for this is where we eat and sleep and work and raise our children. And we cannot understand the built environment without confronting ourselves: not rational abstractions thinking rationally, but embodied persons. Persons, that is to say, with an upright posture that gives us left and right, in front of and behind, down and up; persons who find some rooms oppressive and others uplifting, some spaces intimidating and others cozy; persons who perspire and breathe, laugh or grow angry while waiting in traffic. Persons who cross boundaries and enact them too, in the embodied, temporal being that they are.

Studies in form: the human body under stress.

Buildings are more than edifices; they are locations. They gather the surrounding bodies and landscapes and bind them in relationship, redeploying and repositioning everything around them. A bridge, Heidegger says, expresses the fourfold of earth, sky, mortals and divinities; it crosses a chasm or river and folds two landscapes together, enabling movement and other human projects. All constructions have this potential, especially if linked in some way to the expression of spiritual aspiration or devotion: the temple, the cathedral, the skyscraper. Even the simplest building entails the creation of space, and so of meaning. Buildings structure interiors within an exterior, and although they might be composed of materials such as concrete, glass and steel, they are actually *made of thresholds*; they could exist but for the presumed crossing and recrossing of the boundaries they embrace.

This is the way a building *condenses culture* in one place. Like the body itself, which is always cultural and social as well as physical, it pleats presuppositions and ideas and relationships into a material fold, a container of meanings. Just as persons are not locations (though they may be localized), buildings are not containers (though they may hold things, and persons, secure within them). A house is not a bunker; it contains people only provisionally, and for a moment. All buildings are *open*. They are permeations. That is why, as Heidegger says, you do not get closer to the being of a building merely by going inside it. Nor, he might have added, by regarding it from outside.

Modernist architecture tried, with partial success, to embrace this structural energy of inside and out. Thus its techniques of distortion, reversal, floating planes and massive cantilevers that try to hide or obscure the materiality of buildings. Internal ducting or service gutting may be brazenly put on view instead of hidden. Glass, along with ferro-concrete and tempered steel, the great material of the twentieth century, creates a constant series of threshold experiences: in Philip Johnson's Glass House, in every mid-century glass-curtain skyscraper. As early as the Eiffel Tower, the logic of inside and out was coming to the fore, Roland Barthes suggests. We enter the tower only to find that our experience of the inside is really one of the outside, of structure as such. "This tour of the *inside* corresponds, moreover, to the question raised by the *outside*," he says. "The monument is a riddle, to enter it is to solve, to possess it." The tower forces us to *think like an engineer*, to confront the fact that monuments engage a dialectics of materiality and meaning. That is not always reassuring. The poet Gottfried Benn finds in early modernist architecture evidence of a "displacement from inside to outside"; there is, he says, "spatial feeling" now "projected, extruded, metallically realized." A modernist building is a kind of "discharge mechanism," a dramatization of death that pushes "the spirit of construction ... to the limits of immateriality"—"the final stage" must be near. In fact, as we know, modernism did not so much speed up to the final standstill of death as peter out into mere style.

In our own day, its utopian energies all but spent, its revolutionary potential largely dissipated, modernism has been everywhere reduced to the generation of that generic slickness found between the sometimes new skins of postmodern buildings and their mechanical bodies. New antimodernist buildings, including Rem Koolhaas's "broken-skyscraper" CCTV building in Beijing, say, continue to play with notions of inside and out, but without a sense of liberation, only of

A model of Philip Johnson's Glass House, New Canaan, Connecticut (1949), at the Museum of Modern Art, New York: the transparent inside the opaque.

mischief. (Koolhaas has said that there are three seminal events in the history of architecture: Samson destroying the house of the Philistines in 1100 BCE, the fall of the World Trade Center in 2001, and his 2006 design of this building.) I.M. Pei's Bank of China in Hong Kong is "an aquarium for passing clouds, once again questioning the relation between inside and outside," one critic writes. Norman Foster's design for the Hong Kong and Shanghai Banking Corporation is built as if downwards, a wispy, disembodied form to meet the needs of a client who wanted a building that did not look like a bank. The irony is that, whatever the exterior, the interior business of global finance—wispy and disembodied in its own fashion—is more opaque than ever. There is play but no permeation.

Koolhaas has deplored these developments even as he has, typically, also furthered them. Disaffected with the Manhattan he celebrated in *Delirious New York,* he has lately decided to "Go East" and join the unfettered authoritarian capitalism of China and Singapore. But the

"A building condenses a culture in one place." (Edward Casey)

problems of modernism and postmodernism are not so easily evaded. Koolhaas and other architects of the current supermodern moment would do well to remember Koolhaas's own analysis of the "latent fascism" contained in the pervasive junkspace buildings of the new century. Even in *Delirious New York* he knew that the logic of inside and out had its clamp-down potentials, as well as emancipatory ones. The original skyscraper, he says there, performs a kind of lobotomy on the urban brain, breaking the traditional symbolic link between exterior appearance and interior function. Buildings no longer have to look like what goes on within them. The skyscraper, with its flex-space office floors, "spares the outside world the agonies of the continuous changes raging inside it. It hides everyday life." The resulting "climate of obscurity" is not challenged by the alleged anti-skyscrapers of the Far East. If anything, they make it more alive and well than ever, only this time under conditions overtly hostile to democracy.

One might say that architects would do well to remember these things, but in truth the responsibility is more general. The logic of inside and out belongs to us all—not only because we all must live with and in buildings, those monuments to human desire, but also because, and more profoundly still, it structures consciousness itself.

Evan Penny's multipiece bronze sculpture *Pi* (1992), Toronto: art for the urban interior created by built forms.

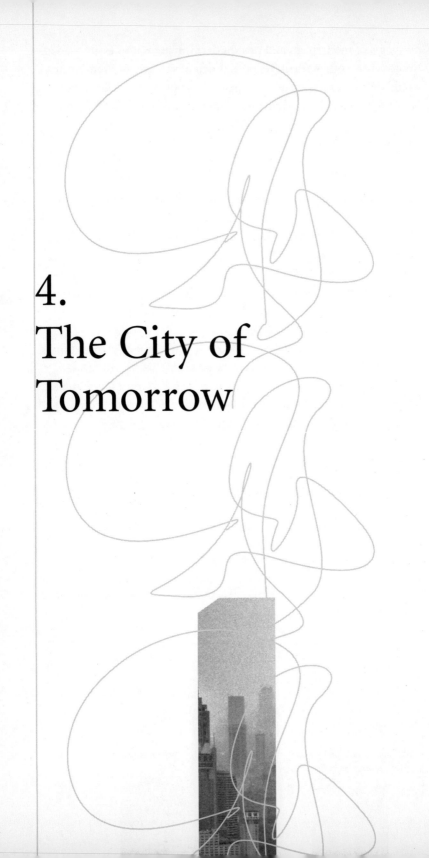

4.
The City of
Tomorrow

i. Modeling the Future

Backed by Beijing's desire for Western portals, Shanghai has
become over the past three decades a turn-of-the-twentieth-
century playground for the world's architects. During the
1990s and early 2000s, it sprouted architectural megaprojects

faster than a child's playroom, structures impossible to imagine any-where else in the world. Whole blocks and districts materialize as though downloaded from an orbiting supercomputer, transforming the mundane big city of two decades ago into a head-turning showcase of material ambition. Virtually every major Western architect, plus a lot of minor ones, wants a crack at this unrestricted landscape, bring-ing a host of ideas both brilliant and bizarre. Ironically, the utopian visions of the West, the soaring towers and radiant cities of the high modern imagination, are rarely possible in the grand cities of the free world. They are realized instead in the authoritarian and dictatorial regimes of Asia, where life and steel are cheap. Europe's dream of heroic architecture has found its material realization in the People's Republic of China.

Always a threshold city, a roiling cauldron of old and new, Shanghai offers an absurd but appropriate showcase for a country at once feudal and hyperindustrial. Since 1993, when Shanghai technocrats became the third generation of Communist Party powerbrokers in Beijing, shifting financial aid from rural maintenance to the astonishing urban reconstructions of the last decade, money and *guan xi,* or connections—the twinned currencies of China—have been mar-shaled more and more to build high and big. Three-quarters of Shanghai's urban fabric has been constructed since 1985, and the dozens of high-rise office towers that now climb into its pol-luted sky have created ten times the floor space of the pre-boom city. Following decades of wariness and disavowal, this is once more the Party's favored gateway to the West, edging out flashy prodigal son Hong Kong (though Hong Kong money remains welcome anywhere). With the Beijing Summer Olympics in 2008 and the World Expo in Shanghai itself in 2010, this city has never been more interested in Western visitors. Government sources estimate that there was a 35 percent increase in tourist visitors during 2004 after the SARS downturn of 2003, and the city built five-star hotels at a brisk clip to

accommodate them and the growing stream since. And not just hotels are being approved. Office towers, residential blocks, shopping malls, stadiums and museums are springing from the ground all over the vast square mileage of greater Shanghai.

Complain as we may about the design compromises forced in the democratic West by overlapping interest groups, setback restrictions, health standards and public financing, the results in the undemocratic East are far more unnerving. At the asymptotic edge of design freedom lies a sparkling, overgrown, hyperscaled city of bright nightmares, sometimes beautiful, often strange, always oppressive. Shanghai is modern urbanism on a speed high, rambling and incoherent, with a lump of shopaholic emptiness at its center. Nowhere else on Earth is

"Architecture is always dream and function, expression of utopia and instrument of a convenience ... [U]se never does anything but shelter meaning." (Roland Barthes)

the promise of architectural emancipation, that dream of modernism, more vividly broken. Architecture will not set us free, no matter how hard—how high and fast—it tries.

Ask anyone here and he or she will tell you: Shanghai is the future. But that is not so. Shanghai is not *the* future; it is *every* future, a palimpsest of urban visions, a history of what is to come. Visiting Shanghai is a journey to the very near future by way of the very near past, a fact that contributes to a strange form of urban vertigo. You may never have been here before, but you are always already here. The result is a fantasyland of architectural grandiosity where any drawing, no matter how insane or adolescent, may come to life almost instantly, without the citizens' committees, building restrictions and expensive labor that hamper architectural geniuses elsewhere—though also, maybe more often, rein them in just enough to force greatness through a press of constraint.

To call the city science-fictional is correct but too general. Yes, there are geodesic domes and massive cantilevers and huge expanses of neon and glass. But the landscape offers a full spectrum of sci-fi echoes and allusions. There are Buck Rogers ray-gun finials on the China Life building in Pudong. Portholed Jetsons-style flying saucers hovering atop the Lan Sheng Building and the JJ Oriental Tower in Pudong. The knifing faceted slash of Tomorrow Tower is like Darth Vader's headquarters designed by Japanese toy freaks. For advanced students, there is Space Ghost whimsy to be found in the Marriott Hotel and in the Bund Center, with its crown of gold spikes, said to recall a lotus blossom but really looking more like a huge pineapple. Or consider the Batman-inspired cowling of the New World Plaza, over near the bustling shops of Huaihai Lu, capable not only of lighting every one of its windows but of making them play a rippling multihued symphony of light, a Laser Floyd extravaganza, every night. There are glass domes on almost every corner, from Meiluo City to the International Convention Center. Down at street level, it is impossible to view the city in anything other than cinematic terms: the *Blade Runner* globalization jumble, with some *Terminator 2* overtones, of rickshaws and noodle stands washed in rain-softened neon or the Technicolor sunsets of pollution—all dwarfed by slabs of steel and glass stretching eight or nine hundred feet into the night sky above.

Above all, a weird recombinant futurism is evident everywhere. The buildings of Shanghai look kooky, overdone, self-consciously bizarre—a skyline conceived by Dr. Evil and executed by Virtucon Industries; but also compelling, witty, sometimes even beautiful. The city's structures are suffused with a peculiar nostalgia, a simulacral allusive novelty, the very slightly advanced techno-cultural melange of Shanghai's plus-thirteen time zone. "He took out his hand organizer and poked a note to himself about the anachronistic quality of the word skyscraper," Don DeLillo writes of a superwealthy investment banker, in the novel *Cosmopolis*. "No recent structure ought to bear this word. It belonged to the olden soul of awe, to the arrowed towers that were a narrative long before he was born." Maybe in Manhattan, but in this cosmopolis the anachronism of scraping the sky is precisely part of the enduring appeal—even as some of the newest designs, like Koolhaas's eighty-story, U.S.\$664-million CCTV building in Beijing or the China Commercial Bank in Shanghai, are crazy deconstructions of the soaring tower, twisted letterform or elephantine structures sitting low to the ground. This may be the last place on Earth where, pro and con, the word *skyscraper* cannot be retired. The narrative of aspiration and emancipation could never be the same as it was in the olden soul of awe—it has indeed acquired its own simulacral rewriting, reducing freedom to something like an allusion—but that says as much about the original narrative as about this metastasizing city.

"Modernity is really taking place in China," Koolhaas told the *New York Observer* not long ago, calling Beijing's West-friendly planning "communism in the form of a state that can still have a purpose," while in America "there is no potential alignment for architecture to a project that could be for the public good." (Koolhaas, who wrote the definitive essay on the Manhattan grid, is building here, not in New York—unless you count the Prada boutique in SoHo.) But it is not so much modernity as Compu-Global-Hyper-Mega-Modernity; an accelerated Version 2.0 of metropolitan life. Design ideas run riot around Shanghai, deployed by imaginations unfettered by a sense of proportion or strict zoning laws. There is no established aesthetic vocabulary, as in New York or Paris or Prague, where new buildings face pressure to respect their context, to fit in. Architects in Shanghai mix and match bits and pieces, drawing from every model and every conceivable style. They are kit-bashers, novelty-mongers, gimmick-runners. The signature buildings of Shanghai, the two dozen highest downtown skyscrapers, appear to have come together the way we used to mess around with scale models and airplane glue: sticking the wings of a F-86 onto a Ford Mustang chassis, dropping a tailfin on a Ducati roadster, fixing the conning tower of a submarine to the fuselage of a 707. You can see this same contrivance-happy exuberance at work in art high and low, from the exploded toy-store installations of Kim Adams to the wacky Gerry Anderson *Thunderbirds* television series of the 1970s: the overelaborate launch schemes and implausible aircraft, the go-go uniforms of Supermarionation. In this skyline we can recognize, with a pleasure equal parts kitsch and delight, the very same kooky Moonrakerish, Octopussified gadgetry-fetish.

That kind of what-the-hell design sense is usually confined to the rec room or the special-effects studio. In Shanghai, it is called urban planning. In fifty years, perhaps twenty, this riot may well resolve itself into the kind of cherished whole that Manhattan's variegated skyline offers visitors today. At the moment, it is as close to time travel as the globe allows.

ii. Modernity at Ground Level

"It is glorious to be rich," Deng Xiaoping famously said, and Shanghainese have always enthusiastically agreed. But never more so than now. There are few places on Earth where the bustle of urban life is more concentrated or unabashed, the sense of urgency so overpowering. Down at street level, there are times when it feels like every single one of Shanghai's millions of pedestrians, bicycles, scooters, mopeds and cars is heading right for you. Cross Sichuan Nanlu at 9 A.M., or dodge through the rat's nest intersection of Nanjing Donglu and Xizang Nanlu anytime, and a spiky roaring mass of traffic bears down on you like a semimechanized army division on chaotic maneuver. Above, there is a thick tangle of power lines, and telephone cable is thickly festooned with laundry airing in the toxic yellow air. Hundreds of boxy early-model air conditioners hang strapped to the sides of every wall, lending even the newest buildings an instant slumland air.

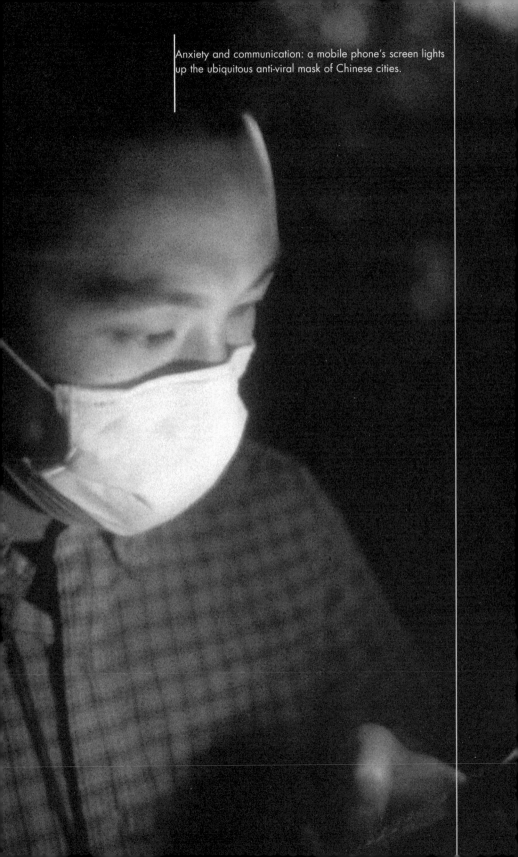
Anxiety and communication: a mobile phone's screen lights up the ubiquitous anti-viral mask of Chinese cities.

Pink and yellow and sky-blue apartment blocks march away to the west and south in close-packed orderly slabs.

The press of humanity here is multidimensional, omniolfactory, inescapable and loud. Like its citizens, Shanghai's sights, smells and sounds crowd in from every direction, thick walls of sensory noise that snap out signals as fast as your learning-curve brain can take them: an English sign in purple neon, the mingled scents of frying pork dumplings and rotting watermelon rind, the unmistakable *hrnfft …* *hrnfft* of a businessman in gangster-cut suit and broken-down leatherette loafers voiding his nostrils onto the sidewalk, thumb pressed to either side in turn. Dirty water and fish guts spill into the street from sidewalk stalls that cluster under spaceship high-rises and five-star hotel ballrooms, all washed in KFC and McDonald's neon, Prada and Gucci signage, everywhere the inevitable green of that globally ubiquitous coffee chain.

A tiny man with the weathered face of an ancient god under a Nike toque huddles in a corner selling seven mismatched batteries and a bundle of wilted scallions. Touts with knock-off luxury goods are so persistent, repetitive and hectoring that you may begin to think your name actually is Rolex Montblanc. Toddlers in embroidered split-crotch pants, imperial hats and decorated surgical masks stare at you and point. In fact, everyone you pass stares hard, with an indecipherable mix of curiosity and what probably isn't but sure as hell feels like hostility. *Roundeye go home.* The city buzzes and stinks and knocks you over if you don't step nimbly. The Chinese are used to less personal space than almost anyone on the planet, and especially on the streets of Shanghai, largest and fastest of its cities, body contact is not optional. Unlike the deft dancers of Tokyo or the sweet-feet dodgers of Sao Paulo, people here make no effort at all to avoid sidewalk collisions. Jaywalking and people-dodging techniques that might work on lunchtime Fifth Avenue are here badly in need of an upgrade; accidental slams that would prompt an offer of violence in London or an abject apology in Vancouver are here merely ignored, the routine tolls of walking the streets of the city. Shanghai is not for strollers, no refuge for oneiric Parisian *flânerie*.

Always a city of self-conscious newness, nothing at all like the ancient cities of Suzhou or Changzhou to the west, Shanghai really dates from just the 1840s. The various concessions—French, British and International—divided up the land along the west bank of the Huangpu River, building gateway houses known as shikumen and alleys in an East-meets-West fashion found nowhere else on the planet. More than twenty thousand Chinese fled into the International Concession after the Small Swords' Rebellion of 1853, and profits from shikumen rentals, often sublet and subdivided over and over, were mostly raked offshore—not the last time that would happen. Shanghai's heyday was the 1930s when, as a free-movement zone where no visa or passport was required, it was a haven for crime and high life. A decade ago it was big and dull, a moribund hulk filled with people but no life, honored as the birthplace of the Chinese Communist Party but distrusted, even reviled, by doctrinal hardliners in Beijing and distant peasants alike.

Then, in the wake of Deng Xiaoping's rule, a cadre of influential Shanghai technocrats, schooled in Western efficiency, found favor in Beijing and put urban improvement on the national agenda for the first time. Jiang Zemin, once Party secretary in Shanghai, was made president; a former mayor, Zhu Rongji, was elevated to prime minister. The smart, go-ahead Shanghai boys replaced a conservative, suspicious and corrupt leadership, mostly from Hunan and Szechuan, which had ruled in an unbroken line from Mao. China was changing, and Shanghai's legendary taste for novelty was a central focus, accelerating beyond all precedent with huge injections of cash from the central government. Individuals began to flash their money too, with most of China's estimated population of 236,000 U.S.-dollar millionaires calling the city home.

And yet, the city, for all its newness and international sophistication, remains irremediably Chinese, which is to say suspicious, even provincial, and racked by ancient conflicts and attitudes. Even the conspicuous consumption has a peculiarly traditional flavor, an expression of the golden dragon of Chinese wealth—part of the Middle Kingdom and therefore without limit on tackiness or ostentation. Most of the city's inhabitants, meanwhile, are, by North American standards, poverty-stricken, creating a disturbing first-world/third-world dynamic found also in many other of the globe's largest cities. Money and poverty combine uncomfortably with the city's familiar-but-strange visual field—like advertising on the moon—to destabilize your judgment constantly, shifting from premodern to postmodern in a blink. Shanghai allows, or maybe forces, a species of urban time travel, collapsing the centuries in the manner Trotsky noticed of the grandiose architectural projects of 1930s Germany. "Today, not only in peasant homes but also in the city skyscrapers, there lives alongside the twentieth century the tenth or the thirteenth," he observed. "A hundred million people use electricity and still believe in the magic power of signs and exorcism.... Despair has raised them to their feet; fascism has given them the banner.... Capitalist society is puking up the undigested barbarism. Such is the physiology of National Socialism." The vertiginous nausea of observing this process, a form of political time travel, or time collapse, effected by mixing technical marvels and cultural darkness, can still (or again) be felt in Shanghai, towering skyscrapers casting long shadows onto peasant homes, sometimes occupied by the very people clambering over the rickety bamboo scaffolds of the supermodern building sites.

The Shanghai of cultural legend is still here, maybe most clearly in the shabby-elegant Peace Hotel on the Bund, Shanghai's celebrated riverside strip. The Bund skyline is an essay in Art Deco solidity, a rank of squat banks, customs houses and hotels, mostly sandstone, that curves along the busy bend in the Huangpu, a tributary of the mighty Yangtze, about fifteen miles upstream. Shanghai means "up from the sea" and, while not a saltwater port, retains a sense of connection to the East China Sea—the route by which the Japanese came and devastated the city in 1939, part of a reign of terror unforgettably depicted in J.G. Ballard's novel *Empire of the Sun*. The Bund defines Shanghai's last boom, the cinematic interwar vogue of gangsters, flappers and opium-fanciers, when the city attracted bankers and financiers as well as the dissipated, criminal and bored. Noël Coward, for example, is said to have written *Private Lives* while living at the Peace Hotel; even now its ancient wood-paneled jazz bar features a six-piece band whose players probably knew him. The band stayed, but the gangsters either died or moved on to larger stages, the most famous of them Chiang Kai-shek—"Shanghai Czech"—who brought the same streetwise business sense he displayed while dominating the sex and drug trade to running the Kuomintang.

The local taxis are all bright VW Santanas with uniformed, white-gloved drivers, innocent of both geography and regard for life, and with a pronounced proclivity for blind left turns. I got in one, and we drove through the usual insane traffic to Yuyuan Garden, a combination cut-rate tourist mall and traditional Ming Dynasty garden. If taxis weren't so cheap, Shanghai's day-long traffic jams would be excruciating; as things stand, they're merely ridiculous and toxic. As I got out in a crush of people, street wardens began adding their piercing whistles to the standard cacophony of traffic noise and music. One of the pedestrians yelled at a street warden to stop the whistling, and then the two had a brief stylized argument about it, as if rehearsed for a bet. It ended as quickly as it started, with no apparent animosity on either side. Shanghainese are rarely physically violent, and the crime rate for such a large city is virtually nil by North American standards. Pedestrians or cyclists knocked to ground by roaring cars or mopeds shout but don't push or punch. I witnessed just one shoving match in Shanghai, and that was at a Sunday matinee of Beijing opera attended mostly by music students and old men in Mao jackets. For all I know, it was a dispute about the purity of the singer's otherworldly falsetto. It was over quickly and the larger of the two grapplers was then hissed and scolded by the old men nearby.

There was the usual incongruity of a KFC sign next to an ancient pagoda—a cultural juxtaposition, once possibly arresting, which now resides firmly in the realm of cliché. To notice it is to notice nothing except the creeping ease of thinking notation equals analysis. There are more Christmas decorations and Muzak in Shanghai than in most Western cities, neon and fur coats and fast food everywhere. Shanghai revels in what Westerners schooled in upscale lifestyle porn would want to call tastelessness. Here excess is the point, conspicuous wealth like the clanging gold jewelry of an old-school rap star and his entourage. Yuyuan is China the way Times Square is America. The gardens themselves are an essay in grace, however, every passageway exactly proportioned, every space metaphorically charged and heavy with meaning. There is very little traditional Chinese architecture left, as the building boom has swept away the old city like so much floor dust, but what remains is a keen reminder of the deep human genius of an ancient culture, its centuries of aesthetic refinement and spiritual investigation. You can never entirely forget the hordes of aggressive merchants and junk purveyors outside the garden, but for a moment the sights and sounds of hypercapitalist free-for-all recedes into the background.

Not far away is Renmin Square, the People's Plaza. Once a racetrack for the moneyed Westerners of Shanghai, it is now a grand sweep of parkland and civic architecture, far more urban and enclosed than Tiananmen Square, like something you'd find in Chicago or Houston. Shanghainese tend to be less political than their counterparts in the capital. When an upstart lawyer, Zheng Enchong, organized a class-action lawsuit against the Communist Party over the massive enforced relocations demanded by the Pudong development, the protests happened largely in Beijing. Land has no official dollar value in China, in principle owned collectively by "the people," so the deals offered to the displaced Shanghainese were dismal at best: some cash, maybe a chance to bid on a tiny expensive apartment in a new high-rise a dozen miles away. As the Canadian consul-general, Robert Mackenzie, put it to me dryly, "The compensation certainly does not satisfy any Western notion of human rights." According to most human rights organizations, Zheng is in jail.

The jewel of Renmin Square is the new Shanghai Museum, a squat puzzle of a building clad in Spanish and Italian granite, pink outside and gray within. The exterior is hard to digest, a sort of circle-square affair intended to symbolize rectangular earth surmounted by circular heaven; also to resemble an ancient bronze *ding,* or three-legged vessel, a class of artifact in which the museum is especially blessed. This is all more pleasing in theory than in practice, but the interior is probably the nicest museum space I have ever seen—serene, intelligent and polished. (Contrast this postprosperity institutional luxury with the old Shanghai natural history museum a mile or so away, a deserted dilapidated shop of horrors now standing under a concrete overpass near the Bund, with glass cases full of moth-eaten taxidermy, gruesome biological samples and questionable science.) The north side of the square is more impressive, if also weirder. A forbidding civic administration building is flanked by two white steel contraptions, the famous Grand Theatre, Jean-Marie Charpentier's futuristic glass-and-plastic extension of traditional Chinese upturned eaves, and the Urban Planning Exhibition Centre, with four huge metal florets on its roof meant to resemble magnolias. I got a coffee in the basement of the theater, then climbed the stairs of the urban planning building to visit one of Shanghai's most wonderful places, the floor-sized urban planning model constructed as part of the hard sell for Expo 2010.

The model is at a scale of 1:500 and covers roughly 6500 square feet, about the size of a couple of tennis courts. Steel viewing platforms are constructed around its perimeter, so the gaggles of Chinese tourists and visiting Hong Kong developers can stand in turn and eye the part of the city they want to denude. Little signs say "Don't jump." Like the Panorama of New York constructed for the 1964 World's Fair, now housed in the Queens Museum of Art in Flushing, New York—its sole major attraction—the Shanghai model is the ultimate in idealized panopticon vision. Clean plastic residential towers march away in tiny orderly rows from an elegant city center around Renmin Square. All white, the towers sprout no laundry lines or air-conditioning units;

Shanghai's Urban Planning Exhibition Centre: modeling the city to scale.

their roofs are uniform and pristine, with no trace of the hash of styles and hues actually to be seen in the Shanghai suburbs. Neither cars nor people crowd its little streets, and the air is, of course, unwashed by pollutants or noise, as though the miniature city has been neutron-bombed, swept for all mechanical contrivances, then abandoned.

Like most visitors, probably, I stood on the viewing platform that offered the vantage nearest the heart of the model and located the urban planning building on its little grid, then imagined myself inside it, looking at a model of the model, and then at a model of the model of the model, and so on: the *mise en abyme* of inside and outside, representation and represented, model and source. Standing dumbly there, I had a sudden desire, probably just as common, to vault the white railing of the platform and stomp around the model in my Pumas, going *errrr! errrr!* while crushing blocks of Identi-Kit apartment towers, shooting death rays from my eyes, snatching up the Nanpu Bridge in one hand to hurl it across the room.

A poster near the model said: "Shanghai is a sparkling pearl of the East, a colossal earth-shaking dragon soaring the skies, a city where excitement is created. The target population of Shanghai is to be sixteen million by 2020. It will have become a world-class metropolis." Too late. The local English-language newspaper, the *Shanghai Daily News*, had reported that very morning that the population of the city, migrant workers included, had just topped twenty million.

iii. The New Economy

Western architecture firms love the massive Chinese market almost as much as electronics and running-shoe companies once did. With 1.4 billion people and growing, there is no shortage of highly skilled labor, and it comes cheap. Sometimes the very people being displaced by a new high-rise work, often for pennies a day, on the scary bamboo scaffolding that shrouds the emergent skeleton. But the market picture is far from simple, not least because the Chinese are selling goods back to Western countries even as they keep their currency tightly controlled and sell off nonperforming loans and other devalued paper to American and European banks. Morgan Stanley already has U.S.$500 million in Chinese bad debts, and the estimated total held by foreign banks, sixty of them from nineteen countries, is U.S.$200 billion.

Meanwhile, the change from labor-intensive to capital- and knowledge-intensive growth has been steady during the past decade, a shift mirrored in the rural-to-urban building spike and a new encouragement for people to spend hoarded hard currency from the old days when only dollars could be used to buy consumer durables such as TVs and washing machines. Westerners often find doing business in China tricky, prompting an MBA-program boomlet in handy guides to understanding face, diversionary politeness and a host of related style matters baffling to the go-get-'em American negotiator. People are estimated by wealth, sure, but *guan xi*—a combination of social position and personal leverage—operates more readily and often. Relative degrees of *guan xi* are intelligible to Shanghainese on a superfine scale, attended by minute modes of face-loss and respect. Communism has done nothing to level this ancient hierarchical economy, merely changed the direction of its flow.

China's trade surplus with the United States hit a whopping $2 billion a week in 2005, totaling $400 billion during the three years from 2002 to 2005. This is not the wonderful market for Western goods that Americans were promised back when George Bush Sr. granted China most-favored-nation status during, of all things, a Yale convocation speech. On auto parts, for example, the ratio in China's favor is 6:1. China's recent entry into the World Trade Organization will only increase that imbalance. Unless, that is, the WTO forces China to lift some of its tariffs, or something drastic happens in a float of the RMB, or new yuan, against other currencies. There's a lot of American dollars salted away in China. At the moment, Beijing holds something like $122 billion in U.S. T-bills and bonds, and nobody knows what the private holdings, once illegal and now an open secret, might be. Individual foreign banks are taking China's bad debts, and multinational corporations are buying China's cheap labor, but the U.S. government is actually borrowing from the Chinese to finance the stability-threatening debt Washington is busy running up via tax cuts and foreign invasions. Which means more U.S. money is flowing into China, and Washington can't stop it. This is one reason George Bush Jr. is so accommodating to Chinese premier Wen Jiabao's denunciations of democracy in Taiwan, a face-saving policy that Washington likes to call "strategic ambiguity." Meanwhile, the Communist government in Beijing is maintaining the same attitude to foreign investment the Chinese have always had: Come. Bring your money and your talent. Just don't expect to stay around for the payoff.

There may not be one, of course. While the automotive and electronics sectors are healthier than ever, and Shanghai shimmers every day with renewed boomtown energy, it is still far from clear who is going to inhabit much of the new square footage being thrown into the sky. Most of the country's population is still too poor to buy the goods they labor to make, and, unlike in India or Malaysia, there is almost no middle class to bridge the unstable gap between the slick superrich and a vast peasantry. Worse, in a nation where *bourgeois* is still a real term of abuse, there can't ever be a large middle class: Social aspiration dies at the moment of its waking. Despite what Western investors—and tourists—seem to believe, you can't just shop your way out of a half-century of communism.

I mentioned some of this to Brian McCluskey, a Toronto-based landscape architect, as we rode a chilly bus out to the farthest reaches of Shanghai. Here the city gives way to bottling plants, windswept industrial plazas and forlorn amusement parks flanked by big swatches of elevated highway sweeping away to nowhere. Brian's firm, like many of the smaller Western outfits working in China, was busy chasing down a tender for a new commercial-residential development in a town about two hours' drive southwest of Shanghai, one of the small centers about to be swallowed up by the city's sprawl. In an effort to ease congestion in the city proper, planners were subsidizing projects that would in effect fashion nine new exurban downtowns, all with 35 to 40 percent green space. The mayor of this town had received a subsidy and wanted to deliver a contract within a few weeks—an unheard-of schedule in normal architectural practice. If the firm was going to compete, the architects would have to work overtime during the holidays just to come up with the preliminary drawings.

Shanghai overpass in the rain: concrete arterial.

"Yeah, anything goes here," Brian said of the effect the building boom was having on his own practice. "Huge glass cubes. Hundred-foot-long reflecting pools. If you did any of that in North America, the client would say, okay, next firm. Here the main problem is figuring out just how far they're willing to go."

That morning we were attending the opening of a new environmentally friendly house on the outskirts of Shanghai. Brian had done the landscape design. After years of shoddy, heedless construction in the approved Soviet mode—ranks of instantly old, effluent-belching concrete sheds found everywhere from Vladivostok to Prague, with walls that come to pieces in your hands—the Chinese were catching on to green building.

Or so they said. The experimental house was located where almost no one would see it, miles from the city center, past the mind-numbing expanses of pastel-colored apartment towers, each surmounted by every conceivable style of decoration, from Greco-Roman to French colonial. Clusters of useless columns, gables and dormers crowded the sky, floating high above industrial parks and deserted roads. You'd have to be either a truck driver or desperately lost even to pass within five hundred yards of the house.

Brian and I stood with a few dozen others in the bone-chilling morning air, looking at what all buildings are at the start of their unpredictable lives: a hole in the ground.

"They put it right beside this main road," he said, over the sound of reversing trucks and heavy traffic on the nearby dual carriageway. "And they didn't take down these other buildings." A couple of deteriorated warehouses stood hard by the site. I looked at the billboard drawing of the projected house. It was set next to a hardhat warning featuring the angry, determined face of a Chinese construction worker, who was wearing his protective gear in the heroic style of a Maoist propaganda poster. The drawing showed a futuristic glass-and-metal edifice nestled comfortably in lush green parkland, inevitably reminiscent of an old *Star Trek* backdrop.

"See, I've put a berm between the house and the road," Brian told me. I tried to imagine this desolate roadside hole, a place you might go to dump bodies, transformed into the image on the board.

We turned to sign a guest book. In accordance with Chinese tradition, we were handed little loot bags, as if at a New York fashion opening or film festival party. I looked in mine. Two pairs of cotton long johns. I wished there was a place to put them on. Also a plastic corsage. I left everything in the bag and later left the bag in my hotel room.

We waited, shivering. A loudspeaker began to blare uplifting martial music at an unreasonable volume. A man came and had his picture taken with me for no reason I could see. Long minutes later, four men wearing dull gray suits and sweater vests mounted the small stage. Five pretty girls in long wool coats stood to one side with ribbons and bouquets. The man on the far left approached the microphone and began barking harshly into it. Chinese speech-makers do not tell jokes, move their bodies, smile or talk with their hands. They never gesture or josh; they just stand, arms hanging straight down, and shout. The speech, predictable boilerplate about the joy we all felt at this new dawn of environmental sensitivity, was nevertheless suffused with imperative urgency, like a desperate battlefield briefing.

We looked around, bored, cold, counting the minutes of life we would never get back. An ear-splitting wave of noise started up behind us— celebratory fireworks, rolling on for a minute or more of rising intensity, absurdly overdone as if intended as sound effect for a film firefight. Everyone clapped furiously. The pops and cracks died slowly away. Smoke and sharp cordite odor wafted past.

"I'm not sure how environmentally friendly that is," Brian said.

The Chinese contingent trooped off to the bus, to spend the rest of the day watching presentations about the green house. Brian and I exchanged a glance of mutual horror. Neither of us had had any breakfast or even coffee. Juliet Chang, the representative of two Toronto architecture firms, Brian's landscaping outfit and a builder of large-scale stadiums and towers, came over to us, and we prevailed on her to get us a ride back to the city. Juliet is short, fiftyish, with a smooth face and head that looks too big for her body. Her English is good, polished by a couple of years in the graduate education school of the University of Michigan, which has become a kind of clearinghouse for ambitious Shanghainese. Her cell phone was never far from her hand, though she stopped short of hanging it around her neck on a cord, as some Shanghainese do.

"I think this is good time to look at apartment, Brian," she said once we were moving. Juliet had a scheme to buy a not yet constructed flat, near the center of Shanghai, then rent it to Brian's firm. The car snaked its long way back to the city, narrowly avoiding two serious accidents, with no visible reaction from the uniformed driver. We approached the edge of the French Concession. This is probably Shanghai's most popular neighborhood, at least among Westerners, site of numerous restaurants and cafés and, along Hengshen Lu, the neocolonial and Latinate mansions that once defined the best of the city's East–West grace. These sit comfortably alongside the few remaining shikumen structures in Shanghai, lovely terraced houses and alleys dating from the early twentieth century that are not long for this world unless smart developers get to them soon. It's easy to get lost here and so experience what Benjamin celebrated as an underrated gift of urban life, *losing your way*. In Shanghai it feels more like a curse than a gift, though. The last section of Kazuo Ishiguro's haunting novel of Shanghai in the 1930s, *When We Were Orphans,* describes the mesmerizing disorientation of these close-packed streets, and there is nothing happy about young Jim's terrified movements through the French Concession in Ballard's novel. My own adventures were less intense but, wandering one afternoon, I did manage to walk two miles in the wrong direction before I came upon Shanghai Stadium, former home of the Houston Rockets' star basketball forward Yao Ming, then with the hometown Shanghai Sharks franchise, and realized my mistake.

I saw through the car window a rising residential tower of surpassing ugliness, with absurd neoclassical doodads on top, as if a cheesecake model of the Parthenon had been flung across a room to land on a filing cabinet. Brian laughed when I pointed to it, then stopped laughing as the car, silently directed by Juliet, swung into the tower's parking lot.

"This building is by Charpentier," Juliet said, looking back at us, referring to the flamboyant Frenchman who designed the stunning theater on Renmin Square. If so, he must have been out of the office that day, or else in the grip of some fast-onset dementia. As yet another pretty girl in an overcoat guided us through the showrooms and model condos of the complex, known as Louis Triumphal Palace, the overwrought Caesars Palace sensibility, heedless of reference or coherence, grew more pronounced and punishing. Concrete statuary of dryads and warriors lined the gravel walkways. All the interior floors were slick polished marble, hard and unforgiving. Gilt fixtures sprouted from every inside corner: gilt phones, gilt faucets, gilt doorknobs. Gilt-edged mirrors attempted to expand claustrophobic, gilt-wallpapered one-bedroom modules. The playground of the new Shanghai moneyed class, cut up into one-thousand-square-foot gilt chunks. A place to go quickly and comprehensively haywire, overwhelmed by the dead weight of desire.

But also, from the Shanghai perspective, a dreamspace, clean and shiny, hovering in the air above the filmy surfaces and dirt at street level. "I think is very beautiful," the guide said, smiling at me.

iv. The Potemkin Shopping Mall

I left Puxi, the original city, the next day to experience the other side of Shanghai, the fresh-from-the-box vastness of Pudong New City. At one point in the mid-1990s, it was estimated that between a quarter and a half of the world's high-rise cranes were in Pudong, lifting piles of I-beams high into the sky one after the other like giant insects, hanging floor on floor from thin steel spines jabbed into the earth. In Berlin during the 1990s, the vast International Style towers of the Potsdamer Platz development, all thrown up in apparent minutes, were billed as "die Stadt von Morgen"—the city of tomorrow. You could stand on the edge of it and see a sky filled with cranes, like trees in winter, for miles. But Shanghai's tomorrow has come sooner and bigger. Pudong is less frenetic now, but only barely: fewer cranes, more buildings. And more to come.

Here the wide stretch of Century Avenue, carved out of what used to be fishing villages and small farms, is an almost deserted, pedestrian-hostile slash of asphalt. Science-fiction office towers climb fifty, sixty, seventy stories into the air, all of them dwarfed by the eighty-eight-story vertical pagoda of the Jin Mao Tower, China's tallest building and—as of this writing anyway—fourth tallest in the world. The Oriental Pearl Tower, a concrete and pink-glass phallus reminiscent of a chem-lab model of molecular structure, thrusts stupidly into the air near the river, attracting a scatter of visitors and vendors hawking fruit, meat grilled on tiny braziers fixed to bicycle fenders, and novelty Polaroids of people apparently leaning against the tower as if it were a lamppost. Still more people are pushing into the Super Brand Mall across the street, ten stories of sweeping marble vistas and designer-clothing stores, most of them deserted, with a bright fast-food court and vast Western-style supermarket in the basement, both jammed.

The reasons for the bifurcation are simple and once more typical of the Möbius-strip economies of new China. Prices for luxury goods in Shanghai are so high that nobody shops in the branded stores—not even Western tourists, who prefer to hunt for knock-off bargains in the street markets, thermonuclear versions of Manhattan's already insane Canal Street. One boutique shopping mall, Plaza 66, is perpetually deserted, while the shops don't even carry much stock. As one observer noted, there is a structural irony here: "Just as Stalin erected Potemkin villages to display the glories of communism to outsiders, Shanghai is creating its own illusion of prosperity out of the world's most luxurious brands." In an effort to compete, at least in appearance, with Milan and New York, the city offers cut-rate rents to top-tier fashion houses. Burberry, Hermès and Chanel happily take advantage of the legerdemain, since advertising is almost as important as sales. "Most leading luxury brands will need to have a flagship store in Shanghai if only to put Shanghai along with London, Paris, Milan on their bags," said Paul French, founder and China chief of Access Asia, a marketing research firm in Shanghai. The resulting shops, even more spectral than most branded enterprises, which already sell identification and position more than merchandise, either have little in the way of stock or carry only sizes too large for the average Shanghainese.

On the streets of Pudong, the contrast to Puxi, with the neon-overloaded pedestrian mecca of Nanjing Lu, Shanghai's famous old shopping drag, or the heavy midtown-consumer feeling of Huaihai Lu, is stark. No shops, no dumpling or omelet vendors, no early-morning clusters of middle-aged Shanghainese doing tai chi, sword art or ballroom dancing. None of the kite fliers, kids, Red Army soldiers or people walking backward for their health who give the hazy sunrise along the Bund its untranslatable charm. Just big chunks of nothing. Pigeons and squirrels seem barely to exist in some parts of Shanghai, and the rats, thankfully, stay mostly out of sight. An empty street is really empty—vacuumed clean, denuded, void. Shanghai boosters love to tell you that Century Avenue was modeled on the Champs Élysées, and it certainly possesses the grand dimension of a Parisian street, but it is an elegant boulevard in the way Hallmark verse compares with Donne. There is no residential surround, no urban life to flank this broad conduit running from the side of the river and off into eternity. The sidewalks are narrow and windswept, leading into concrete cul-de-sacs that force you to backtrack into eight-lane intersections, themselves impassable without a panicky last-minute run as traffic curves in from the side.

The avenue itself is, like a superhighway, more a river than a street; its natural movement is along rather than across, sluicing cars and buses from the sprawling new suburbs to the east and slamming them into the bottleneck valve of the Yan'an Donglu Tunnel, site of some of the city's worst traffic jams, as everyone tries at the same time to get to Puxi for work or leisure, like Jerseyites off to Manhattan on a Friday night. A few shops are scattered along its length—offering electronics and food and cheap clothing—but there is nothing that smacks of urban life. True, this is a financial district and therefore likely to be deserted now and then, but if the designers of the urban experiment of Shanghai imagined that Pudong would be a vibrant mixed-use cityscape, they are badly wrong. The residential towers are here, and so the people must be too, but there is no sign of them. The Legoland blocks of high-rises range away to the south, toward the site of the 2010 Expo, and to the east, toward the new international airport, creating bleakness nodes, one after the other, at their feet. Like the bad dreams of Le Corbusier's garden cities, where stacked apartment buildings isolated in greenspace, meant to be Edenic, merely establish vertical slums with people-free danger zones at the base, these blocks make the usual utopian mistake of normative modernism: Good on paper too often equals bad on the ground.

But they also project the even deeper utopian melancholy, the empty promise of modern living, the banality of comfort. You get your room in the sky—and then what? In *Delirious New York,* Koolhaas revives grand dreams and old drawings of one-hundred-story fantasy sky-scrapers that would lift whole suburban-style tract houses into the fir-mament, a vision of heaven on earth. But there is always a worm coiled in the core of the utopian fruit. No matter how high up you go, no matter how fantastic your space, it is always yourself you meet there.

I had checked into the Grand Hyatt in the Jin Mao Tower, a hotel whose lobby is on the fifty-fourth floor and rooftop bar is on the eighty-seventh, making it the highest above-ground hotel in the world. In between floors fifty-four and eighty-seven is an open columnar space around which the rooms are scattered along small corridors, so you don't exit your room and come immediately face to face with the yawning expanse of space, like a huge air vent in hell. Although the doughy concrete and tainted steel of the pro-Soviet era is long gone in these newest buildings, there are numerous incidental dangers in the land of instant architectural fantasy. Stories circulate of plate-glass curtains popping out of their frames and plummeting sixty stories to the ground, and Jin Mao has become notorious for an alleged design flaw that creates air currents so powerful, because of the length of the shaft, that hapless maids and guests are routinely sucked in and maimed. I could find no evidence of this phenomenon, which likely lies in the realm of urban myth, but there are certainly plenty of dan-gerous spots in the tower. The very luxury of the place, so wonderful but finally so prosaic, is one of them; one can imagine a desperate Japanese salaryman prompted into sudden existential flight by the emptiness of all this wealth. Xing Tonghe, who also designed the Shanghai Museum and is guiding the Expo project, was behind the inspira-

tion for the small corridors and glass railings, neat design tweaks that kept both architects and developers happy. It saved the open column but minimized the danger. I had met him the day before, and he acknowledged that his solution, while imperfect, was practical. "Drunks will fall over anyway," he told me, not smiling. "You can't design the whole thing for drunks."

The registration form at the Grand Hyatt asks you if you prefer a "high room," which is a joke no one here seems to get. I ticked the box and was given a room on the sixty-sixth floor, which didn't seem that big a deal. But height envy becomes an inevitable preoccupation in a place where height is the point. Every time I got on the elevator, I would check out the guy next to me to see if he pressed a higher number.

Would you like a high room? The Grand Hyatt, Jin Mao Tower, as viewed from the eighty-eighth floor.

Like all of Shanghai's dozen or so five-star hotels, the Grand Hyatt is an exercise in bizarre economics, the complicated mix of import taxes, controlled currency and ridiculously cheap labor. Unlike the Peace Hotel, there were no discarded carpet samples or piles of insulated cable strewn in the corridors. Instead, the hotel delivers the complete James Bond postmodern global luxury experience, with hand-wave-triggered light switches, a "sky pool" that floats above the old city like a bath in heaven, and a glass-box shower sporting controls worthy of a nuclear submarine. Phalanxes of beautiful smiling girls greet you at every corner, exit or elevator, and a gang of strapping six-footers, clearly chosen for their chiseled profiles as well as English proficiency, fold you into waiting cabs and deliver rapid-fire directions to the drivers. Waiters in the jazz bar actually *run* to get your order in, and a cigar request prompts an elaborate geisha performance over the humidor, complete with low-cut dress, miniature jet-engine lighter and ritual-ized waving to test draw. All this with rooms for less than it would cost to spend the night in a mid-range Manhattan hotel.

At the same time, the drinks and sandwiches and coffee run more than in London or Paris, which is saying something. A martini costs as much as a locally purchased winter coat, a cigar the equivalent of a four-hour taxi ride or enough pork dumplings to feed a block. You can walk out the front door of Jin Mao and, beating down the stares of lunching businessmen and ignoring the giggles of the tag-team wait-resses, for less than the price of a coffee, order a feast of Shanghainese food in one of the nearby restaurants.

Jin Mao Tower was designed by a team from Skidmore, Owings & Merrill, the Microsoft—or maybe McDonald's—of architecture firms. It cost U.S.$540 million. SOM are masters of the skyscraper, probably most famous for Chicago's Sears Tower, and they are everywhere, a firm so huge and powerful they have managed to get a finger in many a pie both east and west. David Childs of SOM successfully muscled his way into the World Trade Center reconstruction at one stage, shoving aside the then-central Daniel Libeskind—who, to be sure, has never built a high building—with an arrow-smart design called Freedom Tower. That project too eventually fell to the side amid accusations of plagia-rism from a disgruntled former graduate student, replaced more lately by a falling-water memorial, which looks to be the main new structure on the Lower Manhattan site. Rem Koolhaas, speaking in New York a few years ago, called Childs's firm "architectural colonialists" and complained that its design for Jin Mao was "so infantile and regressive that they should be sued."

In fact, it is a clever update of traditional skyscraper vocabulary, and not bad at all. Ridiculously tall, yes—1380 feet—but retaining a sense of proportion. Clad in a complicated steel-cage curtain, like chain mail over glass, it has a distinctive latticed-metal appearance reminiscent of bamboo and pagoda details on top and sides, even as every room has a spectacular glass-curtain window. Jin Mao's total number of floors (eighty-eight) and thirteen horizontal bands, meanwhile, are references to Buddhist numerology. The name means prosperity, finance, gold— the usual Chinese wish list. If this is global architecture, it could be a lot worse. The tower occupies a wide-open site big enough to support its height, like an open book to its vertical stylus—though this will change when two taller buildings, already modeled at the Urban Planning Exhibition Centre, rise up next to it. One, the $750-million, ninety-story Shanghai World Financial Building, is a sort of elongated glass spinnaker, like a knife blade embedded in the ground. It is projected to rise 1518 feet and thus beat Malaysia's Petronas Towers by 35 feet, though that will still fall short of the Taipei 101 in Taiwan.

The surrounding district is so far a bust. On a bright, cold morning I walked, a lone pedestrian, through a crumbling concrete plaza of abandoned Western-style restaurants. I dodged crash-happy taxis across the broad avenues. I was on my way to the Shanghai International Convention Center, the space-age site of the World Top Architects Forum, an event whose English publicity material oozed the funny, semiliterate grandiosity of all such documents that have been ground though an imperfect translation, like speeches from the opening sequence of the television program *Iron Chef*. "Historically, every nation's renaissance will give birth to a glorious city," it read. "Every glorious era of a nation is always represented by its big city. For instance, Rome, New York, Tokyo, Paris, they are all alike. The essence of global economic competitiveness is always about the vibrancy of a city's brand. Now, the intelligence of the world top architects will gather in Shanghai basked in the time of China's Renaissance. In this glorious era, opportune location, and grand venue, the World Top Architects Forum shall convene."

I looked around the grand venue for the intelligence of the world top architects, but in vain. The forum drew maybe a hundred black-clad men and women, most of them Chinese, all eagerly collecting their loot bags of glossy magazines and CD-ROMs. The major Western architects, so far as I could tell, had better things to do.

Which was too bad, because there was more to learn here than just how to take multiple cell-phone calls during a lecture or perfect the ostentatious don't-mind-me roadie crouch, scurrying unnecessarily before the peopled stage. There was naturally much pre-2010, glorious-era branding hype, Beijing's chosen line on Shanghai, but mixed liberally with criticism of the ham-fisted central planning and penchant for hugeness that have marred the city's boom—a refreshing dose of candor in face-obsessed China, where nothing is ever an error and nobody can ever say they're sorry.

The Hong Kong architect Chen Jianbang, one of the designers of the much-praised Xintiandi shopping district in the French Concession, a small-scale, pedestrian-oriented cluster of restored traditional buildings, had the last ironic word. *Xintiandi* means, literally, "new heaven and earth," and its small blocks and low-rise scale are gorgeous. It's also within sight of the Communist Party headquarters, where the first People's Congress was held, a standard stop on school trips. The deal with the Hong Kong developers of the Shui On Group, backed in part by action-film star Jackie Chan, was that no commercial signage be visible from the HQ. The Starbucks sign is on the north side, discreetly facing away from it.

"When blocks get too big, people stop walking," Chen said. "And when people stop walking, that's when all the trouble begins." He spoke persuasively about mixed use, integration with the urban fabric and the wisdom of avoiding streets wider than eighty or a hundred feet. "Building is not really building. We are trying to create spaces. Never mind the theory; what truly works is actually quite apparent: People know how to use good spaces."

Just as well, I thought, that the opportune location of the forum was a windowless cube. A glance outside the auditorium would have taken in a bleak vista in direct contradiction to every word uttered there. Zheng

Street scale, Shanghai.

Shiling, then president of the Architectural Society of Shanghai, spoke after lunch. "We must make sure that the foreign architects respect the traditions and values of China," he said, after praising the raze-the-ground buildings of Pudong. "Many foreign architects treat Shanghai as a blank piece of paper." Not only them.

Back at Jin Mao, I rode two elevators to the hotel's fifty-sixth-floor jazz bar, being greeted repeatedly along the way. I sat at the bar, ordered a drink, and looked over the split-level, couch-filled acreage of the place. A few Chinese couples canoodled under dim light. A middle-aged Western man with an outgrown white mullet sat side by side with an absurdly young Chinese girl, on whose knee his big, bejeweled paw rested. A table was set up with a bottle of Chivas Regal, an ice bucket, and cut-glass tumblers—luxury *mise en place*. No one ever came to sit there. Groups of wealthy Shanghainese began to arrive. They shoved tables together and shouted orders for cosmopolitans and layered liqueur confections, sending the waiters hustling across the carpet at the trot. They spoke to the hovering bartender in a manner that suggested he had offended them in some deep, unspecified way. A few of China's quarter-million millionaires. A torch singer in a long white dress, backed by the obligatory lazy trio, began to sing Cole Porter in Chinese from a low stage in the back, ignored by everyone at the tables. When she took a break, strains of the Chipmunks' Christmas album leaked from the sound system.

I waved off the cigar girl and lit my own smoke. I looked out the window at the view nobody was paying attention to. It felt like we were on a spaceship, a low-ceilinged, cozy cruise liner to the future, cocooned by money and the biggest lucky break of them all, the lottery of birth. Brought there by the brute reality of the six-and-a-half-billion-human globe, the indifferent energy of material injustice.

Shanghai, wonders and all, still seems a version of Ballard's "terrible city," gorgeous and awful at once. As material rendering of hypercapitalist desire, it makes a forever-deferred promise of novelty and wealth that also says, just as loudly, that nobody's that special. The Chinese know what we don't, that Western individualism is a myth of significance in a world where you're really nobody and nothing. Even the millionaires aren't one in a million, just one of a million. You can build the buildings, but they stand as empty as the ideas of freedom behind them. The whiff of truth remains. Unlike New York, whose own eight million souls, buoyed along by trillion-dollar debt and confused protectionist imperialism, keep crazy faith with a narrative of success, the false consciousness of social mobility, Shanghai is forever taking away with one hand what it gives with the other. Not a new New York, more like the anti–New York.

"How long is the future?" Xing Tonghe had replied when I asked him what Shanghai's future held. His point was prosaic, but the question itself is not. Shanghai's lesson is the lesson of all futurism, modern architecture's dominant trope, the chancre at the heart of utopia. Much as you might like to, you can't go home again. Not again, not ever. All future-desire is revealed as degrees of nostalgia. Because—look, look up—home has already been bulldozed to make way for another half-empty skyscraper, another simulacrum of wonder.

5.
Consciousness and the City

i. Are You?

Are you conscious as you read this?

Presumably yes, for no other option seems either credible or coherent. How do you *know* you are conscious? Presumably, again, because you are aware of yourself as, we sometimes say, being here: The knowledge of your consciousness is coextensive with your experience thereof. Consciousness in this sense of bare self-awareness is, like a will in law, self-proving; it is its own argument. There is no possible gainsaying of a claim, which we might be inclined to call internal, that "you"—the you of self-awareness—are here, for the only reliable, indeed relevant, witness is that very same you. Denying the existence of one's own consciousness, as Descartes saw, is logically impossible; the very attempt proves the opposite. That inviolability of internalist awareness is a key part of Descartes's achievement. In the familiar argument, he isolates

"The city is as irrational as any work of art, and its mystery is perhaps above all to be found in the secret and ceaseless will of its collective manifestations." (Aldo Rossi)

not only the mere fact of mind via its inability to doubt itself (because the act of doubt establishes the very thing doubted, namely mind) but also the contents of that mind as indubitably present as well.

This is what we mean by the *incorrigibility of the mental,* the Cartesian point that, although they may lack external referents, internal ideas themselves are straightforwardly there. Present, as it were, if not yet accounted for. Thus the main thrust of Descartes's argument: Once mind has been, through hyperbolic doubt, isolated and self-proved, it must attempt to reattach itself to an external world that might or might not resemble, maybe *exactly* resemble, the ideas of that world we have in mind. With the aid of some rather slippery arguments about the existence and nature of God, he does it. This is a world-recovery project that does not alter anything in the world—except the foundation, which it once and for all establishes.

There is another problem, however. You say you are conscious as you read this. I am prepared to believe you. But can you do me the favor of *proving* it: not to yourself; to me. You speak, sure, but how do you know that I hear? You gesture, but how can you be certain that your mental thoughts, which by premise have no location or dimension, are accurately conveyed to the material world? And why do you suppose that "I" am here anyway, an entity possessed of another consciousness

There is no mind, and no pain: Descartes's duck.

more or less like yours? For all you know—indeed, as per your own method of doubt—I might simply be an elaborate automaton with no awareness at all. (This, notoriously, was how Descartes viewed nonhuman animals, as machines lacking in any kind of mental properties, including pain. Hence, there could be no more logical objection to kicking a dog than to pounding a desk, if one were so inclined.)

And now we see that, on this picture, the largest mystery is not consciousness itself but relations between consciousness and the other— what philosophers call the problem of other minds. This difficulty, which cripples Descartes's epistemology, is linked to, but distinct from, the more commonly discussed mind–body problem of the Cartesian model. I might be able to forge a tenuous link between my ego and my mechanical body; I might even extend that connection to the rest of

Descartes at work: the desk as machine for thinking.

the material world my body inhabits; but how can I ever be confident that another mind is present? The initial benefit of self-proof turns into the eventual solipsistic cost that no other kind of proof is possible, and so I would appear to be alone.

The link between benefit and cost lies in the same initial error of isolation. Descartes attempts a philosophical revolution by gaining knowledge through moving in rather than out, pursuing doubt rather than fleeing it. The resulting primacy of mental interiority is, moreover, the key to his influence as well as his errors. An interior consciousness begets an interior identity and solidifies a mental suspicion of the body that predates Descartes by millennia, from Plato's denigration of it as the body-prison in the *Phaedo* to the Christian account of sin. That suspicion also postdates Descartes, of course, in the rationalism of modernity and technology's attempted denial of the body's constraints, part of a general mastery project with respect to the natural world. In this, as in so many ways, his thinking is the hinge of modernity.

Mental interiority is a powerful picture. How many of us, for example, have wondered what it would be like to be possessed of a body made of some other material? My brother, an engineer, used to talk about the benefits of having a titanium shell as the hardware for consciousness instead of the vulnerable carbon-based flesh we know. The flesh may have associated pleasures, but these are more than offset by attendant grotesqueries—or so any of us might think in a cynical mood. Now that he is aging and immune from overpowering sexual desire, Leonard, a character in an Iris Murdoch novel,

> can see it again for what it is, a pitiful awkward ugly inefficient piece of fleshy mechanism. And consider flesh too, if it comes to that. Who could have dreamed up such stuff? It's flabby and it stinks as often as not or it bulges and develops knobs and is covered with horrible hair and blotches. The internal combustion engine is at least more efficient … While keeping flesh in decent condition is almost impossible even leaving aside the obscene process of aging and the fact half the world starves.

Leonard's rant neatly combines the body disgust of Gulliver confronted by Brobdingnagian wens and warts with Cephalus's resigned morality in Book I of Plato's *Republic,* which celebrates the sunset virtue of waning desire. How tiresome and awful our bodies, with their needs and fluid, their ingestion of dead animals and bare forked posture! A titanium body would not require sleep or food, would not wear out or break when struck or sliced, would not, above all, feel pain. Such a body would not be susceptible to the degradation of torture, a measure formerly reserved for evil regimes but now, in the age of terror, an eventuality that even allegedly just regimes reserve the right to use. In a twist worthy of Kafka, torture is subdivided and redefined with academic subtlety, such that inflicting pain is justifiable if connected to the extraction of information and forbidden only if done for its own sake—a cynical use of a good point, that torture is rarely about anything other than itself.

But torture in the name of information is still torture; it is still the depraved interest in, as novelist J.M. Coetzee puts it, "demonstrating to me what it meant to live in a body, as a body, a body which can entertain notions of justice only as long as it is whole and well, which very soon forgets them when its head is gripped and a pipe is pushed down its gullet and pints of salt water are poured into it till it coughs and retches and flails and voids itself." All torture has this end, whatever the stated intentions—and tortured justifications—of its artists. We may recall here the critic Elaine Scarry's formulation of war as *pursuit of policy through the destruction of human tissue.* From this vantage, torture is the pursuit of tautology through wicked attention to human tissue. Torture works not because we have bodies but because we *are* bodies.

Wittgenstein says that the body is the soul's image: not a repetition of Cartesian dualism but a reminder of its incoherence. The claim was presumably conscious mirroring of one from Plotinus, namely that memory is the image of the soul—a common sentiment still, but nevertheless somewhat misleading. Memory is itself lodged in the body, not just in the muscle memories of a fishing cast or free throw, but in the senses whose stimulation, with odor or tune, carry us back to another place and time. The claim about the body's primacy does not erase the importance of memory to self-identity but, rather, grounds it, provocatively, in the concrete particular flesh. This fleshly person meets others so constituted in the shared places and occasions of the lifeworld.

Wittgenstein's use of the word *image* is perhaps a little misjudged; the body is not a representation of the soul or mind, a picture of something existing somewhere else. It is not a matter of making the soul present again. It is instead an image in the sense of being the only way we experience soul, that is, through the presence of embodied consciousness. We encounter neither bodies nor souls; we encounter persons. That is why objectification of the body, as in pornography, is experienced as a violation: It does not take seriously the personhood of bodies.

A titanium body can be posited but it cannot be imagined. The life-world of that entity is not the one we know because, among other things, it is one without the meaning-structures associated with pain. Also without sleep, hunger, desire and the thousand nuanced conditions, bodily through and through, we call the emotions. But pain is not enough. Would it, further, have the visual dominance so characteristic of human experience, especially since the valorizing efforts of the Enlightenment? Étienne Bonnot de Condillac, that perceptive philosopher and psychologist, considered how to bestow human senses on a statue—a creature of earth to be brought notionally to life, a rationalist golem project. Condillac decides to begin with smell "because, of all the senses, it contributes least to human understanding." This prejudice against smell, rooted in the upright posture and the human ascension away from the earth, leads to further ones. The smelling statue, Condillac suggests, can experience pleasure and pain in the form of agreeable and disagreeable odors, but that is the only discrimination of which it is capable. Like Freud's infant, whom it predates by almost two hundred years, the olfactory statue cannot conceive of matter separate from itself. It is overwhelmed by smell and so in effect *becomes* smell. "Our statue limited to smell puts us in mind of a class of beings whose understanding is the most inferior," Condillac writes. The statue has no ability to shape or exchange signifiers; it is barred from the realm of epistemology because it cannot conceive of itself as a subject—which is to say, as something other than the remainder of the world.

For better and worse, perhaps, our own sensory arrays are more complex, and more aligned to identity formation. Given the fortunate fact that most of us rarely experience extreme pain, the emotions are the features of everyday life most likely to limn the complexity of our embodiment. That is why they will feature prominently in the discussion that follows—correcting, or at least beginning to, an imbalance all too common in the literature about cities. Emotions remind us that we are our bodies, and more than our bodies: not simply there, as merely material things are, but living and acting and moving. To use metaphysical language, we are becoming rather than being, never simply situated or still but always in motion—and so always in a state of responsibility, whatever our evasions. Notice, as the critic Terry Eagleton does, the wealth of moral-physical terms in our daily discourse, the adjectives of embodied personhood: "tender, prickly, callous, warm-hearted, ticklish, bruised, feeling, sensitive, sharp, thick-skinned, full-blooded." These words, and the states they describe, carry us back to ourselves, to (we might say) a more full-blooded sense of existence, the sort of fleshly complexity to be found in what eighteenth-century moralists such as Adam Smith and Samuel Richardson called "sentimentalism," or the theory of the moral sentiments. Such a theory is understood to work in contrast to the Kantian rationalism, with its disembodied imperatives and sense of abstract duty, which would come to dominate modern self-conception.

I have said *fleshly,* but it is not precisely the flesh that is at issue; rather, it is *the body*. Saint Paul offers this distinction to isolate flesh as sinning and the body as part of the person, and so subject to resurrection. This complicates the usual story, repeated above, of Christian denigration of the body. Wittgenstein and Saint Paul are actually saying the same thing: The body is how we encounter a person. It is not separable. The flesh is that part of embodiment that leads us to sin—diseased desire, let us call it, the sort that all of us know at the edge of addiction or other forms of self-harm, where second-order longing conflicts with first. The flesh is what remains when the soul is gone—when, as a non-Christian like me would say, the person is dead. The moment of that change is mysterious and terrifying to experience, as when the light dies from a beloved's eyes or a heart ceases to beat beneath your hand's touch. She is there, and then, an indefinable moment later, she is not. The flesh remains, but not the body; for although we use it often enough, the phrase *lifeless body* is a contradiction. That is not her, just the carapace of who she was.

Cartesian influence encourages the dangerous thought that we are alone, struggling to bridge the gap between one isolated consciousness and another with structures of language and gesture and institutions. "O Philosophic reader," Thackeray says in a characteristic formation, "answer and say—Do you tell her all? Ah, sir—a distinct universe walks about under your hat and under mine.… You and I are but a pair of infinite isolations, with some fellow-islands a little more or less near to us." But the structures of language and meaning themselves should remind us that we are, paradoxically, only alone together, at once outside and in, equally interconnected and isolated. Isolation is a function of the shared lifeworld, a breakdown or a willed retreat as it may be. It is not a function of solipsistic mind, for there is—there can be—no such thing.

Reading Giovanni Battista Niccolini, marble sculpture, National Gallery of Art, Washington, D.C.

Consciousness shapes cities. They are built places, the results of human imagination and planning. But planning has limits even as it works to draw the limit lines of the street or right-of-way. Cities outgrow their limits, expand beyond their boundaries. Cities also shape consciousness, then, becoming the places of our dwelling and occupation and love affairs. They house our thoughts and guide our flow. A house, Le Corbusier famously remarked, is a machine for living in; but the machine-thinking of functionalism succumbs to its own limits when we see how entangled and unplanned, sometimes, is the realization of place. Our tools and implements, extensions of the upright posture as well as infections of the body—blurring, then overcoming the threshold between flesh and steel—do not *solve* the problems of self. Technological systems, and systems-thinking, will not answer all our needs, and the implicit technological project of overcoming the body's limits through instrumental reason meets its own final boundary, at least for now, in the fact of individual death. We arrive, and we must leave—crossing the final threshold. Built things were here before and will remain after us, not permanent but, at their best, both a reflection of and an occasion for our best and most interesting thoughts.

Our consciousness is always embodied, and thus it is always somewhere in particular. Moreover, our embodiment is of a particular kind, bipedal and suspended, with a large cluster of our sensory array held five or more feet above the ground on which we stand. Freud hypothesizes in *Civilization and Its Discontents* that the upright posture pulls our noses from the ground and, hence, into a conceptual realm of sanitization and control, the new limit-thinking that separates garbage from food, stenches from perfumes. But the upright posture is as much an achievement in phenomenology as it is an underwriter of the idea of civilization. For, in addition to taking our sensory array away from the ground, it gives us a special orientation to space—the six personal vectors of up and down, left and right, in front of and behind. In turn, and we might say even more fundamentally, the upright posture *demands and allows* an orientation to place. We only rarely, and probably in conscious acts of abstraction, stand in space, feeling the vectors as vectors of a theoretical spatial field. Instead, we are in place: reading in a chair, writing at a desk, walking along a street, perhaps sleeping on the grass in a park.

You are somewhere in particular as you read this, as you and I together perform another sortie on the shared fields of meaning. What kind of place is it? A living room, with a couch or chair, a fireplace, a table covered in magazines? An office, with desk and shelves? An airplane, the cramped place we go in order to move those large distances in our apparently endless rounds of place exchange? Maybe a beach or deck or garden? Inside or outside? Somewhere in particular, anyway; as I am, as we both must be, one to write and the other to read. Sharing this moment, this connection. I cannot, of course, *prove* that I am here to anyone's satisfaction but my own, but, in a limit-case usage that carries more weight than we often suppose, given the centrality of language for negotiating our inside-outness, I will ask you to *take my word for it*.

ii. Consciousness and the World

For some years, philosophers interested in epistemology, justice theory and the idea of public space have struggled with three linked frustrations generated by three kinds of disciplinary blindness—no uncommon fault in certain forms of intellectual effort. They are legacies of, respectively, the theory of consciousness, modern architectural theory and liberal political theory. These frustrations explain the motivation and intent behind any political critique of architecture, and so it is worth dwelling on them now, mindful always that there is a degree of caricature operating in any generalization of the following type.

The errors to be found in these views resemble, though fall short of identity with, the kind of dilemmas or category mistakes seized on by some philosophers of language. That is, they are not errors that can be solved with more effort of the same kind that generated them, and we will look in vain if we merely look again. Such errors are, in other words, species of category mistake that can be cleared up, if at all, not by further investigation, still less by adjudication among options or rival versions, but, rather, by conceptual shifting alone. To use a metaphor first deployed with effect by Gilbert Ryle, the philosophical error of the category mistake is to employ the wrong harness for the particular animal we are trying to drive. Admirable for the horse, per-haps, but not for the camel; and freer use of the crop, a tighter grip on the reins or imprecations of mounting urgency are all useless or worse. We must dismount and rethink.

First, then, this almost truistic point: the theories of consciousness that have come to dominate the field, especially the reductionist and some-times eliminativist accounts inspired by neuroscience, seem at best unhelpful and at worst actively distorted. Even when a conscious entity survives the fine-edged attention of our tribe's sharpest minds, there is a lingering sense that the entities so explained or illuminated do not exist anywhere in particular. Since we *do* so exist, the link between dis-cussion and discussed is difficult to span. As William James said more than a century ago, at this stage of the debate, the category itself seems to come apart in our hands: "I believe that 'consciousness,' when once it has evaporated to this estate of pure diaphaneity, is on the point of disappearing altogether. It is the name of a non-entity, and has no right to a place among first principles. Those who still cling to it are clinging to a mere echo, the faint rumor left behind by the disappear-ing 'soul' upon the air of philosophy."

James's pragmatist alternative to a metaphysics of consciousness involves the claim that consciousness, like breathing, is a presumption of human life that lies beneath conscious attention. There is a *stream* of it, as he famously said, but no concrete entity. Consciousness as such does not make itself available to us for analysis; it is not a concept or substance susceptible to isolation or investigation. Although appeal-ing, perhaps especially to the Proustian or Woolfian imagination, this conclusion is unfortunately vague—not to mention subject to immedi-ate objection. Consciousness comes and goes in a way that other presuppositions of life do not. I breathe when I sleep, but I am not conscious. There is clearly a difference there, but what, exactly, is it? We typically assume that consciousness is a desirable state, something to strive for or be cherished, but sometimes we resent having con-sciousness thrust upon us, as when we are rudely awakened, or rise to remembered grief or are propelled into a hangover. Consider Kingsley Amis's description of a morning after in the 1954 novel *Lucky Jim,* the best such in the language and therefore worth quoting in full:

Dixon was alive again. Consciousness was upon him before he could get out of the way; not for him the slow, gracious wandering from the halls of sleep, but a summary, forcible ejection. He lay sprawled, too wicked to move, spewed up like a broken spider-crab on the tarry shingle of the morning. The light did him harm, but not as much as looking at things did; he resolved, having done it once, never to move his eyeballs again. A dusty thudding in his head made the scene before him beat like a pulse. His mouth had been used as a latrine by some small creature of the night, and then as its mausoleum. During the night, too, he'd somehow been on a cross-country run and then been expertly beaten up by secret police. He felt bad.

Now there's a concrete account of embodied consciousness!

James does not go far enough in his dismantling of philosophical ambition: The logical consequence of the pragmatist position should not be the formulation of an alternate account of consciousness, however attentive to embodiment and immersion in language, but to forebear from *all* talk of consciousness. Contemporary thinkers do not make James's mistake, but their results are no more convincing, nor are they able to solve the mind–body problem any more effectively than he. Indeed, increasingly the entire investigation seems predicated on a necessary abstraction and isolation of the alleged concepts: "mind," "world," "consciousness," and perhaps even "explained"! So, for example, even Daniel Dennett's inventive multiple-drafts or center-of-narrative-gravity models of consciousness do not seem to possess the sort of concreteness, in particular of embodiment, that we associate with our own experience of consciousness. I mean the experience you are having *right now* of being here, in your room or out on the street, drinking a coffee or scratching a finger, sounding these words while also thinking about dinner and noticing the cat rubbing against your ankle …

Approaching consciousness as a property or condition to be explained—at least, explained in the outside-in way typical of modern science's presumed models of validity—is to make an error that can generate only further errors. The consciousness these theories uncover is everywhere and nowhere, a generic neutral nonparticular property (or perhaps entity) that bears no relation to the embodied consciousness that is alone a matter of our experience: From the inside out, you might say, but using such language only as a handy first stab at metaphor, since the very notions of inside and outside are the questions consciousness as we really know it perpetually engages, and undermines. The abstracted outside-in consciousness is not real but instead a philosophical fiction—as much a philosophical fiction, despite argumentative improvement and small-grained problem solving over three and a half centuries, as the disembodied consciousness whose "discovery" (which is to say, invention) started the confusion.

Such a consciousness does not sit or stand or dance a meaningless jig; it does not walk or eat or void itself; it does not live in a house or drive a Jaguar or smoke a cigar in the garden. It has no existence of its own. It is instead sustained alone, and solely, by the philosophical attentions of its creators, those mad scientists of the thought experiment. We could not ask it over for dinner, offer it the best walking route by which to come, serve it a gin and tonic on arrival. This consciousness is not from anywhere and does not long to return there. It can't tell you about its hometown's parks, the fragrance of blooming eucalyptus on steep bayside streets or sweet fresh-cut grass mixed with blacktop tar in the schoolyard where only summer sunsets have power of death over an otherwise endless baseball game.

Second, then, a parallel frustration. In the theoretical discussions of architecture, often enough in the practice of architecture itself, there are, to put it bluntly, no people. Often despite genuine effort on the part of some, the drawings and models of the built environment's creators act to reduce the streets surrounding a building to blank white avenues, denuded, pedestrian-free, neutron-bombed. Too often, despite Rossi- and Jacobs-influenced rhetoric of new urbanism, buildings are conceived and planned not as felt responses to need but as ordered patterns of intersecting planes and masses. Stylized plastic couples, a dog-walking hausfrau and a lone briefcase-toting businessman are glued down to show scale, but there is no sense of the teeming mass of people who might rush toward those doors every morning, jam together in those too-narrow corridors at break time or, perhaps worst of all, simply abandon that hopeful courtyard for the dead space it is.

The logical extension (or apotheosis) of this people-free universe is the large-scale model of a town or city, as for instance in the Shanghai Urban Planning Exhibition Centre, rendered in white plaster or painted wood, abstracted and clean, that marches away in orderly rows that give no hint of the tangled intersections, laundry-draped wires, ubiquitous smog and, above all, roiling odor and noise of a real city; no whisper of the dopplering sirens, angry horns, swishing tires and gunning engines, the rising buzz of conversation, garbage stink and wafting fuel fumes, sticky roasted nuts and damp hot dogs.

Here architecture follows, or perpetuates, the same kind of rationalism that generated what rebellious students at the Grandes Écoles in Paris called "autistic economics": the economics of rational-choice modeling under whose a priori conditions all desires reduce to choice and all choices are rational. In the fine-grained theories of the Chicago School, *homo economicus* exists but only as a creature of expressive selfishness and complete self-transparency. Because investigating desires invites moralism, even perfectionism—*why* do you want that good or service?—the model eschews all evaluations except those of efficiency; which is to say, given presupposed motives and limited means, what makes sense for me or you to do under given circumstances. Neither the circumstances, motives nor means can be questioned by the model (though more sensitive economists allow the constraints of contract and criminal law on the issue of means).

The model's only interest, and sole offer of critical purchase, is to evaluate rational action within these conditions. That people often act irrationally, in efficiency terms, is neither surprising nor without humor: the man who drives across town for cheaper gas, burning more than he will save along the way; the teenager who will pay more in real terms for a garment if presented as a sale item; and so on. These routine irrationalisms do not overturn the model but reinforce it. The rationality model is now revealed as a far more normative schema than anything imaged by the Aristotelian or Rousseauan virtue theorist. In forbearing from judging people bad, economics ends up judging most of them stupid. (Easily parodied, I realize. An old cartoon shows two economists appraising an intricate formula on a blackboard. One says to the other: "I find it works better if you leave the people out altogether.")

That hidden moralism is not the main failure here, however. It is, rather, that such models are, like Cartesian space, rigid and self-sustaining abstractions: alluring casts of thought generated by thought's own arrogance. The model generates enough interesting results to obscure its relation to deeper and unspeakable desires—all the more effectively if the model itself abjures desire. The prim rational-choice model, for example, actually sits on a secure foundation of liberal individualism. Early modern state-of-nature thought experiments, whereby private property is defended, are an extension of this ideology of self-generated personal interest. Property is seen in these originary myths as a by-product of self-preservation and self-defense. And yet, there is no real evidence that this was the case in the historic development of the institution. As Thorstein Veblen notes, "with the exception of the instinct of self-preservation, the propensity for emulation is probably the strongest and most alert and persistent of economic motives proper." Emulation—a social function that we share with all our primate cousins—is at the root of comparison and position. I imitate you because, in some sense, you occupy a more desirable position than my own. Given the social ability to generate goods, imitative behaviors are soon supplemented by imitative things: I want to dress or eat or live like you. I need a structure of reliable ownership in order for this emulation and position to function. So, while private property is not strictly necessary for individual survival, it is necessary for invidious distinction. I can go on living without owning anything, but I cannot establish social position without doing so. "The desire for praise," Eric Hoffer notes, "is more imperative than the desire for food and shelter."

Private property is therefore far more likely a *function* of social position than a *cause* of it, based on the drive for self-preservation. Of course, once there is a structure of property in place, goods and services become more and more entwined with social success. Wealth is made coextensive with honor, inherited wealth considered better than earned, and complex systems of distinction are generated. These extend beyond mere ownership, as we know, soon including a vast aesthetic realm deployed under the rubric of taste, and subtle mechanisms of recognition and exclusion associated with issues of deportment and etiquette. Because work forms a large part of human life, it too maps out a large potential territory of judgment, in particular in its absence. That is, leisure time and the conspicuous consumption of its apparatus—hotels, airplanes, sporting goods and "useless" appendages—offer opportunities for establishing position. Indeed, to say this territory is large is not quite correct; in fact, it is theoretically infinite, because there is no limit to the finer and finer distinctions that can be made to display, however briefly and freneti-cally, my superiority over you.

Furniture as consciousness.

This would not be the case if property were a function of need or even of consumption in the simple sense. In the complex sense, consumption is rooted not in bodily requirements but in social ones: my desire to secure a foothold in a social hierarchy. A social hierarchy that may even, and quite effectively, deny its stratification. There is no more efficient boost to the economy of positional goods than a pervasive ideology of social mobility—in some parts of the world this is known as the American Dream. The point here is not to denigrate the desires of individuals, however confused they may be in failing to see positional goods for what they are. (A positional good is still a good.) Rather, the point is to analyze the motives that lead to a theoretical structure that denies the embodied and social character of human desire. We live in a circulatory system that tends to generate, metasystemically, a view of the system as rational and individual when in fact it is neither, or is only so under controversially restrictive versions of those concepts. As long as we employ that view, we fail to see ourselves as we are; perhaps we fail to see ourselves at all.

iii. Public Space, Junkspace

Architecture as a practice is dominated by similar blindness, but not because its practitioners are themselves blind or insensitive. For every architect who perpetuates this exterminator's approach to the inhabitants, viewing humans as vermin unfortunately given access to the pristine edifice of imagination, there are likely hundreds of well-intentioned architects who try, with the best will in the world, not to take people for granted. Yet, these efforts too often fail, demonstrating that this issue exceeds any question of intention. We cannot blame twentieth-century modernism, or its various postmodern appropriations, entirely for these failures. They are, rather, the residue of a much older modern project and ambition. I mean the unlived, and unlivable, abstractions inherent in the necessary (or seen as necessary) move from two dimensions to three, the insuperable conditions of building on the basis of drawing. This is a legacy, let it be added, of the very same Cartesian revolution that skewed the vision of philosophers of mind, only now that part of the revolution that lays down, not the isolated disembodied consciousness, but the foursquare plan of abstracted planar space, the grid of rationality imagined as draping over everything from the island of Manhattan to the page on which these words appear before you. The fictional Cartesian exterior, which models sites rather than real places, is a mirror image of the fictional Cartesian interior, which models thoughts rather than lived experience.

In a common irony, the discussion of cities has over the last few decades reached a theoretical impasse at just the moment we most need liberating thought about the circumstances governing the bulk of human life. By the eighteenth century, theories of the city had developed the now common circulatory model, the stone version of flow and health otherwise realized in flesh by William Harvey's maps of the blood-laved body. Adam Smith was among the first to view people, ideas, commodities and wealth as elements that flow and exchange, the physical conurbation a material host to notional but powerful markets. Streets were seen as arteries, a usage still to be heard, and people or vehicles conducted without cease from place to place, held up by congestion or rubbish clogging the line. Hygiene was realized by scouring the conduits and, in a later development, first speculating then succumbing to the insatiable logic of faster flow. Then, more lately still, the current began to slow and, sometimes, cease: gridlock.

Likewise, unfortunately, in the stream of ideas about the problem. Widening freeways destroyed fabric without easing traffic, and exurban sprawl created faceless housing tracts where rich versions of place and dwelling are difficult, if not impossible, to achieve—though we should always be careful with wide-swath denunciations of suburbs, given that people still want to live in them! Certainly, in far worse and more populous conditions—I mean the largest cities of the late modern world, most of them outside the so-called developed world—these trends have created vast warrened slums of cheap concrete high-rises and makeshift shanties.

Nowadays such complaints about the problems of the city are uniform, to the point where it seems only logical to declare cities over and start again. "After a century's criticism of the large city," Jürgen Habermas writes, after innumerable, repeated, and disillusioned attempts to keep a balance in the cities, to save the inner cities, to divide urban space into residential areas and commercial quarters, industrial facilities and garden suburbs; private and public zones; to build habitable satellite towns; to rehabilitate slum areas; to regulate traffic more sensibly, etc.—the question that is brought to mind is whether the actual notion of the city has not itself been superseded.

The average hyperindustrial modern city is a cluster—or more likely, sprawl—of diverse and unconnected interests, linked by phone lines and shared sewage systems but otherwise exclusive and mute. The city center is a site of mixed functions layered over one another, no longer, as in early modern cities, differentiated by a formal architectural vocabulary but all inhabiting the same multipurpose function-boxes and distinguishing themselves by logos or brand identities. Which identities, however spectral and merely graphic, sometimes outpace or

Labor into order: *Der Herbst* (1607), oil on wood panel by Abel Grimmer, Koninklijk Museum voor Schone Kunsten, Antwerp.

supersede the original function, becoming, in a now familiar postmodern twist, the focus of our attention.

Much of what surrounds us moves toward a deadening sameness, the banal luxury of what is sometimes called super- or hypermodernism but what is actually more often the sort of building Koolhaas includes in his condemnation of junkspace. The term is rather elastic. Sometimes Koolhaas means the interstitial "fatty" spaces between artful facades and airless interiors, the inevitable result of designing from the outside in: airless and soulless atria, elevators and malls. Sometimes he means the block after block of standardized in-fill that blights our cities, isolating monumental buildings in gray surrounds of mediocrity. Sometimes, again, he means the generic, airport-style designs that seem to colonize the entirety of the contemporary urban experience, those clean and deliberately boring spaces through which we wish to move as quickly as possible, the city as circulatory machine taken to its logical conclusion of movement without motive.

"Junkspace is political," Koolhaas argues. "It depends on the central removal of the critical faculty in the name of comfort and pleasure.... Junkspace pretends to unite, but it actually splinters. It creates communities not out of shared interest or free association, but out of identical statistics and unavoidable demographics, an opportunistic weave of vested interests." The result is not dystopia but atopia—the Identi-Kit no-place structures of the new century, where every departure lounge, shopping mall and hotel lobby is indistinguishable from the last. It might be suggested that this is an insight, indeed a condition, available only to someone with a great volume of frequent-flier miles; but that underestimates the reach of the atopian experience. It has been said that the mogul-hermit Howard Hughes went mad because he was the first truly postmodern man, living everywhere and nowhere at once. A half century later, this is an experience common to at least a fifth of the world's population, maybe more (and it is craved by an even larger number). Places become spaces, then become junkspaces, no-places, by the very ubiquity of design itself. The Generic City, as Koolhaas calls it, is a perverse result of modernism's stylistic revolution and the resulting democratization of design. Now Singapore, Houston, Beijing and Melbourne all look significantly the same, like their airports. Unsurprisingly, it was briefly jet-set slang to refer to cities by their

The departure lounge between flights at Narita:
space that is not place.

three-letter airport call signs: YYZ for Toronto, OHR for Chicago and so on. This, Koolhaas notes, realizes one strand of modernism's dream, the constancy of dynamic movement. This is "Schwitters' Merzbau at the scale of the city," he says, "the Generic City is a *Merzcity*."

Our relationship to these cities is likewise increasingly spectral. We arrive and leave by air, touching down at an airport miles from the city center and itself a node of passage hardly distinguishable one from another, despite attempts at domestication or aestheticization. The airport has become, in fact, the twenty-first century city: not merely an extension but the most vivid expression of the consumption/movement imperatives of current urbanism. No one needs to be told that cities are no longer centers of production or manufacture but of shopping, food and entertainment. The airport is not merely a gateway but a placeless apotheosis of this truism, a nexus in which we always spend more time than we would wish, our aroused fears and security consciousness dulled by familiar retail shops themselves designed to palliate our unease. Anchored only by portable laptops and email connections, we are at once there and not there, traveling and immobile, suspended not over the open road of romance but the interchangeable gates and carousels of life, waiting, always waiting, for a row to be called, a bag to appear: the tiny miracles, alone apparently magical, of postmodern existence.

Or perhaps we still drive into the city, our fossil-fueled sports utility vehicles, ever expanding in size, sizzling along on concrete expressways whose very signage signals the uniformity of our automotive urban experience, unchanged from Vancouver to Brisbane, from Miami to Hong Kong. Rare, except for backpacking Euro-travelers or weary commuters, is the Industrial Age experience of entering the city from within, via the vaulted neoclassical expanses of the downtown railway station. Impossible, to be sure, is the daunting threshold experience of being allowed passage through the premodern city gate, exchanging wilderness for civilization and plenty—that drama of judgment and approval is now shrunken to the velvet-rope boundaries of nightclubs and bars, the inner glow of noise and revelry offering invidious contrast to the dark, lonely street.

Always the city represents both hope and danger. There are many ways of being in the city, together and alone. Isolation can sometimes be a function of density, not sparseness. Melville's *Bartleby the Scrivener*—"a Story of Wall Street," as its subtitle indicates—illustrates one version of this dialectic, Bartleby refusing to cooperate with the demands and reasons of market capital, going ever more silent and still in a hostile takeover of the street's financial logic. Philip Marlowe's nocturnal prowls through the garbage of Los Angeles and Bay City offer a cynical, wounded morality of cramped integrity versus general corruption. The city can be straightforwardly romantic, as in *An Affair to Remember,* say, with its celebrated thwarted skyscraper rendezvous. The city can offer mean streets and sunny parks, smooth exchanges and clever heists. City/country or city/town dialectics have proved a powerful conceptual tool for generating cultural influence, most of it negative. City = corruption, sin, deceit. Country = bucolic simplicity, bliss. At the present moment, the conflict is even taking on a vicious apocalyptic tenor, pitting Christian exurbs and subdivisions against the perceived perfidy of old downtowns.

In the 2004 U.S. election, Christian fundamentalists in Georgia toppled Democratic incumbents by offering this coded mantra: "Shorter commutes. More time with family. Lower mortgages." Which is to say, *move out of the city and save your soul.* This despite that many exurbs are parasitic on the urban tax base, with its density of people and exchanges, of which they are so condemnatory; and that the "community" exurbs offer is often really the avoidance of conflict and cultural innovation that results from proximity. The city, and as ever the megacity of New York, has come to represent everything the Christian Right believes is evil: same-sex relationships, ready abortions, strong drink and swearing. Not to mention racial diversity, artistic energy and the sense of possibility that we happy members of species *homo ludens* usually call *fun.* When an evangelical Christian from Colorado was told that a writer interviewing him lived in New York City, the man stared hard at the writer and just said, "Ka-boom!"

The dichotomy is dangerous, but it is also false: its image of the city is inaccurate as well as pejorative. That is, the forms of our urban interaction have, so far from being the happy jostle of art and commerce, actually lost concreteness. It is not only, as Habermas says, that "the urban habitat is increasingly being mediated by systemic relations, which cannot be given concrete form." It is also that those systemic relations themselves are impersonal and virtual. Cities are nodes of population, but they are no longer the nodes of power, which exist rather in a placeless universe of networked exchange. The central tension of postmodern life is not the lack of a governing narrative of meaning, though that afflicts too many of us, and empowers the violent narratives of meaning told by others. This familiar collapse of narrative coherence is merely a symptom of the larger malaise, an unease rooted in the placelessness that is a logical outcome of the modern experiment, where time and space are first abstractly created, then systematically annihilated by the pursuit of speed and the cult of efficiency. The first casualty of that annihilation is awareness of the real facticity of life, what the phenomenologist Edward Casey calls "embodied implacement."

We are incapable of imagining experience without our embodied selves; experience is always of embodied self. And embodied self is always somewhere in particular, in a place. And yet, as Casey argues, place is the most overlooked—indeed, the most comprehensively denied—category of philosophical analysis. We are busy destroying our feeling for place even as it remains the one constant, the fundamental precondition of all human experience. The resulting spread of *atopia,* or placelessness, is the real postmodern condition—an affliction we share with certain modern and indeed premodern peoples, but with the difference that we now actively pursue our own displacement in the form of a cure worse than the disease, the ultimate iatrogenic illness.

Even if we accept that a project of renewed implacement is appropriate (or even available) to the public sphere, we must be careful not to fall into a simple exchange of space-dominance for place-dominance. There is such a thing as an experience (not just employment) of abstract space—as when, for instance, I "find myself" on a map or grid and experience the low-level vertigo, itself a product of modernity, of whipsawing between my sense of myself as a body and my sense of myself as a point of location. The pleasurable, almost erotic feeling of bird's-eye surveillance and dominance afforded us by the very abstraction of three-dimensional space is almost an out-of-body experience. I float above places, and myself in them, to view the world from two perspectives of place and space at once. The map, per convention, offers me a location and, hence, an orientation: "You are here" below an arrow and dot. Such maps, if oriented so that the dot is anywhere other than the bottom or the center, risk orientation failure. The errors fail to take into account the complex dialectic between my embodiment in place and its relation precisely to my experience of abstract location: the way *up* in maps translates to *in front of* in place.

In an old cartoon, the label below the dot and arrow on the map of the Institute of Philosophy is not the typical one. It says: "Why are you here?" An even more pertinent question for our purposes, one which works by enfolding these others, mundane and satirical, is, How can you be here? What is it to be in a place within a world of space, both embodied and disembodied, both inside and outside? Spatial influence is vast and cries out for countervalence, but we make a grievous error if, in challenging Cartesian conventions, we simply replace one unbalanced account with another.

iv. Translation of Dreams

The contemporary discourses of consciousness, architecture and politics are almost completely unknown to one another, despite that their interdependence seems obvious. The overarching paradox is that their respective shortcomings are, in part, a function of that ignorance. The realities of the built environment impinge on the reigning model of consciousness just as seldom as the thought of personal awareness is allowed into the foreground of architectural creation; and architecture and consciousness, in turn, are but rarely taken as basic concerns of the political theorist. All three will benefit from further contact with the others, the consciousness of the philosophers at last finding itself somewhere in particular, embodied and situated; the abstracted space of architectural imagination recast, reshaped by working from the inside out rather than the outside in; the resulting conjunction revealing, finally, why architecture matters so very much to us, our consciousness as citizens.

It would be rash, not least because simply untrue, to suggest that a full solution to these concerns can ever be achieved. Forays into the spaces of inside and outside, the crossing of limits and thresholds, the bracketing of assumptions both powerful and many, are baby steps at best in a phenomenology of cities, a sort of anti-Cartesian reflection about the places and ways we live, that is always necessarily incomplete. Husserl acknowledges the need to be, as he said, an absolute beginner before the fact of experience—though he also demonstrated, in a familiar paradox, that the notion of absolutes is itself the reigning philosophical fiction to be dethroned. "No thought can lead to an absolute beginning," Theodor Adorno says of this insight. "Such absolutes are the product of abstraction." Adorno's particular concern at the moment of making that point is, coincidentally, architecture. Speaking of functionalism's challenge to "spurious" or "degenerate" eclecticism—the challenge issued by Adolf Loos, that form should follow function merely as the technical solution to technical problems—Adorno reminds us of a deeper wisdom, which is that neither function, nor form, nor materials nor even meaning is fundamental. Beauty is never a mere decorative superaddition to utility, though the functionalists were right to see that, in the modern division of aesthetic and technological

Intersection: the skin of the street, dead space, surveillance space.

realms, this becomes a practical danger. But to insist on that division—whether pro or con—is merely to perpetuate it. Failing to see that beauty and utility are inseparable is to commit another error of abstraction, violating the true nature of lived experience by trying to derive the whole from a part, an Ur-phenomenon that grounds the rest.

"[Great] architecture asks how a specific purpose can become space," Adorno says, "through which forms and materials; all these moments are reciprocally related to each other. Architectural fantasy would thus be the ability to articulate space through the sense of function, and let the sense of function become space; to translate purposes into formal structures." Nothing is fundamentally given, guiding all the rest; building, like life more generally, is not a project of sovereignty but of mediation: of functions and purposes as well as materials and forms. Building is a project of finding our way, not solving a problem or decorating a shed. The key concept in that mediation is, notably, one that derives from the lived experience of an embodied person: *Raumgefühl*, or the feeling of space. "The feeling of space has grown together with the purposes and functions," Adorno adds. "Whenever in architecture this feeling of space asserts itself by surpassing mere functionality, it is at the same time immanent to the sense of function." A valid functionalism does not reduce to mere functionality; it is not a one-sided rejection of "style" that becomes a style of its own. It is—or rather, would be—a practice of building ever mindful of the inseparability of form, function, materials and purpose, the four-sided causality of Aristotle.

There is, however, a defensible aspect of the very same modernist vision, indeed in a sense premodern in its conjunction of ethics, politics and craft, of citizenship, projection and construction. Here the "aesthetic radicalism and boldness" Albrecht Wellmer notes in the early modernist architects, qualities we may still discern beneath the scalar excesses of some supermodern ones, can be foregrounded again. "It is not only people who dream," Wellmer says; "cities and landscapes, and even materials also dream, and perhaps it is the task of architects to interpret these dreams and to translate them into built space." Indeed, but not perhaps. And then the rest is up to us, each and every one responsible.

Only close attention to the complexity of lived experience can redeem us from one-sidedness, abstraction and reduction, in architecture as in politics—the lingering traces of a discredited yet still present modernist cast of mind (and narrative). Only here, in the crucible of embodied consciousness, do we reacquaint ourselves with the wonders of existence, the astonishing fact of myself in the world *somewhere in particular*. Language, including the present deployment of it on this page, is an attempt, necessarily limited and partial, to mediate one person's feeling of place. But, just as necessarily, to attempt that mediation is already to transcend the limits of what one person thinks—and so already to cross a boundary, to find a way.

6.
The Thought of Limits

i. Inside Outside

Before we can fully appreciate the importance of embodied consciousness, we must enter more fully into the metaphysical and, we shall see, metaphorical space of "interior." Whether it is to be protected or transgressed, interior is always defined by at least three working parts: inside, outside and, most important yet least noticed, the threshold setting off one from the other. Properly speaking, this threshold is neither outside nor inside; rather, in setting the limit between them, it partakes of both. Like the skin of a body or the cladding of a building, indeed like any surface, the threshold comes into contact with what lies on both sides of it, linking the two environments in the act of separating them. A character in Don DeLillo's novel *Cosmopolis,* considering the exterior of his skyscraper home ("he thought about surfaces in the shower once"), muses: "A surface separates inside from out and belongs no less to one than to the other."

The threshold is an ontological anomaly, a space outside of space, existing only in its vanishing. The word *threshold* invokes the wide stone that separated inside from outside in early European dwellings, a tread or thrash that secured the boundary and thus had heft; but in theory, a threshold, as with any line in geometrical definition, has extension but no dimension; it is zero degrees thick. The function of the threshold, therefore, is not to *be wide* but to *separate,* and thus to *be crossed.* Every limit is also its own negation. Drawing the limit line inspires the desire, or demand, that the line be crossed. Once established, boundaries "ask for" breaching—traditionally, a task for heroes.

"The passage across a dialectic threshold," says John Llewelyn, "is negation and affirmation" at once. It seems to offer a spatial version of the sublation, or *Aufhebung,* found in the Hegelian system: taking up and forward the previous moment, but also transcending it. Often enough, to be sure, this process goes entirely unremarked. Crossing a threshold is no simple matter, though we may blithely perform it dozens or even hundreds of times a day. Indeed, the mundane act of unself-conscious crossing is a good example of what Heidegger means by *Zuhandenheit,* the readiness-to-hand of potentially revealing acts or spaces, whose revelatory possibilities are held in check by their very everydayness. They are nevertheless intimately related, you might say implicated, in the importance of another Heideggerian theme, the idea of dwelling: being at home, finding a place where thinking is possible. To see this, we must interrogate the line that separates inside from out, pay attention, as Kafka so often does, to the sometimes cramped and airless spaces of inside, attics and offices and passageways, and the thwarted desires we feel to throw open a window or break through a door.

What is involved here? That is, what relationships of time and space, of consciousness and identity, of necessity and freedom are created by the move from outside to in and back again? Let us approach liminal spaces by tracing the idea of interior to its geometric inception, a philosophical ground zero: the drawing of lines and circles. Once inside, but only then, we may begin to ask, What do we seek in this crossing over, this transgression. Is it comfort? Security? Control? Or perhaps something deeper and more challenging: the act of thinking itself?

ii. The Pull of Geometry

The inscription above the entrance to Plato's Academy, the first school of philosophy in the Western world, read: "Let no one enter here who does not know geometry." The lines of thought to be pursued inside the academic space are extensions of the lines in mathematical space pupils were already to have mastered, the enabling conditions of higher philosophical thought. And in the famous defense of philosophical education nestled in the heart of *The Republic*, where Socrates claims

Layers of perception: the street outside.

that cities shall know no justice until philosophers rule as kings, geometry is one of the courses of study demanded before true knowledge is possible. Even the archmodernist Le Corbusier could not resist the pull of the geometric. The plan, he says, is everything. And the plan is composed of regulating lines: "The regulating line is a satisfaction of a spiritual order which leads to the pursuit of ingenious and harmonious relations.... [It] is a guarantee against willfulness. It brings satisfaction to the understanding." The classical harmonies of circle and right angle figure their way from the two dimensions of a plan to the four dimensions of a lived building. The plan remains essential throughout the building and throughout the ages, even for what Le Corbusier calls "primitive man," who marks out his plot with cubits, hands or feet—the imprecise but necessary measurements of early building. Nothing much has changed except a greater shared precision in measurement, and thus the ability to reiterate designs.

Oddly, as he goes on in this vein, Le Corbusier begins to sound more and more an unapologetic premodernist in the manner of Pythagoras: "Geometry," he says, "is the language of man." In a claim reminiscent of Plato's *Meno,* in which an unschooled slave-boy demonstrates the Pythagorean Theorem, he notes that "children, old men, savages and the learned" are all given, spontaneously, to tracing out the golden section, that 21×34 perfect proportion, based on the Fibonacci Number Series, which also happens to inscribe the propagating spiral, or nautilus curve. Geometry meets nature. And this should be no surprise, for the forces and options are equivalent: "The creations of mechanical technique are organisms tending to a pure function," he says in a very optimistic statement of technological naturalism, "and obey the same evolutionary laws as those objects in nature which excite our admiration."

Let us call the Platonic reasoning in play here *transcendental functionalism,* in contrast to the naturalist functionalism of Aristotle. Plato suggests that geometrical concepts—where, for example, a point has location but no dimension, or a line has infinite extension, still without dimension—are already more abstract, and thus more real, than any line you could draw, let alone any line observed in the shifting shapes of the perceived world. Geometry is on the way to truth by virtue of its distance from what we choose, nowadays, to call the real world but which is for Plato merely a shadow-play of appearances and variances. Our knowledge of it, when secured, may be presumed to be, as in the slave-boy's recapitulation of the Pythagorean theorem in *Meno,* psychologically a priori; which is to say, pregnant in the soul and awaiting delivery into consciousness by the probing intellectual midwifery of the Socratic elenchus, or method of questioning.

We do not need to accept Plato's controversial metaphysics to appreciate his challenging epistemology. Points and lines and circles are powerful tools of insight, not just of representation. They inhabit our language of meaning and, hence, our sense of ourselves, far more than we often appreciate. This is true not merely in the three-dimensional space of our modern imaginations. This is the space of triaxial occupation, where a body can be mentally mapped—and its volume mentally calculated—by measurement of regular lines in height, width and depth. The Greek geometers thought there were various regular solids that structured the universe, including cubes and tetrahedrons, and these solids were extensions of the various two-dimensional figures, including triangles and squares, themselves natural conjunctions of line. Irregular solids, of which the world was inconveniently full, posed greater problems of measurement, but, as so often, a single brilliant insight solved the problem in a flash. When Archimedes sank gratefully into his bath and noticed the water level rising an amount that must correspond to the displacement of his no doubt quite irregular body, he of course cried "Eureka!" and dashed down the street to collect his reward. He also, maybe more importantly, managed in a stroke to subsume any and all irregular bodies to the relentless logic of regularity.

We also consider time a dimension, a word meaning to measure off, and so we conceive of time as a line that extends in just one direction. Thus the branching time trees and gated logic of temporal choice. Indeed, choice is for us frequently conceived as a fork in the road, from the fated "place where three roads meet" that initiated Oedipus's downfall to the two roads in Frost's scene of choice, the one not taken that has made all the difference. Although both share a metaphor of branching lines, a significant shift is enacted here. On the one hand, there is the terrifying, inescapable structure of Sophoclean tragedy, where any attempted avoidance of a foretold fate only tightens the noose of inevitability. There are three roads, not two, suggesting a mystical press of circumstance, a range of supernatural forces. And the three roads *meet,* signaling that the point thus established is a matrix of fate, a significant location. On the other hand, we are given a melancholy but insistent celebration of free choice in modern self-conception: a line branching outward, not meeting, in two directions, not three. Oedipus is pulled toward his converging roads; the Frost narrator stands free to push himself along one of the two available paths.

Oedipus acts in a social and spiritual web of relations, a complex system whose equilibrium is upset and must be restored, at great cost to himself. His actions are public and publicly assessed. His shame and downfall are carried out in the streets of Thebes, with commentary offered by a chorus articulating, and shaping, the sentiments of the audience. The narrator of Frost's poem is neither public nor, in this older sense, capable of shame. He offers an interior monologue of isolated choice and equally isolated judgment. He tells us what he thought, what happened, and what a difference it made. He does not tell us what the difference is and so does not allow us to judge him. We judge, and are meant to judge, only ourselves: our relation to choices, to decision, to regret. This is no chronicle of a fate foretold, only a report of a free choice committed. The winter traveler is coming from somewhere, we know not where, and going somewhere, *he* knows not where, and that is what human choice means, at least for us moderns.

Thus the difference symbolized by two different linear metaphors: the place where three roads meet (fate) versus the proverbial fork in the road (free choice). Both metaphors offer reflection on the nature of individual action. The differences between them reflect their eras and audiences, but, digging deeper, we see that they each arise as a response to that which they cannot master, namely, the place of individual action in time when conceived as linear—a conception we need to challenge. Convergence (or fate) and divergence (or choice) are both, at bottom, *linear* metaphors of time, and both confess, in their distinct fashion, an inadequacy or perhaps an irony—tragic or reflective, as the case may be—about how we fare when we try to tack along the lines of possibility in this life. Fate and free choice, in short, are two nonsolutions to the same basic nonproblem—a nonproblem, that is, not in being less troubling but in not admitting of solution.

Both metaphors steer clear of a full confrontation with contingency. Although the two concepts are frequently confused, fate and luck are not synonymous, and the fated encounters of the conventional Aristotelian narrative may serve merely to obscure the difference. By emphasizing the cathartic possibilities of the tragic arc, Aristotle suggests that we are made to face the terrors of mortality and living in time, where all actions have consequences, even or especially those actions undertaken in the hope of avoiding predicted, or merely dreaded, consequences. But these frightening conclusions mask insights more frightening still, namely that there may be no intelligible connection at all between action and consequence. The pull of dramatic narrative is not that it is like life but precisely that it is unlike it, conclusive in storytelling where experience is not. "In a world in which everybody would be free to change Oedipus' story," Umberto Eco has said, "they would lose the real force, the real lesson, the real wisdom, of *Oedipus Rex*. Which is that the gods make blind those that they want to ruin."

But, of course, there are no gods but those of our own imagining, and so no wanting here and no ruin. Or rather, there is only a confrontation with mortality and the limits of acting in time, therefore only ruin in our attempts at making sense. "The experience of a linear 'organic' flow of events is an illusion (albeit a necessary one)," says the philosopher and critic Slavoj Žižek, "that masks the fact that it is the ending that retroactively confers the consistency of an organic whole on the preceding events. What is masked is the radical contingency of the enchainment of narration, the fact that, at every point, things might have turned out otherwise. But if this illusion is a result of the very linearity of the narration, how can the radical contingency of the enchainment of events be made visible?"

The answer is, paradoxically, this: "By proceeding in a reverse way, by presenting the events backward, from the end to the beginning." Thus the second-order disturbances and cathartic possibilities of Harold Pinter's *Betrayal* or J.B. Priestley's *Time and the Conways,* which proceed along back-to-front timelines, or the films *Memento* and *Run Lola Run,* which jumble both timeline and the uncertainties of unreliable narrators. By playing with narrative conventions, these efforts denatu-

Circles of falling water at
Johnson and Burgee's
Williams Tower, Houston.

ralize them. But even so, they cannot avoid a general economy of acceptance. Contingency may be briefly glimpsed, but it is in its nature not to be accepted. We shift from a fate model to a free choice model without either one taking full stock of the play of sheer luck—which is reducible to neither.

iii. Around and Around

Notice the influence of linear-narrative metaphors in life. They structure our sense of time, however illusorily, and so influence our sense of ourselves as timely. It might be said that circles are just as important to this fiction or hypothesis as lines, if not more so. Of course, a circle is, we might say, just a line bent gently back on itself, the shortest possible journey out and back. ("Of course" has itself a geometrical echo: It means to stay on the expected line.) Once joined, the circle immediately represents not just a particular journey—say, the one of its inscription on paper—but every journey, starting and stopping at any point, because it is unbroken and therefore complete. Circles symbolize, for us, commitment and wholeness and perfection. It can be no surprise that the Greeks conceived the movements of celestial bodies as a symphony of circles and their three-dimensional extensions, spheres. They went to great lengths, as did geometers long after, to reconcile observable anomalies such as the apparent retrograde motion of Mars with the desired conceptual neatness of circular orbits.

Circles even more than lines cut deep to the heart of our self-conception. They embody movement and stillness at once, the closure of completion and return. We long to come full circle, to return to where we started, to get safely home. The very drawing of a circle tells us this, as in Donne's poem about parting and returning:

> If they be two, they are two so
> As stiff twin compasses are two,
> Thy soul the fixed foot, makes no show
> To move, but doth, if th'other do.

And though it in the centre sit,
Yet when the other far doth roam,
It leans, and hearkens after it,
And grows erect, as that comes home.

Such wilt thou be to me, who must
Like th'other foot, obliquely run;
The firmness makes my circle just,
And me end, where I begun.

There are difficulties afoot. Jacques Derrida probes the circles presumed by Hegel and Heidegger, among others, noting that here they,
and all philosophers seduced by essence, will find exactly what they are
looking for, the answer contained within the very terms of the question: the Absolute, dialectic, Being, truth as *aletheia* or the clearing.
Heidegger and Hans-Georg Gadamer warn that the task of philosophy
is not to escape the hermeneutic circle but to enter it in the right way,
and so acknowledging prejudice as a necessity of interpretation, and
hence of understanding itself. Gadamer writes:

> If we see this circle as a vicious one and look out for ways of
> avoiding it, even if we just "sense" it is an inevitable imperfec-
> tion, not to be reduced to the level of a vicious circle, or even of
> a circle which is then the act of understanding has been misun-
> derstood from the ground up … it is merely tolerated. In the
> circle is hidden a positive possibility of the most primordial
> kind of knowing.

Derrida shows that this self-aware, virtuous circle, so far from being
open to rehabilitation, is fatally tainted. The circles of interpretation
are bewitched spaces of presence, self-authenticating fillings-in of what
is called empty. For Derrida, every presumed philosophical circle, no
matter how subtle and interpretive, is revealed as a vicious one. The
general project of metaphysics is an "attempt to view the totality by
escaping it," he says, an "excessive and deranged" ambition that succeeds only in denigrating the world of our experience as "merely
apparent" in hot, and impossible, pursuit of something imagined to be
more real (or, rather, Real): the world as it really is. Here the only out-

come is a gesture "in the direction of infinity or nothingness," and so reason (or, rather, Reason) reveals its inescapable tinge of madness, its unreasoning desire. Unreason is always linked to reason as what reason wants to, but cannot, say. In this sense, Derrida says, reason is "more mad than madness" because "ordinary" madness, mere insanity, lacks this deeply lunatic delusion about transcending limits.

We may have cause to doubt Derrida's diagnosis, or perhaps to doubt the usefulness of it if true. What is left to do or say if all our deeds and thoughts are pre-condemned *and* the deed of saying so has already been performed? Whatever their necessary relation, reason is not identical with unreason, not least in reason's ability to do things with words, *to get things done* through communication and the coordination of action. Moreover, is not the desire to transcend the presumed limits of this world a central feature of this world? Human consciousness is, we might say, the world becoming aware of itself, and at precisely that moment, the world both wants to go beyond itself—and, in a sense, already has. The world realizes that it is not itself a function of limits even as we in the world attempt to draw those limits. Language cannot speak all of what is, cannot succeed in the implied rational project of complete signification, not because it lacks power but because it retains it—because language is part of what is, and so cannot signify itself. This is a point to which, like a circle, we will return.

In any event, the self-to-circular relation can crack under much less sophisticated pressure also and so quickly become fodder for parody. An episode of the animated television show *The Simpsons* mocks a purveyor of cheap self-help techniques, Brad Goodman. "Let's say this circle is you," the suave Goodman says to cheesy infomercial host (and perennially out-of-work actor) Troy McClure, drawing one on a chalkboard. "My god," marvels McClure to the audience, "it's as if you've known me all my life!" Circles are an easy trap. Still, for just that reason, they are hard to resist and impossible to avoid, in life and games alike. Consider the diamond shape of the infield in baseball, that most metaphorical of sports. The diamond is a modified circle, and the bases are mere way stations, or points of temporary safety, along the perilous journey out and back, to home, where one's happy teammates are waiting, fists and spirits high. A home run in baseball is called, not

What the coffee tells you.

coincidentally, "circling the bases," the opposite of that basic metaphor for the impossible task, foolishly undertaken, of squaring the circle. When it is a matter of judgment, as when the ball just barely makes it over the fence, and, hence, out of the magic semicircle of the outfield, a 90-degree segment of the available 360 degrees called fair rather than foul, the umpire signals by stirring the air above his head in a counter-clockwise circle. Time may be measured on the circular face of the modern clock, but baseball, where time passes only in outs and innings, not minutes and hours, knows better. Like the umpire's finger, we circle the bases against the clock.

Once there is a circle, there is a boundary—literally a binding, as with rope—and therefore an inside and outside. Velvet ropes mark us off from the happy partygoers inside the club. Gates and fences keep us from trespassing on private property. Walls in Berlin and the West Bank, fences in Mexico and Belfast enact controversial political realities. Every line is a claim, an insistence on some form of belonging that, categorically, excludes as well as includes. It is always significant to go *beyond a boundary,* as in the title of C.L.R. James's book about cricket, which is not really about cricket. A cricket boundary may even be literal, that is, a circle of rope, so that a fast-moving ball will jump at the edge and indicate, in its movement, the four runs just tallied. It is interesting that only cricket and baseball, of all the world's major team sports the least territorial and most linear, have a central place of success reserved for sending the ball out of play. It is as if their sense of linearity's demands in running the bases or scampering between wickets leads to a buildup of psychic pressure that must be discharged in the explosion of going beyond the threshold of play itself, outside the final line, past the limits of the game. In baseball, a home-run ball is literally gone forever, becoming some fan's souvenir—except at Wrigley Field in Chicago where, famously, fans throw home-run balls hit by visiting teams back onto the field, like garbage. Well, they are garbage. The throwing back makes them so.

Home runs in baseball, fours and sixes in cricket, can turn the tide of a game in an instant. They are powerful, often majestic: the act of a border-crossing hero. They are also anomalous. In the 1988 baseball film *Bull Durham,* a veteran catcher excoriates home runs to his baffled teammates. They stop the game, they exclude every other player on the field, they involve no action. They are undemocratic and unjust. Heroes, boundary-breachers, thus have a dialectic relation to justice. The boundaries of the city define the limits of the political, such that what lies beyond the pale, past the lines of defense, is barbarian. The city is, metaphorically, the ambit of justice, the sphere of law. Entering the city, via the gates of ancient and medieval cities, say, is to acquire the protection of law and even, sometimes, the rights of citizenship. But this is by no means guaranteed, and the dynamic tension of all cities is their simultaneous enactment of security and threat. Law exists, but its reach cannot cover the range of law-breaking the city enables.

Moreover, the law itself may be corrupted and made tyrannical, and then the heroic move is back outside the city, the disobedient lawless gesture that is, paradoxically, a reaffirmation of the law's sovereignty. As Hegel saw, Antigone's mourning of Polynices in defiance of Creon's dictum is a synthetic move that rises beyond the conflict of atavistic familial devotion and abstract political authority in a powerful, tragic critique of both. She needs to obey her father the king and bury her slain brother against the explicit order not to do so. Antigone embodies—she enacts with her body—the impossibility of reconciling these two claims on personhood. The psychoanalytic theorist Gillian Rose has suggested in a similar vein that Poussin's painting of the wife of Phocion gathering his ashes outside the limits of a ruined city tells us something about the dialectics of boundary. The painting does not, as it may at first appear, depict a rejection of the city's rational legal authority, embodied by the soaring classical columns and entablature of the city's architecture. It is, Rose suggests, instead a paradoxical affirmation of the city in legitimate form. Here, going beyond the boundary of the city in order to mourn means that mourning becomes a political act, a rearrangement of boundaries through the breaching of boundaries.

Instead of an endless unresolved melancholy at the fact of tyranny, Rose argues, an anarchistic nihilism that cannot unite the disparate demands of Jerusalem (devotion) and Athens (law), mourning *becomes* the law. And, as with Elektra's mourning of her too-beloved father, this is at once a progression and a befitting. Mourning *both* works its way toward law *and* is appropriate to law. Consider Antigone's dilemma of what to do with the body of her brother Polynices: She can neither bury him nor not bury without violating custom (family duty) or the law (in the form of Creon's prohibition), respectively. As Hegel again suggests, she forces consciousness forward by dwelling in, but not fully resolving, this dilemma about the most basic of lines: the rotting, unburied body, the lifeless corpse that becomes, without a soul, a kind of garbage. Thus, among other things, the creepiness of zombies: not the dead or the living, nor even the resurrected, they are the undead. They remind us, in their postmortem ambulations, that buried bodies are invisible but not gone.

The dialectical overcoming achieved by Antigone is only ever partial, however. Dialectical overcoming can only ever be partial, because consciousness alone cannot solve the problem of its own conditions and limits. The *third city,* the city of our dreams, the just city that is neither Jerusalem nor Athens, is reinvigorated in the heroic grief-work of walking bravely past the limits of the given. But the issue that remains (the issue *of* remains) is this one: How to realize that city except in hope?

iv. Beyond Boundaries

There is an inside, so there is an outside, and even if the outside means danger or risk or the unknowable, we long to explore it, to spill out. (Samuel Beckett: "The whisky bears a grudge against the decanter.") The desire is structural, not merely incidental; it is inscribed in the very act and art of inscribing. Immanuel Kant noticed in his transcendental philosophy how the drawing of limits was always, inescapably, to go beyond limits. To say what was beyond knowing was always to say something about how things lay on the other side of the boundary. Thus the celebrated distinction in critical metaphysics between limits and bounds, where the first is crossed in its drawing, the second a sign of canceled possibilities, like the literal bounds of a trussed prisoner. Ernst Cassirer summarized the Kantian project of critical idealism this way: "To step into the infinite it suffices to penetrate the finite in all its aspects."

Well, fine—and no one did it more thoroughly, if not necessarily better, than Kant. But to plot the limits of what we can know *completely* or even *incompletely but exactly,* you want to say, is always to characterize what we cannot know, and therefore to know it: An act of humility becomes an act of unwitting arrogance. Compare this telling remark from the *Tractatus Logico-Philosophicus,* which firmly sets in its place the common desire, among philosophers and others, to speak of the entirety of existence. That is impossible, Wittgenstein says, "for that would appear to presuppose that we were excluding certain possibilities, and this cannot be the case, since it would require that logic should go beyond the limits of the world; for only in that way could it view those limits from the other side as well." Lines and circles work to circumscribe, to draw around, to establish position, but they cannot really contain us unless we let them; nor, however, can we exceed them unless we are willing to ignore logic and indulge a flight of fancy. It is a flight we often long to catch, however. That is, we always wish to get out, to escape fate or exercise choice, to pass beyond *circumstances*—which are, as the word suggests, just the things standing around us.

Hegel sought to move beyond Kant by employing a modified geometrical trope, the spiral, which is really what a circle becomes when it remembers that it used to be a line. A spiral is a line circling upward or downward. It returns, but not to the same place, and, hence, shows both familiarity and strangeness. But it does not *solve the problem* of inside and outside any more than the circle, because sooner or later we must get off the merry-go-round, escape history's complex imprisonment. And at this point Hegel's elaborate spirals are likely no more convincing than Plato's heavenly forms or Kant's transcendental realms of speculation. In all cases, escape velocity is reached only at the cost of putting ordinary experience firmly in its place as inadequate, rather than embracing the flawed desire that leads to those feelings of inadequacy in the first place.

We can see this more concretely by considering what is at stake in boundaries and their violation. Conceptual contrasts are fundamental to human projects of sense-making, in everything from the primitive spiritual geographies described by Lévi-Strauss—the raw and the cooked, ashes and honey, artifice and nature, the sacred and the profane—to the fine distinctions of a careful analytic philosopher. We are addicted to taxonomy and line drawing, the creation of distinct spaces to match distinct ideas. It is a way of marking out our place, of finding a form and an orientation. Temples and courts and theaters are all interiors whose function and integrity are maintained by a separateness from what lies without, the generalized public space of secular

A spiral is a line circling ...

life. The home, that most basic interior, is likewise protected as a distinct space, an ambit of privacy and comfort as against the chaos and commerce of the outside. When we bring a Christmas tree into the house, we enact a pagan consciousness of this distinction, the artificially comfortable world of the interior as distinct from the natural world outside—a line, and a set of categories, themselves both artificial.

These mundane boundaries are related, on one side, to the traditional distinctions of Platonic metaphysics—appearance/reality, sensible/intellectual, written/spoken, made/found, margin/center and, finally, theory/practice itself, the womb of the West. This logic of distinction is a powerful force in human thought, the drawing of lines that serve to impose not just a division but an evaluation, the ultimate in positional goods, such that philosophy teaches us to distrust and demean the given, the apparent, the everyday. Deconstruction, the strategy of reversing the polarity of these distinctions and so undermining their authority, is a form of threshold erasure. But it confesses its own assimilation to the logic of duality: By reversing polarities, it reinforces them, thus often failing to illuminate what Rose, a more dialectical kind of late modernist, calls "the broken middle" or "the third city."

On the other side, the household boundary is related to seemingly trivial but actually deep human feelings concerning, for example, food and garbage, health and contagion. Most people are familiar with the iron-clad children's law that no two foods may touch each other on the plate, lest the liver-born juice cooties, say, infect the otherwise acceptable mashed potatoes—a distant juvenile cousin to the more serious scriptural commandments to keep milk separate from flesh. We are probably all familiar with the so-called "five second rule," which stipulates that any piece of food dropped onto the floor or into the sink is still edible, that is, does not become garbage, if retrieved within five seconds. (Recent scientific studies claim to find this rule sound: Contamination of common sorts is avoided if food is retrieved quickly from a dirty surface. As so often, rival studies show the opposite.) Perhaps less well known is the term, but not the practice, of *disconfection,* which is the sterilization of a piece of candy retrieved from the floor by blowing on it, assuming this will remove all the germs.

Amy Vanderbilt does not have to tell us not to pick food out of the garbage, as the character George Costanza does in a notorious episode of the television show *Seinfeld,* presumably because we know this already. But we know it in the way we know other second-nature, rather than first-nature, things. It is a distinction, a threshold, into which we have been initiated. Our feelings of disgust, rooted in the body and its wet limits of blood and pus, contagion and disease, are often extended in just this way, just as the household interior is an extension of our embodied consciousness. We are ever on the lookout for evidence, or even just the bare possibility, of infiltration, contamination, pollution, corruption. Food off the floor or out of the garbage is hardly likely to be always harmful, and yet this boundary is considered inviolable. Except, that is, when it is considered desirable to violate, as when, says Freud, disgust becomes a veiled form of desire; or, as we might suggest instead, the actually disgusting is actually desirable. Especially in sexual contexts, another kind of boundary is crossed, so that we want, and do, things we would not normally consider doing, and often cannot easily talk about. Disgust, often enough, goes undiscussed.

In general, though, we *fear* the foreign object, or *xenocyst* as Gadamer vividly calls it. Foreignness in the imported object violates the imagined coherence or sanctity of an interior space. Such violations are deep and often unsettling, if also now and then comical. The gouging tool or file sneaked into the ring of cheesy professional wrestling is invariably referred to by announcers, in appalled tones, as a *foreign object,* giving this choreographed thuggery a mythic, threshold-breaking significance. Any newcomer to a house brings a disruptive alien presence, as when, to take another television example, the grumpy father of Frasier Crane moves into the psychiatrist's immaculate—that is, literally, *spotless*—Seattle apartment. His hideous broken-down, duct-taped easy chair is an immediate point of contention, a symbolic foreign object that forces a reordering of that interior. A possibly less amusing outcome might be imagined in the violation of a burglary, in which the taken-for-granted security of an interior space is breached and so undermined well beyond the actual incident. You may catch your burglar, but that will not allay the feelings of unease in knowing that your interior, your private space, has been violated.

"The center is the threshold."
(Edmond Jabès)

Such an encounter may only enhance the weirdness of such an event. The sound of footsteps down the hall, waking you from sleep, is not soon forgotten.

v. Between Inside and Out

Other constructions formalize this ever threatened violation of the threshold by creating, in effect, liminal spaces as part of the dwelling. I mean such things as open porches, verandahs and stoops. These spaces, traditionally the sites of leisure, are neither fully inside nor fully outside. Instead, they embody the liberating movement from one to the other, and it is never a surprise (though it is always a pleasure) to notice that people tend to gather in such spaces whenever circumstances—including, crucially, the weather—allow. In this sense, the porch or verandah is an expanded version of the window, that feature which, as Le Corbusier noted, is at the very center of architectural history. A material permeable by light but not by air, constructed from a ubiquitous substance nevertheless commonly found in quite different form, glass is a kind of architectural miracle, and its stable production changes human life as few things have. From the dark dwellings of the West's adolescence we emerged into a bright young adulthood, where windows were taxed, so valuable were they considered, and then eventually into a singing maturity in which glass and its true-solid relation, crystal, allowed us finally to build the spun-sugar towers and soaring cathedrals of our postmodern imagination. But the window, especially in the form of the glass-curtain walls of generic modernism, can also obscure the useful dialectic of inside and outside. "In our time," says Yi-Fu Tuan, "the desire for a picture window and for the expansive view suggests a need not only to command space but to see into the future and command time." This warped utopian impulse, so liable to pathology, can serve only to distance us from the chastening reminders of natural limits, the presence of ineradicable dangers outside. It replaces irony with certainty and hope with lust.

The porch is like a window that allows the outside to come inside, to add air to light without opening up the dwelling, with its sanctity and privacy, to the full blast of exterior gaze and contagion. "The true porch," writes Garrison Keillor,

> strikes a balance between indoor and outdoor life. Indoors is comfortable but decorous, as Huck Finn found out at the Widow's. It is even stifling if the company isn't right. A good porch gets you out of the parlour, lets you smoke, talk loud, eat with your fingers—without apology and without having to run away from home.... You should be able to walk naked onto a porch and feel only a slight thrill of adventure. It is comfortable, furnished with old stuff. You should be able to spill your coffee anywhere without a trace of remorse.

The porch is both free and stable, open and protected. Unlike the true outdoor picnic, which is conventionally a site of disruption, where natural forces upset the social order (the Box Hill picnic in Jane Austen's *Emma*, say), a meal taken on the porch is nicely poised within the balance of human claims. It allows but does not demand. It asks but does not require. "It is," says Keillor, "our reviewing platform and observation deck, our rostrum and dais, the parapet of our stockade, the bridge of our ship."

Because we can be inside the porch, which is neither inside nor outside, we can begin to glimpse here the nature of thresholds more generally. The porch is a good place to think, perhaps on a long evening with summertime drink in hand. It is not named with a specific purpose, as other spaces within the house may be. It embodies, instead (to borrow a phrase), purposiveness without purpose, a reflection of the house upon the fact of itself. More so even than the garden, which has its own store of insights to offer on inside and outside, natural and artificial, the porch allows room for thought about position and permeation and boundaries without insisting that those thoughts submit immediately, or maybe at all, to the pervasive logic of instrumental reason. The *Stoa Poikilé*, the Painted Porch in Athens, was the covered colonnade to which the paradox-fond philosopher Zeno and his followers resorted. Thus their school of thought became known as Stoic, a resonance worth recalling.

The rabbis of Talmud Torah delineate the threshold space of the *eruv,* the house—sometimes notional—that allows Orthodox Jews to engage in activities such as carrying keys, pushing a stroller, or walking the dog, which would otherwise be forbidden on the Sabbath. There is an *eruv* in Manhattan, defined by fishing line strung between lampposts, that runs from 125th Street all the way down to the fifties and clear across the island from the East River to the Hudson. One in Toronto, which took more than a decade to complete, covers a large chunk of the Greater Toronto Area (as it is invariably called), including the neighborhoods of Forest Hill and Bathurst Street north. It uses the handy walls of Highway 401 as an obvious boundary on one side, supplemented by fencing, poles and fishing line. This *eruv* replaced an earlier one, first constructed in 1922, which was located downtown, where the city's Jewish population was then concentrated.

Even a house this large—the Manhattan *eruv* currently encompasses about sixty-five million square feet, or four thousand acres, which is to say more than one-third of Manhattan, and set to double when the *eruv* is extended down to 23rd Street—needs a controlled threshold. A house is not a house if there is no way in or out. In this case, the threshold is established by means of gates placed at various points along the line, small compartments that contain cords that can be stretched across streets. For the rabbis also say that a house without a porch or vestibule lacks warmth. We must enter a full living space directly, as from the busy street outside, without any transition. We have no separate time to divest ourselves, to enact literally the meaning of vestibule, the place where outer clothing is donned or shed. ("Again the little vestibule which frees your mind from the street," Le Corbusier says of a temple.) A porchless house is therefore not just awkward but incomplete, broken, not least because it does not allow that moment of anticipation—the anticipation that is this life, this mortal vestibule— before going in to find the banquet that awaits.

We lose thereby a degree of explicit formality, and so of awareness, about the complex functions of the threshold. In warmer climates, it is common to pass from inside to outside without thought or change of clothes, and we may see a greater degree of ease in other manners too, a sort of generalized porch where there is no need to insist on the strictures of what Don DeLillo calls *roombehavior,* or that favorite of nettled mothers everywhere, *your indoor voice.* Public and private may blur at the edges, altering our sense of possibility. Not for these dwellers the sober airlock considerations of entering winter's chill on the prairies, for example, where no venture outside is ever casual. Not for them the controlled climates of air conditioning, which can create their own air-locks—and, indeed, those expensive blasts of chilly air into the sweaty sidewalks of downtown streets, calculated to turn strollers into shoppers, changing idle movement into cash-nexus exchange.

No room is just a space; it is always a *place* we are either entering, occupying or exiting. "Thanks to the double horizon that body and landscape provide," Edward Casey says of this implied movement, "a place constantly overflows its own boundaries. Uncontainable on its near edge, it flows back into the body that subtends it; uncontainable on its far side, it flows outward into the circumambient world. Place's inflow and outflow are such that to be fully *in* a place is never to be confined to a punctuate position; it is to be already on the way out." We do not have positions; we are activity. This is far from obvious and even farther from obviously easy. Movement makes for projects, but projects can succeed or fail: Logic demands that, if we can find our way, we can also get lost. Our suspension in time means, further, that the not-yet of happiness forever teases us with its collapsed utopian urges: the cosmic joke of the bar sign offering "free drinks tomorrow," an appropriate slogan not just for a culture but for humanity. "All of human unhappiness stems from one thing," Pascal says in *Pensées*: "not to know how to remain in repose in one room." The thought appeals—a sort of generalized externalization of comfort in one's own skin. And yet, the idea is incoherent, for we cannot stay in one place. Edward Albee, making the point cynically, says the key to happiness is "to know one's limits and aim a little bit lower." But limits are understood, categorically, as what holds us back from where we wish to go. Even when the task is impossible, limits are meant to be broken.

That combination of categorical impossibility is, finally, illuminating if not liberating. A fundamental irony of human existence may be captured in the fact that repose in one room is also a definition of prison. Happiness taunts us with its lack, a lack both feared *and created* by all of our desire. We keep running back into ourselves: exiting rooms only to find ourselves in new ones; crossing boundaries just to find that new ones have been created. Escape is impossible because no matter how fast we travel, we cannot outstrip the *horizon of concern* we all carry with us. We cannot leave ourselves behind, for there is no behind except the one that we define by being here, standing somewhere in particular.

7.
The Limits of Thought

i. Crossing the Threshold

The ordinary household threshold embodies all these possibilities of limit and insight, and so crossing it, though usually performed without thought, should be a little act of heroic dimension. That we do this without much thought is not the

most obvious symptom of our dis-ease with thresholds. In focusing so much on the details of the interior, rather than on its enabling and highly contentious metaphysics, we have lost sight of the necessity of the relation: the understanding that a vigorous public realm is possible only when the private realm has its proper place. Unlike the ancient Greeks, who saw the private dwelling space as the realm of mere necessity, where food and shelter could lay a practical foundation for more important matters of citizenship and public discourse, modern individuals often see the domestic interior as an end in itself. We seem to want to make the domestic realm not merely an extension of one self among others, an heroic democracy in fact, but the whole of the world: an inside that feels the outside that makes it possible. And that is a grave oversight of the interior's power.

Nor can you allow yourself to be dominated by the geometrical regularity that is implicit in the house. As an acute phenomenologist of interiors reminds us, a house is not merely a building. "A house that has been experienced is not an inert box," Gaston Bachelard says in *Poetics of Space*. "Inhabited space transcends geometrical space." That is, the space of home, of the dwelling, is space from the point of view of concern, of lived experience. It fluctuates and condenses with no regard for the straight lines and right angles of drawing. The bedroom looms larger and closer because you are in it, say, waiting for me. The nook or cranny becomes immense, threatening (or, conversely, close, protective) because of its role in my dreams. All parts of the house work to establish this space.

Even the lowly basement, itself the merely functional foundation, becomes a space of wonder. Like the attic or the garage, that crucial annex to the space of the house, a weapons-cache for the sleek automobile, the means of our fast escape or weary arrival, the basement can be used to store the bewitching odds and ends of life, the discarded toys and rusted yard tools, the collections of LPs or comic books, that can, overturned by accident, effect a vertiginous time travel. Or the basement can be finished, made into the suburban rec room with its suspended ceiling, shag carpeting and fake wood paneling, site of Ping-Pong games, television marathons and make-out sessions; or the workshop, where plastic models may be painstakingly glued together, rickety tables constructed, bicycles repaired. "The basement workshop is the greatest blessing of the twentieth century," the graphic designer Thor Hansen said, in extravagant praise of this mundane site of craft, this democratic forge.

And yet, this kind of space is too often taken for granted, left uncelebrated; and so our task as phenomenologists of the interior is to achieve understanding without resorting to the reductive explanations of geometry even as we honor the influence geometry has exerted in creating our spaces. A house, says Bachelard, is always at once open and closed. A seat in a bay window gives us a view of earth and sky, mirroring our own "half-open Being" in the moment of revealing and concealing. There is always inscribed here a possibility of transcendence, a line of hope extended. Outsideness represents alienation or aloneness, Lear's ordeal on the heath, contrasted with the belonging or immersion of insideness, the comfort of the hearth. But we need to think both to think either.

To be sure, the carving out of this interior from the rambunctious shared spaces of the European Middle Ages, along the way making possible a more abstract defense of individualism, is one of modernity's great achievements. Nevertheless, we should probe both its limits

Andrea Palladio's Villa Capra (1566–71), also known as the Rotunda, viewed in section.

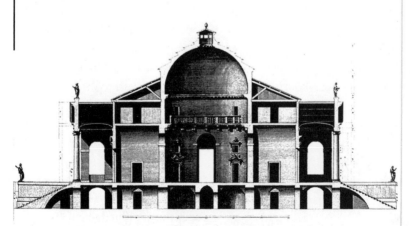

and its variability. Michel Foucault, for example, warns us against the temptation to naturalize individual consciousness, to see it as driving history forward to the "rational" end point of free individuals in well-decorated detached dwellings. In history, Foucault says, we must remember that "nothing is fundamental." Material innovations, as when the life-sustaining fire moves indoors through advances in masonry, often change the web of social relations. Now we have a hearth, and so gathering around the hearth, and so hearth and home, and so on. But material change of this sort never occurs in the social vacuum of theory's own abstraction. Rather, it responds to complex motivations in a series of escalating feedback loops. "Why did people struggle to find a way to put a chimney inside a house?" Foucault asks. "Or why did they put their techniques to this use?" Indeed, why? Desire and change are intimately related, and far more complex than even Hegel's ascending dialectic could account for.

Architecture more generally, says Foucault, is best conceived not as a baseline material fact but as "an element of support, to ensure a certain allocation of people in space, a canalization of their circulation, as well as the coding of their reciprocal relations." It may be reactionary or liberating, or neither. Liberty itself is a practice, not a static condition. We are free individuals only in the exercise of our highly contingent, luck-bound freedom, not as part of some biological or, still less, God-given nature. So-called natural limits are not, as we know, entirely uncrossable thresholds. We defy gravity, outwit genetic code and revise bodies all the time. Likewise, on the opposite side, we submit to luck and contingency, the fine acid of chance. We must exist in time and space, apparently and (Kant would say) a priori; but time and space are not rigid grids of necessity; they bend to our will in countless ways, and mind meets world always halfway or better. Every threshold noticed is also a crossing anticipated.

ii. The Truth of a Map

That crossing, in turn, always puts us somewhere in particular. Position, sheer physical location in space, cannot be overcome;

it always leaves its trace. You are here, I am here. There are lines and vectors, and so there are boundaries and insides. There is, too, a new map of space itself: the infinitely flexible grid of Cartesian planar space.

What Descartes adds to traditional Greek geometry is the systematic biaxial—eventually triaxial—plotting of position. The basic fact of human existence in space is that there are always six directions created by being: in front and behind, above and below, left and right. These are not always the terms of directionality but its possible namings. The grid takes that irreducible three-dimensional reality and renders it two-dimensionally. But it does more than this. In its various acts of dimensional reduction, the grid is also creative; it alters our idea, and therefore our experience, of space. Now we can map and grid virtually anything—or, to be more precise, virtually map and grid anything.

The very idea of the map, though preceding the Cartesian moment by long centuries, is given new life and direction now. The map no longer embodies the conceptual fantasies or cautionary fables of earlier ages, where it might express the rule of Fortune's wheel or the chastening fears of the dragons lying beyond the boundaries, but, instead, a cluster of imperatives about "precision" and "accuracy." And as with space, so

Cartesian coordinates: space made, space mastered.

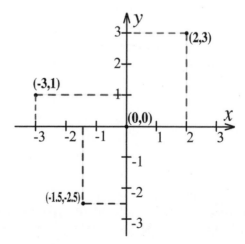

with time. It is well to remember that the navigation and charting of the seas would not have been possible without the reliable timepieces that enable useful longitudinal measure. You can fix latitude by the stars and thus get a reading on north and south; but east and west resist measurement as long as there is no precise, measured time-telling.

These norms of measurement, as always both driven by and driving political and commercial desires, themselves create a driving inner logic of representation—the need to *get things done*, and to have reliable guides to action. You need to find your way from place to place, make right turns at the church or lefts at Albuquerque, avoid cliffs and locate treasures. Maps are true in just the same way anything is true, namely, just to the extent they succeed in relating to a world through which you are navigating bodily; and you care about this truth just as you care about any truth, which is to say because it allows you to track the relation between your goals and the world. Since the world contains you, and your consciousness, these goals may shift and change as you respond to your experience, sometimes at very short notice. But it is always the case that you must have such goals, must be oriented by them, if you are to care about the idea of truth at all, and with it the subordinate idea of representational truth, where some image copies a landmark or outcropping. A map to nowhere is not a true or a false map; it is not a map at all, except perhaps for the despairing.

At the same time, maps obscure the very ground they seek to illuminate, because they can function only, indeed exist only, by way of abstraction, exclusion and limitation. The truth of a map, like the truth of a painting, is an isolated particular that relies on a rich context of presuppositions; these presuppositions cannot be examined or evaluated, only acknowledged. (Consider the notion of perspective, so indispensable for the act of representation: What makes perspective possible, the taking up of a particular standpoint, cannot itself be made perspectival. We must always stand somewhere!) Hence, the act of representation—putting onto paper a two-dimensional rendering of a three-dimensional face or a topology—is inherently unstable. There is, says Derrida, a *minuscule hiatus* that lies between the thing represented and the representation of it. Traditional illustrations of the birth of drawing symbolize this hiatus by depicting the original draftswoman of legend as blind—even as she transfers to vellum a trace of the shadow thrown by her departing lover. The move from formal universality to informal particularity—what we would call, otherwise, from type to token—crosses a chasm, and retains a gap, of impossibility. The truth of a map, but also the truth of a statement, is negotiated, as it were, across this gap. It is never stable, and it is never general.

Even to speak of the "the idea of truth" is to invite a misunderstanding—just the sort of misunderstanding that leads to apparently interminable debates between advocates of objectivity and subjectivity. A general *commitment* to truth is not the same thing as a general *theory* of truth, a beast of which, in any event, there is no coherent example. A general commitment to truth means simply that you care about whether certain statements match up to states of affairs, or certain pictures match certain features of the experienced world. It does not privilege a presumptive "objectivist" metaphysics, since truth enters the picture only as a result of my having goals and intentions; it is not the

Leo Belgicus, 1611: the Low Countries mapped in the skin of a lion.

naive realism of simply assuming the world, because it recognizes how the very idea of world is a result of my consciousness being part of whatever "world" means. That is, the world is not out there, over against me. The world is right here, all around me and in my horizon of concern. You are concerned with truth, in maps or anything else, because you are presumptively concerned with making your way around the world, with projects.

To be sure, that is not as simple as it sounds. Accuracy in maps is driven first by these projects. But accuracy can, like the spatial abstractions characteristic of the Cartesian picture, begin to control the determination of human ends rather than serve existing ones. The ideal of accuracy becomes self-fertilizing and perverse. We might put the point this way: Abstract space is what happens when a logic of representation takes on a life of its own, rather than serving the projects of life. This is, to be sure, reducible at the margins to absurdity, as in the Jorge Luis Borges tale of the county so bent on accurate mapping that it commissioned a 1:1 map that, when completed, lay over the ground like a carpet. All maps, even highly accurate ones, remain fantasies of representation, and the concepts of accuracy and precision themselves subject to important limits. Maps make sense only insofar as they are used, and use structures the meaning of both precision and the act of representation itself. Fractal mathematics reminds us that a given stretch of coastline, for example, no matter how short in miles, is infinitely long. Every inlet and crevice can be mapped, but then can be mapped again at some even higher degree of minuteness, and so on, and so on. At a certain point, a point which can only ever be determined by our purposes, by what we are up to, the notion of accuracy, with its implicit but wispy normativity, the more accurate map being the *better* map, becomes self-defeating. Accuracy devours itself.

The frank cartographic acknowledgment of "Terra Incognita," meanwhile, which for many years marked what is now known as South America or California or Asia, posts an apparently honest limit to knowledge that really masks the failure, at least for the moment, of conquest. It improves on the more ancient "Here be dragons" by projecting a future knowing that may or may not be dangerous but which is surely inevitable. In this manner, "Terra Incognita" is less a recognition of limit as an unconscious statement of purpose, a vector of

Concrete Reveries

(usually) imperial desire. A lackey of the recent American empire, Donald Rumsfeld, notoriously defended the controversial invasion of Iraq by referring to the limits of thought. "There are known knowns," he said. "There are things we know we know. We also know there are known unknowns. That is to say, we know there are some things we don't know. But there are also unknown unknowns, the ones we don't know we don't know." Although this looks like a reprise of the Socratic *Doctrina Ignorantia,* a commitment to unfettered investigation, it actually confesses a darker and less open truth. As Slavoj Žižek points out, a fourth category is conspicuously absent from the list, the real terra incognita of pedantic—or, worse, political—rhetoric. This, he notes, is "the 'unknown knowns,' things we don't know that we know, which is precisely the Freudian unconscious, the 'knowledge that doesn't know itself,' as Lacan used to say." In this case, as so often, "the real dangers are in the disavowed beliefs, suppositions, and obscene practices we pretend not to know about."

San Francisco: Are the tourists consulting the map, or is the map itself the attraction?

Which is really to say that the notion of *our purposes* is itself unstable, because often based on a false (if natural-seeming) picture. We think we have our purposes first, and then act to pursue them. But this is wrong. We do not select purposes from a notional inward box of them, standing there ready to be taken up or set down. Purposes, like intentions, are shaped as a result of being in the world, often as backformations. Sometimes, that is, you don't know what you were up to until after you were finished doing it. We are always already immersed in a complex field of relations—equipmentality, language, intersubjectivity, *places* themselves—of which purposes are, we might say, nodes or (better) precipitates. A map is not a response to some pre-event purpose, clear and clearly determined beforehand; it is, instead, a feature of the events that unfold within its horizon. Just as, in Heidegger's famous formulation, *language speaks us,* we should be careful to notice that *maps read us* rather than the other way around. (This is distinct from, but perhaps related to, the common experience where, so to say, *maps fold us* into rage by refusing to let us unfold them.)

We should be careful not to fall into other ready traps in this territory, especially when we try to think about meaning or truth in more general ways. We may feel moved to say, for example, here are the *standard* or *ordinary* uses of truth in language: The cat sat on the mat; there is no elephant in the room right now; and so on. These are easy and clear. Other usages are less clear, indeed, may even be marginal to or parasitic on the standard: ironic, fictional, deceptive and so on. This ordering suggests itself likewise with spatial representations, as in the perceived difference between, say, an army ordnance map of Wiltshire and a map of Middle Earth as drawn by J.R.R. Tolkien. This natural temptation is wily, though, because it leads us down a garden path of epistemological dogmatism. Such dogmatism, detectable even in otherwise antimetaphysical "ordinary language" philosophy, restricts "acceptable" instances of statements to contexts, as Derrida says, "determined by an epistemic intention" or "within a horizon of truth." It is a conception of language, and of truth, which allows "no dissemination escaping the horizon of the unity of meaning."

Notice the interesting image of horizon employed here: The ordinary-language advocate would limit our understanding of language by way of a logic of center and margin, a *containment* within the boundary of meaning or truth. And yet, as we know very well, horizons do not function in this limiting fashion. They are boundaries of an especially unstable kind, roving thresholds we might say. They blur at the edges, permeated by possibility and chance. If we shift position in order to, as it were, *reinforce* the fuzzy boundary, we find only that the boundary too has shifted. The desire, so natural-seeming, to contain meaning within a boundary surrenders to the very same embodied perspective that is characteristic of our existence generally. The ideas of *ordinary* and *standard* reveal themselves as (a) far more unstable than "ordinary" usage would suggest, and (b) carrying within them a potentially vicious normativity, a fetish for purity. Language cleansed of the irrelevant or the nonstandard becomes a general goal, backed by law, of the enlightened age, of philosophy itself. It is no coincidence that the routine refusal to speak with regard to the truth is called *bullshit*: The evasion of normativity produces a kind of ordure, a dissemination of garbage, the scattering of shit. This is why, as Harry Frankfurt reminds us, bullshit is far more threatening, and politically evil, than lying. The bullshitter "does not reject the authority of the truth, as the liar does, and oppose himself to it. He pays no attention to it at all. By virtue of this, bullshit is the greater enemy of the truth than lies are."

Truth and lies alike affirm the authority of the truth, albeit on one side by explicit rejection or conscious flouting. Lies are still subject to truth's authority—that is what makes them *lies*. Bullshit does not offer even this degree of subjection; it doesn't bow, it just lies there, epistemic garbage. And yet, as we know, garbage is itself inescapably a boundary phenomenon, a function of moving lines: What makes something garbage is a function of a drawn line. There is no purity without impurity, and so any final purity is impossible; we cannot outstrip the logic of mediation. Authority—linguistic, representational or epistemic—cannot eliminate all otherness. It cannot even pronounce judgment on all of it, encircling it through disapproval. There is always something outside the line. Even death, understood as the absence of all contaminating desires and disorders, fails to solve the problem of impurity, for it is not a problem to be solved. Death becomes the last act of garbage in my life, a disposal project, a mess that by definition you cannot clean up yourself.

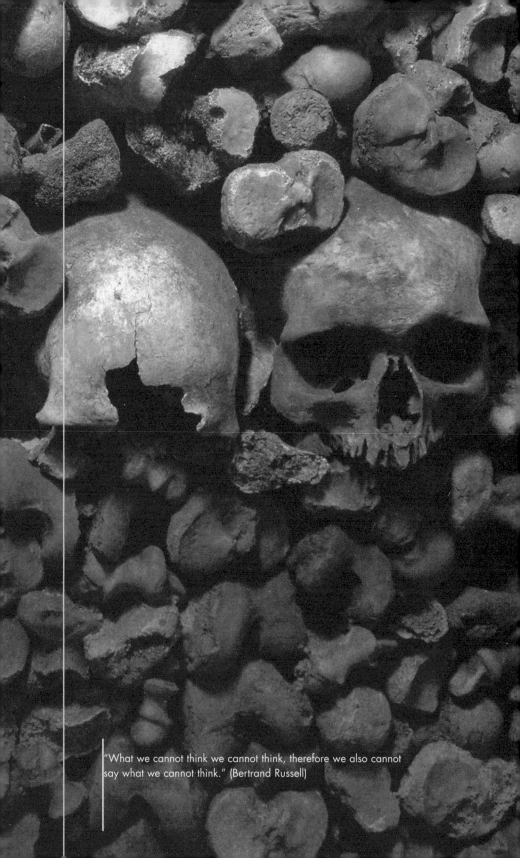

"What we cannot think we cannot think, therefore we also cannot say what we cannot think." (Bertrand Russell)

iii. Where You Are

The Cartesian grid is an abstraction, then, but one of the most power-ful ever imagined. In addition to mapmaking and all that it implies, the grid makes possible the calculus and, hence, the powerful mathe-matics of twentieth-century physics. It structures or, rather, invents, the peculiar space and time characteristic of modernity—a space and time we are here not defending but analyzing. And although its proxi-mate roots are mathematical, its genealogy is more complicated. Just as innovations in optics and epistemology mapped over to bold new techniques in painting after Descartes, enabling the hyperrealism of the Dutch seventeenth century—think of De Geyn or Van Hoogstraten—so earlier struggles to achieve realistic perspective during the Renaissance made possible the abstract refinements of Descartes's notional universe of infinity.

But make no mistake. Infinity, with its swift extensions into trans-national capital exchange and information access, has not really tran-scended the limits of the physical, where body and geography are still inextricable from soul and spirit. A nation-state such as Canada, described so witheringly by Voltaire as *quelques arpents de neige*—a few acres of snow—may be more a state of mind than a sensible territory, but its borders are still lines to be crossed—and defended. A nation defines itself in part by the fact that not everyone can enter. Once again, consider the Berlin Wall, the long corrugated-iron fence along the Rio Grande, the concrete slash dividing Jerusalem—all of these and a thousand others are reminders that freedom is both defined and limited by the drawing of boundaries.

Thus does position become an all-important aspect of human con-sciousness. Even today, when mobile communications have more and more rendered the idea of location irrelevant, the first question most people ask of a cell-phone interlocutor is, Where are you? It doesn't matter, and yet it matters—even as talking on the phone in the first place, that disembodied act, seems to give people a sense of their own solidity, their existence confirmed. Talking to you, I feel myself affirmed. I want, at the same time, to visualize your position, to sketch mentally the distance between where you are and where I am. Are you

Triaxial structure in a chain-link property fence: Is this how Descartes got his inspiration?

in Paris or around the corner? Are you at the top of the Empire State Building or in your basement? Our bodies are oriented to space, and our placement within space is therefore never beneath interest. We communicate with disembodied voices all the time, but we balk at the completion of disembodiment. *Where are you? What are you wearing? What are you doing?*

Marketers and brand consultants know this very well and use their knowledge to track our movements in space. Positional analysis is the subfield of urban anthropology that studies the way humans move through spaces, including commercial spaces. In North America, most people tend to look and turn right on entering a retail space, for example. This is a complicated result of preponderant right-handedness and the way we learn to negotiate movement around stationary obstacles and nonstationary people. Shops can, indeed must, be designed with these positional imperatives in mind lest they lose their ability to surf

Gunnery campaign, 1914: plotting trajectories of pain.

our waves of desire to the shore of profitability. Rem Koolhaas, by the way, although he understands the grid, does not appear to understand this smaller-scale geometry: His design for the Prada boutique in New York's SoHo neighborhood is a space-management perversion, low-ceilinged, alienating and chilly. But perhaps that was his intention.

Margaret Visser, always an acute anthropologist of everyday life, finds the taking of position crucially embodied in the rituals of shared eating. "In the Western world, the metaphor of the ideally inviolable area allotted to each person is daily embodied in table settings," she writes. "Each diner sits on an upright, separate chair drawn up to a table on which is laid his or her 'place.' This is an area bounded by metal slicing, piercing, dipping, and digging implements, or cutlery: the knife, the fork, the spoon, and sometimes more than one of each. The plate with food on it is round—an unbroken ring, holding the diner's portion." We might recall here the elaborate table settings still favored by the devotees of once queenly, then disgraced and lately resurrected Martha—or, my preference, those weirdly compelling abstract diagrams in the etiquette manuals of Amy Vanderbilt and company, some early versions of which were composed by a young commercial artist called Andrew Warhol, who clearly learned a lot about social position, the logic of inside and outside, as a result of the exercise. "The table represents the group," Visser goes on; "its edge is the group's outline. A table, like a diagram, stresses both togetherness among the insiders, the ones given places and portions, and exclusion of those not asked: distinction and rejection or relegation to outside."

Here, with these positions diagrammed, there is to be no reaching, leaning or uninvited taking. "We had to invent plates; to force people never to touch the food with their hands; to create forks, change the shape of knives, and insist that people not point with the cutlery," Visser concludes. "All this artificiality was felt to be worth the effort, in part because it supported the embodiment of that image of ourselves as bounded areas: we were slowly becoming more and more individualistic." This is a daily enactment of positional boundaries, a defense of what Norbert Elias, in *The Civilizing Process,* called "the walls of shame," inside whose limits you may not venture without suffering the adverse consequences of public ridicule, even humiliation.

Position is not always literal, and shopping and dining themselves are often the ligament here, especially in our consumerist days. It is a truism at least since Veblen's *Theory of the Leisure Class* that the motive in the acquisition of commercial goods is not the objects themselves but the social position they confer. Positional goods are troubling, indeed incomprehensible to crude economic analysis, because no amount of expansion will solve the problem of deprivation. That is, they are designed to create deprivation and corresponding feelings of enjoyment in those not deprived, what Veblen famously referred to as invidious distinction through conspicuous consumption. There is no purely goods-based escape from this complex of social relations, since the positional goods of consumption are linked intricately, if falsely, to the positional goods of merit and earned distinction. (An Olympic medal or an A-plus grade are likewise positional goods: They would be valueless if everyone had one.)

In Veblen's jaundiced but penetrating view, the messages of social life are never about what they seem to be about. On the surface, the furnishings of the country house or the high-rise apartment purport to send intricately coded signals of personal taste or sophistication or refinement—and indeed these codes are based on real semiotic

The order of things: formal dinner place setting from an etiquette manual.

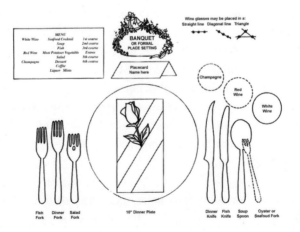

practices that can therefore, in principle, be decoded. I recognize the make of your car or the designer of your sofa and congratulate you, or pity you, depending on my judgment of your judgment. But more basically, these objects are purchased, placed and displayed to indicate, sometimes quite precisely, one's average net worth and margin of disposable annual income: one's social position as measured *and signaled* by wealth. For Veblen, far more than for Marx, all aesthetic judgments reduce under analysis to economic ones. Here is a typical sentence from the early master of consumerist analysis: "The superior gratification derived from the use and contemplation of costly and supposedly beautiful products is," Veblen writes, "a gratification of our sense of costliness masquerading under the name of beauty." Whatever bohemian rebels might like to believe, historically, *taste* is most often just another name for status.

Hence, the key role of design objects in establishing position. Everyday life is structured by how we indicate status, both in our own eyes and in the eyes of others. Indeed, the two perspectives collapse into one under the pressure of maintaining position. That is, we tend to internalize the notional other, who sees and judges and perhaps approves, even as we make our so-called individual choices. Although they feel not only free but constitutive of unique personal identity, these conjunctions of desire and action are in fact nodes in a complex web of intersubjective reality. As Veblen remarks,

> Any consumer who would, Diogenes-like, insist on the elimination of all honorific or wasteful elements from his consumption, would be unable to supply his most trivial wants in the modern market. Indeed, even if he resorted to supplying his wants directly by his own efforts, he would find it difficult if not impossible to divest himself of the current habits of thought on this head; so that he could scarcely compass a supply of the necessaries of life for a day's consumption without instinctively and by oversight incorporating in his home-made product something of this honorific, quasi-decorative element of wasted labour.

Consumer societies, really all societies operating past the subsistence threshold, are adept at keeping alive the link between material goods and the position they render. What the goods are, or what specious claims are made for their so-called intrinsic value, are finally unimportant. Goods may possess intrinsic qualities, whatever that means (*intrinsic* literally means inward and, hence, essential), but that is not why they are valued. If existing positional goods are more widely distributed, in other words, experience shows that new ones will quickly be found, usually involving, Veblen says, finer and finer distinctions in equipment or difficulty or rarity, abrupt creative reversals (what once was cool now is not, or kitsch is suddenly elevated), and secrecy (exclusive clubs, undiscovered shops, hidden restaurants). There is always here an unstable dance between the imperatives of exclusion and ostentation. So, for example, I may tell you all about a fantastic unknown café or bar, but I will not tell you exactly how to find it.

The key to all positional goods is envy. We speak of house-envy, that particular form of marginal dissatisfaction that comes upon people

Envy (1306), one of the Seven Vices frescoes by Giotto di Bondone, at Cappella delgi Scrovegni (Arena Chapel), Padua, Italy.

who cross the thresholds of others, like visiting vampires, to consume the experience that they don't have: those window treatments, that tchotchke, that granite counter or stainless-steel refrigerator. Facilitating envy is in one sense just an extension of ostracism, though today we rarely employ that ancient Greek defense of the practice, namely that it built character and encouraged reflection in the ostracized. No, we practice a simpler version, which is mere invidious out-grouping—thrusting people beyond a new boundary, a threshold of cool or success or taste, as we may choose to call it. And once there is a threshold between the cool and uncool, the good and the evil, it is very easy to shift out-grouping to scapegoating or worse. Indeed, at this point, exclusion, not inclusion, becomes the point of maintaining the boundary. The limit case here may be the schoolgirls' club whose sole rationale is the exclusion of a single schoolgirl.

Such a grouping confers a rare power upon the excluded schoolgirl, as Hegel aptly noted in his analysis of the volatile relationship between master and slave. The master needs the slave to remain a master, to maintain that limit of his identity, just as the mean schoolgirls need their enemy in order to justify their existence as sisters. Unfortunately, this is not a power that slaves or schoolgirls, or ordinary shoppers, have been very successful at perceiving, let alone exercising actively or, still less, overturning.

iv. On the Street Where You Live

Now that we have circled, or spiraled, back to the point from which we started, let us be as clear as possible. We have lost our sense of threshold in an extended fetishizing of the inside. We have, in pursuit of our individual freedom, let slip both the tragic dimension of confronting limits and the robust relation of private to public characteristic of the Greeks at their best. We have misunderstood, and more often merely ignored, the rich politics of interiority. We have allowed misconceived consciousness because we have neglected the true complexity of inside/out.

It was said earlier that Descartes gave us the outlines for the abstract, gridded space of the modern world. In this sense alone he might be considered a creator of modernity, with its science and technology so dependent on the manipulation of those x/y/z abstractions. But Descartes makes another decisive modern move, the point toward which I have been aiming all along, if often obliquely. In the *Meditations on First Philosophy,* Descartes famously tries to solve the problems of error and God's existence by a novel strategy of self-investigation, a series of epistemological threshold-crossings designed to first embrace, then defeat, the dreaming doubt and a possible malicious demon engaged in systematic deception. This first-person process is so familiar to us now that we might not see the genuinely revolutionary import of the interior move, or indeed the fictional status of Descartes's character, his mind's I. Seeking the foundation of truth not outside, in a transcendental realm, but inside, in the nature of the mind itself, Descartes recharts philosophy's course. The resulting

The outlier's meditative gaze.

picture of the mind as a self-conscious, nonmaterial, nonspatial substance dominates the West still, despite its many philosophical problems. The Cartesian interior becomes, as it were, the final frontier of self-narrative, the ultimate inside, where each of us, in our uniqueness, goes through time and space in a sort of mumbling monologue that, occasionally, erupts into articulate speech or creation.

Language is the most obvious way we try to cross this apparent threshold from one interior self to another. But in fact, once we see the depth of our linguistic being, the sense in which, as Heidegger said, "language speaks us" rather than the other way around, we begin to see, too, the limits of the Cartesian position on limits. Consciousness may *feel* itself to be alone, an interior looking to move out, but this is an illusion born of a highly developed skill, central to modernity, of introspection. Descartes, like most philosophers, finds exactly the answer his question contains, and the artful constructions of his asking it only work to conceal this basic circularity.

This was a point seen clearly by Gilbert Ryle, that most acute critic of "the official doctrine" of Cartesian substance dualism. The dualist would have us believe that we are two kinds of thing at once. "It is customary to express this bifurcation of his two lives and his two worlds," Ryle notes in the first chapter of *The Concept of Mind*,

> by saying that the things and events which belong to the physical world, including his own body, are external, while the workings of his own mind are internal. This antithesis of outer and inner is of course meant to be construed as a metaphor, since minds, not being in space, could not be described as being spatially inside anything else, or as having things going on spatially inside themselves. But relapses from this good intention are common and theorists are found speculating how stimuli, the physical sources of which are yards or miles outside a person's skin, can generate mental responses inside his skull, or how decisions framed inside his cranium can set going movements of his extremities.

The dualist, in other words, falls into a habit of threshold thinking where, if dualism is correct, there can be no threshold because there is no space—location in space being a feature of matter only, not mind. And in this particular the official dualist is not far from the common person, who also tends to speak of an inside mind and an outside world. Nevertheless, Ryle says, "the actual transactions between the episodes of the private history and those of the public history remain mysterious, since by definition they can belong to neither series."

The Cartesian legacy is once again vast, because the separation of mind and world thus effected, however mistaken, continues to dominate the epistemological agenda to the present day, despite the efforts of some contemporary philosophers. Awareness of its central contradiction may force us to abandon the official doctrine, but it remains an open question what, if anything, might replace it. Is it not, after all, correct that I am "in here" and the world "out there"? Even a critic unbewitched by the logical faults of Cartesian dualism, Mikhail Bahktin,

Faculty psychology: the mind mapped.

Crux of the problem: the function of the pineal gland in communicating pain.

may fall into error here. "The most important acts constituting self-consciousness are determined by a relationship toward another consciousness," Bahktin says in his *Problems of Dostoevsky's Poetics*. "Not that which takes place within, but that which takes place on the boundary ... on the threshold." Yes, except—is that a threshold *of* or a threshold *between*? Consciousness is here saved from solipsism only at the cost of circularity in the argument, with the nature of consciousness assumed as a proof of the nature of consciousness.

A clue to a more compelling picture can be found in Ryle's question concerning distant stimulus. It is not at all rare for me to be affected by a stimulus that is physically removed; indeed, it is far more common, in everyday configurations of self-in-world, that this should be so. As I walk along the pavement of the street where you live, as the Lerner and Loewe song goes, I am far more conscious of you in your absence than I am of the asphalt beneath my feet or the trees in my field of vision. This is *your* street, and therefore redolent of you, and I care about it because you are within—perhaps centrally within, overwhelmingly within—my horizon of concern. *All at once am I several stories high!* Edward Casey gives a better sense of what is involved when he says this about place and my relation to it: "Thanks to the double horizon that body and landscape provide, a place is a locale bounded on both sides, near and far.... A place constantly overflows its own boundaries. Uncontainable on its near edge, it flows back into the body that subtends it; uncontainable on its far side, it flows outward into the circumambient world. Place's inflow and outflow are such that to be fully *in* place is never to be confined to a punctuate position; it is to be already on the way out."

In other words, consciousness is not a disembodied, nonspatial substance that uses language as a threshold bridge; it is far better conceived as part of a shared lifeworld of which language is just one facet or dimension. We are each of us apparently alone but also necessarily together, existing as ourselves only in a web of relations, "a reciprocity of perspectives," to use Alfred Schutz's phrase. *Pace* the traditional Cartesian-Lockean version of the problem, personal identity does not arise as an issue without this shared lifeworld; there is no possibility of *even the metaphor* of inside without there being also a common outside. The inside is not primordial, though Descartes makes it appear so; instead, inside and outside arise together as functions of a specific form of the world becoming conscious of itself. Even this way of expressing it may obscure the depth of relation here with both traditional Aristotelian metaphysics and common sense—though, crucially, in an insight that is unavailable to common sense so long as it remains commonsensical, which is to say going about its business without attending to the structures underwriting that business. "Everything is somewhere and in place," Aristotle says in the *Physics*—a thought that is contrary to the Cartesian metaphysics of isolated, disemplaced consciousness. Wherever I go, I am always someplace in particular, even (or especially) when my concern-horizon is wider than my literal one.

Language, meanwhile, supposed by the Cartesian orthodoxy to be a bridge from one isolated mind to another, is already a cluster of practices rife with the concept of boundary; it is a series of line drawings

Ernst Mach, *Inner Perspective*: the self as a function of body image.

Phrenological chart from *How to Read Character*, Fowler and Wells Co., New York (1878).

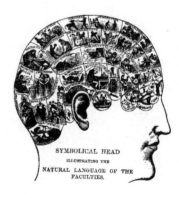

SYMBOLICAL HEAD
ILLUSTRATING THE
NATURAL LANGUAGE OF THE
FACULTIES.

that help consciousness articulate itself. To invoke etymology or the conventions of usage is to plot the limits of a word, the lines drawn by it, as when we in philosophy speak of "the extension of a term," meaning the range of things or instances captured by it. We see the value of language in allowing us to make precise distinctions, by making finer and finer extensions possible as our needs demand. And need is always in play here, though never quite fundamental in the reductive naturalizing sense. There are, according to cliché, dozens of words for snow in the language of Canada's Inuit people, but this is merely a clichéd example of something all cultures allow. How many words are there, for example, to delimit the positions of fielders in cricket, from *square leg* to *silly mid-on*—a fecundity baffling to anyone outside this practice but merely handy to anyone inside. Handiness is itself a key quality of insideness, as these examples show. We want our tools to lie nearby, ready for use. We should not have to go questing for them, but unfortunately sometimes we do: you search your mind for the mot juste, try to flick something off the tip of your tongue and into the shared air.

From the unassailable interior position of mind—unassailable because Descartes is correct to argue the one thing I cannot doubt even in the act of doubting everything is that I am conscious of myself—the world appears to be anything that is not me. Anything outside. In fact, the world is me and vice versa, but coming to see that can take some work. We must move away from Cartesian epistemological limits toward the phenomenological acceptance that limits are always drawn by us, about us. Limits are, we might say, an us-project.

Negotiating and reflecting on the limit between me and the world thus becomes a central task for each one of us. It can be especially difficult when our ideas about limits are so often confused. There is no me without the world, no world without me—using *without* here in both its related senses of "outside" and "absent." The ongoing self/other encounters of human consciousness lead, among other things, to various kinds of discomfort. "Pathology has made us acquainted with a great number of states in which the boundary lines between the ego and the external world become uncertain or in which they are actually drawn incorrectly," Freud writes in *Civilization and Its Discontents*. "The ego detaches itself from the external world. Or, to put it more correctly, originally the ego includes everything, later it separates off an external world from itself. Our present ego feeling is, therefore, only a shrunken residue of a much more inclusive—indeed, an all-embracing-feeling which corresponded to a more intimate bond between the ego and the world around it.… The contents appropriate to it would be precisely those of a limitless bond with the universe—the same ideas with which my friend elucidated the 'oceanic feeling.'"

Freud sees this self-creation as a struggle, an enforced shrinking of self as the sharp edges of the world encroach. This picture is both too negative and too Cartesian, but it does capture that sense of vulnerability we often feel in the face of the world. Because our interior consciousness is wedded to a body, or rather, because human existence is one of *embodied consciousness,* these limits between self and world cannot be ignored or even fixed in a final way. They must always be negotiated and reestablished. The world inflicts wounds both mental and physical, and being an embodied consciousness is no simple thing, as Gregor Samsa discovered when he woke up feeling like himself but looking like a beetle. Cartesian metaphors persist everywhere, our generalized epistemological hangover.

We often congratulate someone for being comfortable in his or her skin, as if accepting that most basic boundary were a rare achievement. In a time when the surgical alteration of fleshly limits has become common, when even the limits of those genetic circumstances formerly called fate may be adjusted, comfort within one's own skin may indeed be rare. We tend to mean something more metaphorical than literal, however—a wisdom in taking what life has to offer, being happy to be here where admittedly the final limit is inescapable (at least so far), namely, the disintegration—the loss of wholeness—in the body. Conceiving the skin as a boundary enriches the metaphorical store no end. It immediately raises thoughts of breaches and interventions and chinks in the armor of muscle and bone, themselves reflected in the actual armor of breastplates and grieves and helmets, the iron and Kevlar of modern protection against violence.

Wounds may be inflicted, and the wound of penetration acquires a richness of unsettling sexual overtones, sometimes relieved by comedy, as in this passage from Don DeLillo's *White Noise,* where the narrator's wife is about to read an erotic story to him:

"I will read," she said. "But I don't want you to choose anything that has men inside women, quote-quote, or men entering women. 'I entered her.' 'He entered me.' We're not lobbies or elevators. 'I wanted him inside me,' as if he could crawl completely in, sign the register, sleep, eat, so forth. Can we agree on that? I don't care what these people do as long as they don't enter or get entered."

"Agreed."

"'I entered her and began to thrust.'"

"I'm in total agreement," I said.

"'Enter me, enter me, yes, yes.'"

"Silly usage, absolutely."

"'Insert yourself, Rex. I want you inside me, entering hard, entering deep, yes, now, oh.'"

I began to feel an erection stirring.

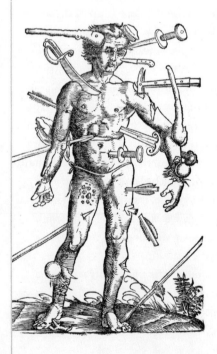

The body in pain: so many choices of vulnerability.

Despite the silliness of the usage—perhaps because of it—the narrator later employs it aggressively and with effect when he learns of his wife's infidelity, rubbing her face in it: *Did he enter you, was he inside you.* The body, like a literal interior of the allegedly separate mind, is seen here as bearing a threshold to be crossed, a vulnerable vessel of life. It occupies space, persists through time, tries to find an arc of narrative, a story, to make sense of its unique, fragile consciousness. It can be penetrated and violated and damaged, broken and, yes, entered. Every body has a sense of its own inviolable, though as a matter of fact often violated, personal space. There is a threshold of comfort that protects the interior self against assault. Crossing that boundary is, under the right circumstances, a crime. The law, we say, lays down the limit of freedom in just these terms, articulating the liberal notion that (as Oliver Wendell Holmes famously had it) your right to swing a fist ends at the tip of my nose. You and I are in this together, together and apart, shaping and maintaining the space we call ours, against a background of space we all must share.

The self's narrative, its self-creation, follows—we like to say—an *arc.* It is understood to describe a plot that unfolds through time, where plot (as Margaret Visser reminds us) is a word that means allotment, the given portion that is one's life, measured by the limit of death. This too is a construction, since the truth of the narrative is that, like happiness or utopia, it is shrouded in not-yetness. But this may prove a necessary and useful construction: fabricated not in inventing death but in giving the baseline "natural fact" of narrative conclusions a particular cultural meaning or meanings. Witness, for example, the Socratic project of *imaginary deathbed psychodrama,* which informs so much of the Western philosophical tradition—and so returns us to the issues of fate and choice. My personal plot and my material plot, my real estate as we say, are deeply linked. My literal interior is an extension of my seeming mental interior, my self as embodies consciousness. Here, inside the dwelling of self as it were, we experience the power of that final threshold, what we call necessity—a word which, in the Greek of Sophocles's time, is *anangkē.* Linked etymologically, it is worth noting, with anguish, anxious, angle and, finally, strangle. Limits squeeze us; they make us feel the edges of our interiority. Every interior you enter or inhabit challenges you to ask who you are, this apparently individual consciousness among others.

An out-of-body experience: *Éxtasis de Santa Terèsa* (1645–52), marble sculpture by Giovanni Lorenzo Bernini, Cornaro Chapel, Santa Maria della

v. A Space That Allows Thought

Exploring the limits of this strange apparent interior, consciousness itself and its necessary negotiations of inside and outside, is life's main task. Carl Jung, the friend Freud had in mind—you notice he cannot quite bear to write the name, an instance of his own self-and-world issues—said the self was not best conceived as a line in time but as a circumambulated circle. We are at work drawing our worlds—a clue to the enduring appeal of children's book characters such as Simon or Harold with his purple crayon, who can create just the lines they like by drawing on the world. We cannot do that, since we inhabit a world where some lines are already drawn, others fashioned at every moment by our fellow travelers.

Even to speak of life as travel may be to affirm once more the misleading, or limited, metaphor of the road, the forking line. If we are reflective—bending our lines of investigation back on ourselves, where they began—we can see that this setting of limits is itself a doubling limit: It limits, and it does not allow us the scope for more robust metaphors beyond limit. We think we proceed along a line, a vector, only to find that we have been walking round and round and return to where we started. Aristotle speaks of the purpose of life as "becoming who we are": not simply transcending the limits we feel, not trying always to go beyond, but learning to abide, to feel the naturalness—and difficulty— of being at home, right here, right now. A new kind of heroism, the heroism of celebrating the contested wisdom that thresholds offer, rather than merely crossing them—a form of free play that, like all the best games and arts, is utopian and paradisal.

As a final etymological gesture, then, let me end by bringing this line of argument back to its beginning. The word *paradise* come from the Avestan word *paridaeza,* or enclosure, meaning the enclosure or park of the king—an enclosure that, as Bartlett Giamatti reminds us in his meditation on baseball, *Take Time for Paradise,* extends its reach through Old Persian, ancient Hebrew, and the Greek and Latin cognates that resound in *Genesis* 2:8, the first and final garden of the Western imagination, the ground zero of hope, the Garden of Eden. John Berger makes the point clear with a concrete example:

In Istanbul, the domestic interior, in both the shantytowns and elsewhere, is a place of repose, in profound opposition to what lies outside the door. Cramped, badly roofed, crooked, cherished, these interiors are spaces like prayers, both because they oppose the traffic of the world as it is, and because they are a metaphor for the garden of Eden or Paradise.

Interiors symbolically offer the same thing as Paradise: repose, flowers, fruit, quiet, soft materials, sweetmeats, cleanliness, femininity. The offer can be as imposing (and vulgar) as one of the Sultan's rooms in the harem, or it can be as modest as the printed pattern on a square of cheap cotton, draped over a cushion on the floor of a shack.

Paradise is not purchased at a fixed price.

Urban wonders imagined: Nebuchadnezzar's Hanging Gardens of Babylon, from *Seven Wonders of the World* (1570?), hand-tinted engravings by Marten Jacobszoon Heemskerk van Veen—now the model for luxury apartment complexes in Dubai.

The domestic interior is never merely an extension of the conscious interior, a thrusting of self into world or assertion of individual choice. Descartes, in the *Meditations,* makes it clear that his domestic scene is not irrelevant to his inner exploration. He describes the warm fire, his chair and desk, his quilted dressing gown. But he misses his own deep point. Thinking happens in places, and places for thinking are necessary to our narratives of self. The interior, domestic or mental, is too often conceived as a place of comfort or security, a cozy escape or a private fastness. That is a mistake, the latter conceptual, the former political. An interior is always far more than a retreat, a contested space, a philosophical wrestling ring where we reflect on the mystery of being a self, a mind, a consciousness, of being here at all. Where the thresholds allow, indeed demand, movement in both directions. Where time and space themselves are up for grabs. Where every crossing is a venture, every return a challenge. Where we take time, not for paradise exactly, but to acknowledge that we cannot overcome the circumstances of thought through thought itself.

8.
The Imaginary City

i. The Limits of Power

What are the political implications of thoughts about limits,
at the limit of thought? Is there a practice to match this
theory?

Let us note, first, something about the nature of the politics, and the state—the structure of political power—that is at their center. The state functions by means of thresholds. It *is* threshold.

The ancient Greek cities established the most basic boundary of all: inside and outside the palings of defense. Inside lies order and civilization, the warmth of the hearth, shared security. Outside, beyond the pale, lies disorder and chaos, the violence of barbarism. Plato's *Republic* stages its discussions of mystical justice in the port of Piraeus, already away from the presumed rationality of the agora: "I went down to the Piraeus yesterday," Socrates says in the opening line of Grube's excellent translation, implying that this out-of-order discussion of civic order requires an exiled location, a location of transaction and danger such as all ports are. Later, discussing the conflicts of the soul, Socrates recalls the story of Leontius, the young man who found himself so fetched by the sight of corpses being burnt outside the city. Struggling between will and desire, he finally gives in and says to his eyes, "There, take your fill of the lovely sight, you hateful things." This is perhaps the most vivid recorded instance of psychic conflict in the Platonic corpus, and the pivot on which turns Plato's tripartite view of the soul: Reason is oriented to the good, but sometimes it lacks the will to control desire. At which point, the human will may even turn upon itself in that special form of anger we call self-loathing.

As inside the soul, so outside in the city. The city struggles to control the desires of its people, to regulate and order them toward the good. When they will not be persuaded, they may have to be forced. And indeed, force is introduced into the picture of the ideal city at many points, not least in the notorious injunction that the entire adult population of any existing state will have to be purged ("sent into the country" is the casual phrase actually used) to ensure that the new story of origin will take root in the people. The state's authority depends upon its origins being shrouded in mystery, the divine obscurity of coming from a moment before time.

Whereas contractarian political thinkers might resort to a thought experiment describing the "state of nature" or an imagined condition behind a "veil of ignorance," a scenario unburdened by claims of historical accuracy, Plato is more straightforward. He insists on what

Jacques Derrida memorably labeled "the mystical authority of the law." The law-givers—in this case, the philosophical interlocutors of Socrates—must fade away as actual people and be replaced by an authority that is disembodied and transcendental. Otherwise, citizens might well ask: By whose authority anyway, this monopoly on legitimate exercise of violence? The law now functions to draw multiple lines of control, right down to the lines that divide the streets, and those that divide the street itself from the sewer below. Infrastructure and ideological structure are mutually reinforced: They become a soft and hard, the concrete and abstract expression of each other.

Think for a moment of that aspect of the city that is habitually ignored or bracketed as unmentionable: its dirt. Everywhere it must be controlled, and thresholds of sanitation—*cordons sanitaires*—established: between food and garbage, product and refuse, body and waste,

The state responds: Activist Midge Potts is arrested on the steps of the U.S. Supreme Court, Washington, D.C., during a 2005 anti-torture demonstration.

law-abiding and criminal, sane and insane, even alive and dead. Whereas an earlier infrastructure of the city would have established all these lines as limit thresholds, and their function as expulsion or purgation, we instead bring the outside in, and the lines become tangled and sometimes confused: the cemetery within the city doubling as a park; the prison or madhouse as public architecture; the toilet within the house; the dump or recycling center within the city limits. Think of the elaborate public urinals that excited Jonathan Swift's imagination, or the Deco and Nouveau stylings that mark famous public pissoirs in Paris. Sewers, dumps and cemeteries now perform the function once reserved, more simply, for the city walls. They become the city. Instead of merely (and literally) ejecting foreign and rotting matter, the corpses and garbage of routine urban sloughing off, defending the boundary as indeed a military necessity, we attempt to manage garbage, and so make it vanish, from the inside out. Bodily waste will be disposed of inside the house, not in an outbuilding; garbage will be removed from sight, but not from site.

Thus do we attempt to manage a necessary threshold by making it, in effect, no longer a simple line but a kind of Möbius strip. And thus, too, our horror when this subtle non-Euclidean geometry of sanitation is broken or ruptured—as when, for example, a hungry rat bursts into a café kitchen and so, from there, into what is known as the front of house. The patrons shriek! Everything is contaminated! And now, wrenched unwillingly in one direction, we must wrench ourselves back. The economy of the *cordon sanitaire,* once exploded, can be restored only by collective forgetting. In fact, "control" is revealed as not control at all but, rather, its opposite, namely, a surrender performed through a willed act of amnesia. Thus Dominique Laporte: "Surely, the State is the Sewer. Not just because it spews divine law from its ravenous mouth, but because it reigns as the law of cleanliness above its sewers." The two functions are not just complementary, they are identical.

Recall the arguments of the previous chapter. Structuralist anthropology offers the crucial antinaturalist insight that, in effect, *nothing is dirt until we call it so*. Dirt is thematized under the rubric of cleaning, which arises as a method of eliminating, or purifying, the unclean or foreign. Therefore without dirt there is no cleaning; without cleaning there is no dirt. Cleaning serves to reassure the social order that it *is* order; dirt makes cleanliness possible, not the other way around, and the anxiety provoked by dirt is forever in need of palliation. Thus inside and outside are drawn, and redrawn, over and over. We may then extend the analysis from the sociology of culture to its underlying religious and metaphysical anxieties. *Purity* becomes a trope of thought, not just of social behavior. The notion of purity, as Paul Ricoeur argues, is formed as an associative network around the ancient Greek words for purity and cleansing. These two words "can express

"All great manifestations of social life have in common with the work of art the fact that they are born in unconscious life." (Aldo Rossi)

physical cleansing, and then, in the medical sense, evacuation, purgation of humours. But this purgation in its turn can symbolize a ritual purification and then a wholly moral purity. The words thus come to express intellectual limpidity, clarity of style, orderliness, absence of ambiguity in an oracle, and finally absence of moral blemish or stigma. The word purity lends itself to the change in meaning by which it will come to express the essential purification, that of wisdom and philosophy." The concrete, mundane purification project of cleansing leads naturally, Ricoeur suggests, to the binary logic and fear of messiness or disorder that comes to be characteristic of the (masculine) tenor of Western logocentric philosophy.

Derrida in turn deepens Ricoeur's analysis of wisdom as purity, a project of sanitation, by suggesting that philosophy's dominant theme since Plato is one of purification by means of applied method, itself a derivation of homeopathic medical therapy: the pharmakon which is at once a poison and a cure. In common with all administered drugs, the Platonic *pharmakon* works by entering the interior of the body and causing an expurgation; magically, the boundaries of thought itself are established as inside and outside, pure versus impure. "The *evil* and the *outside*, the expulsion of the evil, its exclusion out of the body (and out) of the city—these are the two major senses of the character of the [pharmakon] ritual." And so: "The city's body *proper* thus reconstitutes its unity, closes around the security of its inner courts, gives back to itself the word that links it with itself within the confines of the agora, by violently excluding from its territory the representative of an external threat or aggression. That representative represents the otherness of the evil that comes to affect or infect the inside by unpredictably breaking into it. Yet the representative of the outside is nonetheless *constituted*, regularly granted its place by the community, chosen, kept, fed, etc., in the very heart of the inside."

The first conclusion here must be the disconcerting one that philosophy is, as it were, an iatrogenic illness: physician-caused, an infection we contract in the very hospital of our imagined saving. Yet it can be useful to see the authority-project thus turned against itself, contradicting and undermining it. The exercise may force us to other, less stable strategies of thought: the *flâneur*'s or jaywalker's route to desire, rather than the grid-prescribed one. The even more disturbing second conclusion is that the projects of control and sanitation are structurally headed for failure. We cannot ever eliminate dirt or disorder because they, as the enemy we wishfully seek to control, alone establish our control projects as meaningful.

Lately, in the form of security crackdowns of mounting desperation or violence, this failure is revealed in vivid colors. For example: In the wake of the Paris *banlieue* riots of 2004, Parisians began a fearful dialogue about the way the streets and districts themselves might be configured to minimize internal violence—a direct reprise of the *hausmannization* project analyzed by Walter Benjamin. A century earlier, Baron Hausmann had insisted on the creation of wide boulevards inhospitable to guerrilla harassment but well suited to cavalry charges: the lovely Paris we all now know. But the new version of the security project is shot through with contradictions unknown to Hausmann, not least the looming prospect of what Paul Virilio calls the *panic city,* the city structured and premised on fear of the other. A city of portals and barriers, vertical slums and vertical gated communities, security systems and patrols. A city where we witness, in Virilio's words, the *twilight of place,* because there is nowhere that is not already surveilled and secured.

A fine and private place.

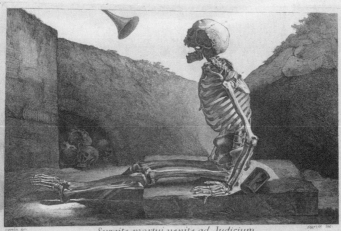

Surgite mortui venite ad Judicium

Louis Althusser gave the name *interpellation* to this form of the state's call, the mystical authority of the law as deployed on the street: *Hey, you there!* This call is, Althusser argued, the basic feature of ideology. So, far from being a specific body of belief or political platform, or even a philosophical position, ideology is instead a web of invisible, presupposed structures of belief, so deeply ingrained that they require critique even to be made visible. For Althusser, interpellation shows that ideology pervades our very sense of ourselves as agents: You are an agent only by being so *in the eyes of the state*. The state grants your agency—subject to limits and constraints, backed by a monopoly on the legitimate use of force.

The police—whose very name invokes the city—are the ones who make the call. Like it or not, we all must acknowledge the force of the law in being subject to it—in being subjects at all. We *believe* we are autonomous individuals, freely acting and deciding. We may even *believe* that we were so constituted naturally, that is, prior to the social. Yet interpellation argues, pessimistically, that these beliefs about individual autonomy are illusions. Their falseness is covered over by their success at reinforcing the current arrangement. Today, to be sure, you are more likely to be hailed not by the police, not by the 4 A.M. knock on the door or the sound of breaking glass, but by the voice of an advertisement or spectacle. *Hey, you there!* Are you the person I have been looking for—the target audience, the buyer? Yes, you may be— you will be, you will always have been—the person I have been looking for! Under these conditions, sites of human interaction are off-loaded to a nonphysical "space" of technology, nodes and networks of an electronic omnipolis: the place that is at once everywhere and nowhere, the city as "omnicenter of nowhere." Life reduces to curating the domestic interior, the last inside, the site of the individual's self-creation—all under the watchful eye of social-networking sites that create the softest of soft surveillance, the kind we sign on to eagerly and of our own volition.

But make no mistake: The state's power remains in play. Ernst Bloch, writing in 1935, noted how the city, for all its apparent comfort and security, even playfulness, still opened up "holes and hollow spaces" of danger, where no door is proof against the knock, no window safe from breaking. The house as private dwelling, bulwark against the outside, dissolves in an instant when the state chooses to intervene. Recall Josef K. in Kafka's *The Trial*, who found that "someone must have been telling lies about him, because early one morning he was arrested in his home." Or, if that seems too far-fetched, too fictional, think of the suburban couple who, not long ago, misdialed 411 as 911. The police came anyway, and the couple's quiet evening ended with a broken-down door and them in handcuffs. Inside the city's threshold, everything and everyone is revealed as disposable, subject to subjection; and then, as Bloch puts it, "the furniture vanishes ... goes to the wall." Now the home is no cherished private sphere but the site of judgment, interrogation, trial.

ii. Imaginary City

And yet, these conclusions are far too pessimistic, and too passive, to convince us for long or finally. Agency is surely not so fragile, or so compromised. And even if personhood is an illusion, it is the kind of illusion we call a necessary fiction, as the previous chapter argues. As I hope the preceding pages show, we have no choice but to start thought about ourselves at the level of the self. The thoughts may

Futurist urban design: *La Citta Nuova* (1914), pen-and-ink drawing by Antonio Sant'Elia.

City of Glass: Vancouver skyline.

rapidly become both unstable and disorienting, but start they must, and nowhere else but there.

These agents are the software that runs on the built-form hardware of any city. The city they create is one of aspiration and imagination, and it is to these agents, past and future, that architectural aspiration and imagination should be directed. A just city is, in part, a city whose hardware and software are compatible, one whose edifices and public spaces offer citizens moments of sustainable joy among the countless overlapping arcs of life and death. Only in such a city can citizens, sharing that space, force the issue deeper and ask how well each of us, and especially the least well off, is faring. Amid all the necessary, even urgent, talk about architectural style, environmental sustainability, carbon-reduction targets and shifts in the materials palette, there must be some room for the specific question of whether an architectural project serves the deepest political aims of the city, the requirements of justice—which are themselves a form of aspiration and imagination. Not just the green city, to recall Frank Cunningham's insight, but the grue city.

We often fail to see this deeper kind of urgency, I think, in part because we fail to understand the nature of desire. What, after all, is desire? It is as much an *avoiding* as it is a *seeking after*. "The paradox of desire," says Slavoj Žižek, "is that it posits retroactively its own cause." That is, we confront, and think we understand, our desires in terms of their immediate *objects*, which we then label as the *origin* of the desire: the woman I cannot have, the car I must own, the victory I long for. Yet these are not the origin of desire, merely its coagulation or fixity, after the fact, in the form of an object. We already realize the truth of this insight, in fact, because of the way desire is constantly failing to be satisfied, even in its satisfaction, and so renewing itself. Indeed, the paradox is deeper than just this one of cause; desire's satisfaction is also its death. We enter into a dangerous game whenever we satisfy a desire. Desire met is desire killed, and so satisfaction is necessarily dissatisfaction. This is more than just a matter of being disappointed with what we get, or finding victory anticlimactic. The economy of desire makes for a constant reproduction of longing in the space we call fantasy—distinct from the freely imaginative, a space structured by what we already want. What we really desire, apparently, is desire itself: the endless circulation around some residue of the real, which fantasy conceals with its array of desirable things and conditions. The real resists complete symbolization, even in fantasy, making it impossible to confront directly. We can see the real only through a skewed view, a looking awry, and even then only a trace.

Desire therefore does not signal, as we often imagine, a lack of object; it signals a lack of obstacle. Desire cannot know its object until it is thwarted; then the object *I do not have* arises for me as the "cause" of the desire. Desire needs the obstacle more than it needs the object—one reason why virtually anything, sometimes the strangest things, can be an object of desire. Having an obstacle allows me to avoid the two terrors that attend all personal economies of desire, and explain why wanting is so important to the very idea of self. On the one hand, we fear the *merging* of our selves with our desires, with the consequence that there is no distance at all left between us and the objects of our wanting. This is self-dissolution, or disappearance. On the other hand, however, we likewise fear the *isolation* of our self and our desires, where we set ourselves against both desire and its objects. This is self-abnegation, or suicide.

Writer's block at scale: Giancarlo Neri's *The Writer* (2005), Hampstead Heath, London.

Both outcomes are kinds of death, in fact, whether we are swallowed up by our desires or so far repudiate them as to, in a final exercise of self, kill off the self. Here we lose our balance and fall, thinking either that death must be either sought or overcome, or, somehow, both. But this seeking for an overcoming always self-defeats. "I think it's a mistake to lose one's sense of death, even one's fear of death," a Don DeLillo character muses. "Isn't death the boundary we need? Doesn't it give a precious texture to life, a sense of definition? You have to ask yourself whether anything you do in this life would have beauty or meaning without the knowledge you carry of a final line, a border or limit." Precisely. But what then is the optimal distance between merging and isolation? Well, that is just the limit-logic that every self must negotiate: the self as *ever unstable* threshold. Personal identity requires obstacles more than satisfactions, because the ego's projects must be both thwarted and satisfied; obstacles are a link to the world, to knowing "where we are" and "where we are going." They tell us who we are, and how we are faring. Without them, we are not just cut adrift, we are literally nothing at all. And so desire must forever renew its dissatisfaction, its being blocked and challenged.

Boredom viewed: *Mariana in the Moated Grange* (1875?), albumen print by Julia Margaret Cameron, George Eastman House, Rochester, New York.

Boredom is one kind of hint at this forever, an illuminating hiccup in desire's otherwise apparently smooth functioning—especially in social economies of desire, where consumption is urged on us at every moment. We all know that this social economy requires a structure of swift discard and inbuilt obsolescence. We must be constantly throwing things out—clothes, tools, trends and ideas—in order to consume new ones afresh each day. The city becomes a mechanism for this economy, a massive machine of desire-circulation. And yet, beneath the dust and chaos of the city, within the forever renewed excitations of longing, there runs a playful current of hope. The imaginary city is more real, in the relevant sense, than the so-called real one, revealed now as a kind of fantasyland of desire's slipknots. The imaginary outpaces the fantastic, exceeds the boundaries of the already-wanted, issuing in reveries about concrete, walking on concrete, being made concrete.

iii. Playful City

The reflections offered here extend a critique of current economies of longing, especially as trapped in various Cartesian hangovers, but they also may do something more valuable. They may exhibit the elements of play that are control's antithesis and rescue. Desire is not vanquished, merely postponed, by exciting a new desire. Only *play*, with its roots in undirected and nonutilitarian desire, its utopian overtones of refusing to assimilate or end or be located, can free us from the stalls of self. We cannot escape the economy of desire, for that is the final limit, but we can renegotiate our engagements. This is where desire transforms itself into the specific kind of nonnihilistic action we call play.

Play is that peculiar and essential form of human activity that possesses many internal (lusory) goals but no external (prelusory) ones: There are things we wish to achieve, and rules or constraints governing their achievement, but the play itself has no end or purpose. There is no point to the game beyond its continuance. It is, as Kant says of beauty more generally, without interest. Thus the affinity between sports and art, since—despite Veblen's sour assessment that an interest in sports is a sign of arrested moral development—both possess the free play of activity and imagination that signifies a human undertaking liberated from use. Thus, too, the rich emotional attachments people form around both sports and art, the lack of ultimate point becoming not a mark against our interest but an essential point in its favor. We care about that which does not matter precisely because it does not. The dialectic of expectation and innovation answers a need in us that is as much spiritual as neurochemical. We watch a baseball game because, although many thousands of games have been played before, even using the very same rules, this particular one has not, and the chances that we will see a play or sequence unique in the history of the game are actually quite high. At the very least, we will see particular plays that are irreducibly novel, that have not been performed before and never will be again. Games ask for, and receive, the very same rapt attention, the *wonder,* that is excited by art. There is no telling how long we must spend giving ourselves over to the game.

The places where this peculiar static action occurs are, perhaps even more than the overdetermined white boxes of the galleried art world, sites of possibility. Enclosed and contained by the city outside, they are ostentatiously different, in the city but not of it, green and separately structured; they tell us openly of their utopian aspirations, their wish to accommodate our desires—if only for a time. In this respect, they are part of that network of otherness that makes any city spongiform and complex, the *heterotopias,* as Foucault calls them, that refuse to surrender to the underlying logic of reasons and exchange: the cemetery, the clinic, the prison, the old-age home, the garden. Heterotopian sites force critical reflection, sometimes unpleasant or undesired, on the general normativity of the city's mechanisms. They are places apart, obeying different rules: often, to be sure, rules of waste or containment or both. (A corpse, notes Dominique Laporte, is just garbage we have buried and sacralized, sometimes forming in the process a city within the city: Many urban cemeteries, including one in my own city, are called "necropolis.") The heterotopia is where we place that which we do not wish to see, or be reminded of—old age, death, crime—but which, nevertheless, we cannot deny or avoid. Constructions of repression, heterotopias generate the usual symptoms of fear and desire that are only partly acknowledged, the urban-fabric equivalent of the contained-catharsis horror films or theme-park thrill rides.

They may also, in sports or carnivals, provide opportunities for bodily *release,* the jouissance of sanctioned outburst, orgasms of cheering, drunkenness and revelry in the midst of the city. Bahktin notes that the operative limit on carnival is time, not space: It is an appropriation of existing commercial areas for noncommercial, indeed nonrational, uses; like the Sabbath, it is time out of time, its church the street and town square. "The main arena for carnival acts was the square," temporarily transformed into heterotopia along with "streets, taverns, roads, boathouses, decks of ships." The inevitable not-yetness of utopia, its insuperable and haunting temporal character—also, to be sure, the banalized commercial versions thereof, in the form of aspirational logic—is here subverted rather than resisted. Heterotopia opens up a time of difference in existing space; it does not defer release to a time that is always still to come.

"Heterotopias always presuppose a system of opening and closing that isolates them and makes them penetrable at one and the same time," Bahktin continues. The threshold must be obvious, its passage controlled in some ritual fashion, entry a transformative experience. We must effect a passage across the *cordon sanitaire* that sets off these spaces as different, alien, even—from the point of view of everyday exchange—contaminated or bizarre. Thresholds may appear obvious but only because we gather up the enclosure of strangeness, not strangeness itself, into the overall city logic, structuring movement thereby: enforced entry (prison), enforced exclusion (club), paid admission (fair). These thresholds are further marked by signifiers of crossing—bars or gate, velvet rope or turnstile—that become symbolic. They indicate where we do time, or spend time, or have a good time or waste time. "All this is time on the threshold," Bahktin says, "and not biological time."

All leisure, according to Veblen's definition, is the "non-productive consumption of time." There are, however, significant potential differences between the ostensible use of leisure time of the leisure

class, which makes a conspicuous and devoted occupation of its non-work time, and the vacation from the reality principle hosted by the open-and-shut time of the carnival. Because it creates a place of pleasure and release, as opposed to punishment or confinement, the carnivalesque is thus a heterotopic reassertion of the body against the pretensions and arrogance of reason. The park or stadium is a concretized carnival or Purim, a place where, according to its rules, the usual rules do not apply. And when there is a championship or other significant victory, the release may itself be released, onto the streets of the briefly suspended city logic. It is often lamented in newspapers that victory celebrations turn violent or ugly, when in fact the truly surprising thing, given the topology of the city and its unconscious, would be if they did not.

The Fight Between Carnival and Lent (1559), oil on wood panel by Pieter Brueghel the Elder, Kunsthistorisches Museum, Vienna.

Entrance to Luna Park: the theme park as incubator of dreams—or nightmares.

The same possibilities abound on the streets, those fluid sites of urban interaction. The thirst for stimulation that Simmel says is characteristic of the metropolitan attitude is best fed here, where there is otherness and spectacle in unlimited quantity. We may even begin to find new forms of selfhood, new subject positions and nodes of identity, by way of our being outside ourselves: the dance of movement on the streets, the kinesthesis of walking, the artwork of self-presentation. The lines of flight that lines of control themselves open up. Creating the self as an ornament offers subjective consciousness a way to reappropriate the urban scene as a realm of democratic play.

The self, conscious of itself as embodied consciousness, crossing and recrossing the thresholds of the city, creating new ones, is a kind of alien body within the civic order. This real imaginary self leaves traces of its swift meander behind, in the form of interactions and encounters. It constantly charts its possibilities. In search of wonder, it opens its gaze to the existence of the others, moving here and there, and shifts the brusque call of authority into a warmer message of shared vulnerability and desire, a shared second-person space.

Hey, you there.

Bibliographic Essay

To keep the main text as readable as possible, I have avoided footnotes and other forms of direct reference. This essay indicates the main research sources, roughly in the order they appear in each chapter. Works not specifically cited but present as general background are found in the sections on Chapter 1 and Chapter 8; certain canonical works, or works mentioned rather than used, have not been cited.

My previously published articles and essays now revised and updated for this book are as follows. Chapter 1: "Concrete's Softer Side," *Saturday Night,* 3 June 2000, 64–67. Chapter 2: "New York, Capital of the Twentieth Century," *The Wascana Review,* Spring 2002, 13–31. Chapter 3: "Space, Place, No Place, and Any Place: Thoughts on Consciousness and the City," *FORM 4,* Spring 2006, 2–7. Chapters 3 and 5: "Meganarratives of Supermodernism: The Spectre of the Public Sphere," *PhaenEx,* Fall 2006, 197–229. Chapter 4: "The City of Tomorrow: Searching for the Future of Architecture in Shanghai," *Harper's Magazine,* February 2005, 62–71. Chapters 6 and 7: "Crossing the Threshold: Towards a Philosophy of the Interior," *Queen's Quarterly,* Spring 2006, 91–104; Summer 2006, 275–89; and Fall 2006, 443–59.

1. Hard and Soft

Lisa Robertson's mesmerizing poems and essays about walking in the city are collected in *Occasional Work and Seven Walks from the Office for Soft Architecture* (Clear Cut, 2003; Coach House, 2006); the text of "Soft Architecture: A Manifesto" is at pp. 13–17. Here Robertson playfully perverts the tendency of architects and designers to indulge in manifesto rhetoric. For more on that, see Jessica Helfand's neat summary "Me, the Undersigned" in her collection *Screen: Essays on Graphic Design, New Media, and Visual Culture* (Princeton Architectural, 2001). Together with a concise history of manifesto from surrealism and futurism to today, she skewers the pretension of Bruce Mau's bafflegab "Manifesto for Incomplete Growth." (For an even more thorough dismantling, see Dean Allen's running commentary,

"An Annotated Manifesto for Growth," at www.textism.com/mau-nifesto/.) It is worth noting that Helfand herself cannot resist offering her own manifesto and, indeed, was one of the signatories of the reissued "First Things First" manifesto for socially responsible graphic design.

Concrete is the second most consumed substance on the planet after water. The ubiquitous material's architectural properties are explored in Jean-Louis Cohen and G. Martin Moeller, eds., *Liquid Stone: New Architecture in Concrete* (Princeton Architectural, 2006). Jonathan Raban's beautifully written *Soft City: A Documentary Exploration of Metropolitan Life* (Harvill, 1998), first published in 1974, remains as vivid and fresh as ever. Among general works on the city, Jane Jacobs has two canonical titles: *The Death and Life of Great American Cities* (Vintage, 1961) and *The Economy of Cities* (Random House, 1969). Other important basic work can be found in Lewis Mumford's magisterial *The City in History* (Harcourt, 1961) and in his earlier study, *The Culture of Cities* (Harcourt, 1938).

Mumford is also important on the topic of utopia, addressed later in this book; see his *The Story of Utopias* (Viking, 1966). Important essays of his are collected in *The Highway and the City* (Princeton Architectural, 1998). On the latter topic, compare Milan Kundera, *Immortality* (HarperCollins, 1991), distinguishing highways from roads: A highway, says Kundera, "has no meaning in itself; its meaning derives entirely from the two points that it connects" (223). As the "triumphant devaluation of space," highways become mere "obstacles to human movement and a waste of time." A highway is all about the getting there, rather than the going. A road, by contrast, is a "tribute to space. Every stretch of road has meaning in itself and invites us to stop." Mumford, like Jane Jacobs, was a staunch opponent of the highway-expansion plans of Robert Moses, losing most of the battles over the plans that resulted in the Grand Central Parkway and Triborough Bridge, among others; projects for Washington Square, Greenwich Village and SoHo were successfully blocked. Robert Caro's monumental biography of Moses, *The Power Broker: Robert Moses and the Fall of New York* (Vintage, 1975), offers the standard evil-genius view of the long-time planner, but a more recent work by Hilary Ballon and Kenneth Jackson, *Robert Moses and the Modern City: The Transformation of New*

Concrete Reveries

York (Norton, 2007), nuances the legacy, noting the many parks, cleared slums, public pools and additions to Central Park that are also Moses's work.

Manuel Castells has written illuminatingly about cities as flow-spaces; see his work *The Rise of the Network Society* (Edward Elgar, 2004), vol. 1 of his massive *The Information Age,* especially ch. 6, "Space of Flows." Specific insights on the economics of cities, a topic that lies largely outside the scope of the present book, can be found in Ash Amin, "The Economic Base of Contemporary Cities," in Gary Bridge and Sophie Watson, eds., *A Companion to the City* (Blackwell, 2000), 115–29; Edward Glaeser, Jed Kolko and Albert Seiz, "Consumer City," *Harvard Institute of Economic Research,* Discussion Paper no. 1901 (June 2000); and Loren King, "Democracy and City Life," *Philosophy, Politics, and Economics* 3:1 (2004), 97–124. See also Richard Florida's widely influential argument on the link between cultural work (or "creativity") and economic prosperity, *The Rise of the Creative Class* (Basic Books, 2002).

"Concrete" is a notion much analyzed in the philosophical literature, though rarely in relation to its instantiation as a building material. Gillian Rose, for example, in *Melancholy Science* (Columbia University Press, 1978) identifies four resonances of "concrete" in the work of Theodor Adorno, especially in his *Negative Dialectics* (trans. E.B. Ashton; Continuum, 1974). They are: (1) concrete as the "hardness" of social determinations on a subject; (2) concrete as distinct from abstract or philosophical, thus to see an object concretely; (3) concrete as the irreducibly material, that which refuses assimilation to concepts; and (4) concrete as the resistance an object offers to us, leveraging utopian possibilities.

The issues of hardness and superhardness in philosophical discourse are raised most compellingly by Ludwig Wittgenstein in his *Philosophical Investigations* (trans. G.E.M. Anscombe; Macmillan 1953). Quotation is from remark 97 ("Thought is surrounded by a halo"). Wittgenstein returned to the issue in his "Lectures on Aesthetics," especially in remarks 26, 27 and 28 of Lecture II; see Cyril Barrett, ed., *Wittgenstein: Lectures and Conversations on Aesthetics, Psychology and Religious Belief* (Blackwell, 1966), 15–16. For more on the deep instabilities opened up by conceiving philosophy as the pursuit of superhard, crystal-clear concepts, see Henry Staten, *Wittgenstein and Derrida* (University of Nebraska Press, 1982), especially ch. 5. Staten also discusses Nietzsche's remark about philosophy being "unconscious memoir," which is from *Beyond Good and Evil* (1886; sec. 1.6), in an essay called "The Problem of Nietzsche's Economy," *Representations* 27 (Summer 1989), 66–91, at p. 66. Like Staten, I also address the problem of how to read Nietzsche as a problem in how to do philosophy, in "Nietzsche's Styles," originally published at www. britannica.com, 29 August 2000, and reprinted in Kingwell, *Practical Judgments: Essays in Culture, Politics, and Interpretation* (University of Toronto Press, 2002).

Richard Sennett's much reproduced essay "Plate Glass," *Raritan* 6:4 (Winter 1987), 1–15, is the source of solid insight about this most intriguing building material, including the quotations from Taut, Schlemmer, Scheerbart and Schoenberg. More detailed placement of this love of glass in early-twentieth-century culture is found in Peter Conrad's admirable and brisk *Modern Times, Modern Places* (Knopf, 1999). Patrick Turmel, "La ville comme un object de justice" (PhD diss., University of Toronto, 2007) offers a novel argument about the politics of urban life under fluid conditions.

Reverie is a word that implies a pleasant daydream, but it also has its darker aspect. In Herman Melville's "Bartleby the Scrivener, A Story of Wall-Street" (1853), the bemused narrator, striving to understand his cadaverous copyist who prefers not to copy, uses the words *reverie* or *reveries* five times: once about himself, stunned into speechlessness, and four times about the increasingly motionless Bartleby. Three of these latter uses are modified by the striking adjective *dead-wall*, as in *dead-wall reveries*. Such is the state of abstract resistance into which Bartleby slowly withdraws, first behind a screen in the lawyer's chambers and then, at the end, before a prison wall. Concrete can also make a cell, and reflect back our despair—or refusal. In "Notes Towards a Politics of Bartleby: The Ignorance of Chickens," *Comparative American Studies* 4 (2006), 375–94, Slavoj Žižek argues that this reverie is a form of political violence: resistance without alternative. See also Žižek, *The Parallax View* (MIT Press, 2005).

The notion that urban planning might count as a form of war crime is vividly raised by Eyal Weizman in the polemical but nevertheless plausible essay "The Evil Architects Do," in Rem Koolhaas, ed., *Content* (Taschen, 2004), 60–63. See also Hal Foster's collection of essays *Design and Crime* (Verso, 2002), which extends Adolf Loos's famous denunciation of ornament as crime. Weizman's argument likewise recalls the critical assessment of *building as fear* deployed by Paul Virilio in his *Panic City* (trans. Julie Rose; Berg, 2005). Virilio's argument begins with familiar readings of gated communities and exurban sprawl, together with an appreciation of the nineteenth-century riot-proofing of Paris perfected by Baron von Haussmann—what Walter Benjamin called the *haussmannization* of Paris, whereby small, barricade-friendly streets were reordered as wide, cavalry-friendly boulevards. But Virilio's provocative analysis goes farther and acquires new resonance in the wake of the Paris banlieue riots of 2005, and of the new urban planning being deployed to prevent recurrence in future—plans which, in the event, may prove even more dangerous to the idea of shared public space under cosmopolitan conditions. See also Lieven de Cauter, *The Capsular Civilization: On the City in the Age of Fear* (NAI Press, 2004).

A basic outline of feral cities can be found in Richard J. Norton, "Feral Cities," *Naval War College Review* 56:4 (Autumn 2003), 97–106. See also James Miskel and Peter Liotta, "Redrawing the Map of the Future," *World Policy Journal* 24:1 (Spring 2004), and Ken Stier's summary in the *New York Times Magazine* "Year in Ideas" feature, 12 December 2004.

Freud's city imagery is found in *Civilization and Its Discontents* [*Unbehagen in der Kultur*] (trans. James Strachey; Norton, 2005; orig. pub. 1921). Kevin Lynch's fivefold schema is found in *A Theory of Good City Form* (MIT Press, 1981), 328–42. See also Jacobs, *The Death and Life of Great American Cities,* 433; this classic volume contains her celebrated disputes with Robert Moses about the Fifth Avenue extension and the tendentious critique of the "Radiant Garden City Beautiful" school of urban planning (see the notes for the next chapter for further reference). Frank Cunningham's as yet unpublished paper "The 'Gruing' of Cities" is the beginning of a larger project in urban philosophy. For the first proposal of *grue,* see Nelson Goodman, *Fact, Fiction, and Forecast* (Harvard University Press, 1954), the original version of the "new riddle for induction." Philosophers remain divided on whether this is indeed a riddle or just semantic sleight-of-hand.

My treatment of public space and the Benjamin–Adorno relationship is in *The World We Want* (Viking, 2000), ch. 4. Georg Simmel's seminal essay on the metropolitan attitude is "The Metropolis and Mental Life," written in 1903, reprinted in Kurt Wolff, ed., *The Sociology of Georg Simmel* (Free Press, 1964), 409–24. The themes of anonymity and getting lost—the things that make cities attractive to the *flâneur*—are central in Walter Benjamin's *Pariser Passagen,* written between 1928 and 1930, in English translation as *The Arcades Project* (Harvard University Press, 1999). "Not to find one's way in a city may well be uninteresting and banal," Benjamin had written of his native Berlin. "It requires ignorance—nothing more. But to lose oneself in a city— as one loses oneself in a forest—that calls for quite a different schooling." This insight in turn influenced Guy Debord and the Situationist International of which he was the main theoretician. Debord's critique/ manifesto *The Society of the Spectacle* (trans. Donald Nicholson-Smith; Zone, 1995) is deservedly a classic, especially for present purposes its defense of the *derive,* or drift, as a way of negotiating the city, subverting the urban program. Contemporary projects of urban space movement are less interested in subversion and more welcoming of technology; see, for example, the headmap movement's documents celebrating localizability at www.technoccult.com/library/headmap.pdf.

Gilles Deleuze and Félix Guattari discuss the machine qualities of the book in "Rhizome," included in *On the Line* (trans. John Johnston; Semiotext(e), 1983), 14 and following. Their favored image of the rhizome, an organic tuber or pile of moving bodies in which all lines may connect, subverts the linear and hierarchical structure of the branching diagram or grid that dominates thought via both language and representation (and language as representation). Note, with respect to a point I discuss later in this book, that measurement itself is an act of repression: "We have no units of measure, but only multiplicities or varieties of measure. The notion of unit appears only when the signifier, or a corresponding process of subjectivization, seizes power in a multiplicity: hence the pivot-unity that founds a set of bi-univocal relations among the elements of objective points, or else the One that divides following the law of a binary logic of differentiation in the subject" (15–16). This short essay is a post-facto commentary on their magnum opus of schizoanalysis, *Anti-Oedipus: Capitalism and Schizophrenia* (trans. Robert Hurley, Mark Seem and Helen R. Lane; University of Minnesota Press, 1983). For more on lines of flight, see the companion volume, *A Thousand Plateaus: Capitalism and Schizophrenia* (trans. Brian Massumi; University of Minnesota Press, 1987). There are many accounts of the comprehensive mediation of contemporary, especially political, life. Todd Gitlin's *Media Unlimited* (Metropolitan Books, 2002) is distinguished for its rich historical erudition and sense of political urgency, though it is more a primer on the familiar problem of media saturation than an attempt at a solution.

Jean Hippolyte studied with Jacques Derrida and is influenced by his thought. The quotation here is from "Structure du langage philosophique d'après la Préface de la *Phénoménologie de l'esprit* de Hegel," in Richard Macksey and Eugenio Donato, eds., *The Structuralist Controversy* (Johns Hopkins University Press, 1970), 343, cited and discussed in John Llewelyn, *Derrida on the Threshold of Sense* (Macmillan, 1986), 4–5.

2. New York, Capital of the Twentieth Century

E.B. White's lovely essay about the city, *Here Is New York* (HarperCollins, 1949), contains a striking melancholy note at its end about the imagined prospect of death-dealing airplanes threatening the survival of the author's beloved Manhattan. Compare with Adam Goodheart, "9.11.01: The Skyscraper and the Airplane," *The American Scholar* 71:1 (Winter 2002), 13–19.

For Kenneth Tynan's relationship with New York, see *The Diaries of Kenneth Tynan* (Bloomsbury, 2001), especially p. 72. Jed Perl's essay "The Adolescent City" appeared in the *New Republic*, 22 January 2001. I discuss Le Corbusier's complicated love affair with New York, especially the skyscraper form, in *Nearest Thing to Heaven: The Empire*

State Building and American Dreams (Yale University Press, 2006). Paul Auster, in *City of Glass* (Penguin, 1987), gives one of the best treatments I know of what it is like to walk one's way to pattern and meaning—or not—on the streets of Manhattan. Auster and artist Sophie Calle are unusual collaborators on a text published as *Le Gotham Handbook* (Actes-Sud, 1999), a fax the novelist sent her about how to walk in Manhattan. Calle later published *Double Game* (DAP, 2007), a compendium of artworks whose central piece is the faxed guide, plus annnotations of an Auster novel that includes a character based on Calle.

Henry Miller's remark is from *Tropic of Cancer* (Grove, 1961; orig. pub. 1934), 67–68. Reporter Marc Santora recorded insights about pedestrian Manhattan in "Think You Own the Sidewalk?" *New York Times,* 16 July 2002. Roy Blount Jr.'s matching discourse is "How to Walk in New York," in *Now, Where Were We?* (Ballantine, 1978), 111–16. Tom Wolfe coined the unimprovable term *pimp roll* in his essay about Dixwell Avenue in New Haven, the main artery of a mostly black neighborhood just past the limits of the Yale campus. P.G. Wodehouse's various terms of pedestrian modes can be found in virtually every story he wrote.

Statistics on automobile-pedestrian conflicts are common, but the mid-1960s numbers relied on here come from Rai Y. Okamoto and Frank E. Williams, *Urban Design Manhattan* (Viking, 1969), a planning manifesto aimed at understanding New York's Central Business District (CBD) in "the year 2000 and beyond." The authors write: "The Manhattan CBD is a machine for bringing together a wide variety of talents and facilitating face-to-face communication," but the prospect faces three central problems:

> First, the growing malfunction of this enormous international business and pleasure machine is causing congestion and friction that increasingly stresses the limits of human tolerance.

> Second, the vivid imagery and distinctive form and appearance created by Manhattan's clustered office towers in the eyes and the mind of the world, are in danger of disappearing under a

spreading "slab city" lacking the variety and identity of the special districts which exist today.

Third, the CBD pedestrian has become the forgotten man.

In this condition, "The pedestrian is relegated to a very low level of importance, with traffic signals being timed for the efficient movement of cars and not people walking. Noxious exhaust fumes as well as an overbearing level of noise caused by cars, trucks and buses constantly confronts the pedestrian." A background premise of the present chapter is that much of New York's 1970s-era decline and 1990s resurgence can be charted as a function of its failure and success as a walking city.

Michel de Certeau describes his experience of walking in Manhattan in the first pages of *The Practice of Everyday Life* (trans. Steven Rendall; University of California Press, 2002). Lewis Mumford's architecture reviews for the *New Yorker* and other publications are collected in *Sidewalk Critic* (Princeton Architectural, 1998). See also Herbert Muschamp, *File under Architecture* (MIT Press, 1974). Rem Koolhaas's *Delirious New York: A Retroactive Manifesto for Manhattan* (Monacelli, 1974) is countervailed by his later denunciations of Manhattan as a symbolic accomplice of U.S. imperialism. See his "White Briefs against Filth: The Waning Power of New York," which first appeared in *Wired* magazine as "Delirious No More," June 2003, and is reprinted, among other places, in Koolhaas, ed., *Content* (Taschen, 2004), 236–39. Le Corbusier struggles with functionalism and modernism in the *circa* 1923 journal essays gathered together as *Vers une architecture,* in English as *Towards a New Architecture* (trans. Frederick Etchells; Dover, 1986).

There is an excellent critical account of the origin of Manhattan's grid, and the influence of gridded cities generally, in Witold Rybczynski's *City Life* (Simon and Schuster, 1996); his volume *The Look of Architecture* (Oxford University Press, 2001) is likewise good, using the block south of Bryant Park and the Manhattan Public Library as a springboard to a general discussion of style and gesture in architecture. Yi-Fu Tuan, *Space and Place: The Perspective of Experience* (University of Minnesota Press, 1977), and John W. Reps, *The Making of Urban*

America: *A History of City Planning in the United States* (Princeton, 1965), are also useful. Kevin Lynch's analysis of "imageability" in cities, including monuments and other landmarks, is *The Image of the City* (MIT Press, 1960).

Two recent urban subversion projects help citizens regain their privacy by showing them how to avoid cityscape surveillance or destroy it. The Institute for Applied Autonomy (www.appliedautonomy.com/isee/) offers an interactive map that shows walkers the path of least surveillance between any two points in Manhattan. For those who want to take the direct route, the anonymous art-anarchy purveyor RTMark explains how to disable inappropriate cameras at www.rtmark.com/cctv/.

3. Public Spaces, Public Places

Edward S. Casey's phenomenological studies are the best examples so far of applying Husserlian and post-Husserlian thought to the question of place. See *Getting Back into Place: Toward a Renewed Understanding of the Place-World* (Indiana University Press, 1993) and *The Fate of Place: A Philosophical History* (University of California Press, 1997). Fredric Jameson's alas too-brief remarks about architecture and the use of the term *postmodern* are found in his Introduction to the English translation of Jean-François Lyotard's *La Condition postmoderne: rapport sur le savoir* (Editions de Minuit, 1979), *The Postmodern Condition: A Report on Knowledge* (trans. Geoff Bennington and Brian Massumi; University of Minnesota Press, 1984). Marc Augé and Hans Ibelings are the influential emergent critics of what has come to be called "supermodernism"; see, respectively, Augé, *Non-Places: Introduction to an Anthropology of Supermodernity* (Verso, 1995), and Ibelings, *Supermodernism: Architecture in the Age of Globalization* (NAI, 1998).

In addition to being an acute critic of postmodern architecture style (and, indeed, pretension), Charles Jencks is the keenest investigator of the condition, also explored by Foucault, among others, of *heterotopia*:

the place of otherness—in his case, Los Angeles. See *The Language of Post-Modern Architecture* (Academy Editions, 1977; 5th ed., Rizzoli, 1987), *Daydream Houses of Los Angeles* (Academy Editions, 1978) and *Heteropolis: Los Angeles, the Riots and the Strange Beauty of Hetero-Architecture* (Academy Editions, 1993). It is worth comparing Jencks's reading of Los Angeles with a more classically negative view such as Kevin Lynch's, in *The Image of the City*. On the question of style in architecture—a bad word, generally—see Witold Rybczynski's *The Look of Architecture,* which usefully punctures the no-style posture.

It is perhaps not surprising that the museum, the public aesthetic building par excellence, the state's democratic cultural gesture, should be the locus of recent architectural megaprojects, and so the site of municipal ambition. See Jayne Merkel, "The Museum as Artifact," *Wilson Quarterly,* Winter 2002, 66–79. We may recall here, too, Arthur Danto's neat assessment of the Museum of Modern Art in Manhattan (MoMA) refusing the institutional grandness of previous art museums, with their neoclassical entrances and intimidating stairs, and opting instead for an unpretentious 54th Street pedestrian entrance, as a decisive modern counter-gesture. See "The Museum of Museums," in *Beyond the Brillo Box: The Visual Arts in Post-Historical Perspective* (University of California Press, 1992).

My own essay on aesthetic tendencies of new-millennium signature architecture is "Monumental/Conceptual Architecture," *Harvard Design Magazine* 19 (Fall/Winter 2004); published and archived online at www.gsd.harvard.edu/research/publications/hdm/back/19_kingwell.html. This essay might best be considered as the more thoughtful companion to a polemical reading of archi-cultural aspiration in my own city, especially Daniel Libeskind's much-abused Royal Ontario Museum renovation, "Redesigning Toronto: the $195-Million Scribble," *Toronto Life,* June 2004, 70–75. I revised my somewhat harsh take on Will Alsop's Ontario College of Art and Design reno, the Sharpe Centre for Design, in a later satirical article called "Stop," in *Bite Magazine,* Summer 2004, 13–15. *Stop* here is a gradual contraction of a nickname for the building, "Stiltslab," and the architect's name, Alsop. That is: *Stiltslab + Alsop = Stiltslabalsop*; this via contraction = *Stiltsop*; further contraction = *Stop*.

Nathan Silver has his own kind of fun while examining "Architect Talk," in Christopher Ricks and Leonard Michaels, eds., *The State of the Language* (University of California Press, 1980), 324–30, which, while undoubtedly dated by subsequent events—and linguistic moves—remains an indispensable primer on architecture's penchant for what I earlier called *philosophical backformation*. Ludwig Wittgenstein's entertaining play of block, slab, pillar and beam as a possible originary language game—building a temple, perhaps, as suggested by the philosopher Norton Batkin—opens *Philosophical Investigations* (trans. G.E.M. Anscombe; Macmillan, 1958), 3 and following, while Alberto Pérez-Gómez's optimistic assessment of architecture's ethical dimensions is found in his Introduction to Louise Pelletier, ed., *Architecture, Ethics, and Technology* (Institut de recherche en histoire de l'architecture, 1994).

Arthur Danto mentions architecture as an example of the third realm of beauty in his linked essays published as *The Abuse of Beauty: Aesthetics and the Concept of Art* (Open Court, 2003). It is worth comparing, on the main point of beauty's abuse and recent rehabilitation, works by Denis Donoghue, *Speaking of Beauty* (Yale University Press, 2003); Virginia Postrel, *The Substance of Style* (HarperCollins, 2003); Elaine Scarry, *On Beauty and Being Just* (Harvard University Press, 1999); and especially the brilliant essays by Hans-Georg Gadamer collected in English by editor Robert Bernasconi as *The Relevance of the Beautiful and Other Essays* (trans. various; Cambridge University Press, 1986).

Hannah Arendt's influential notion of the space of appearances is first explored in *The Human Condition* (University of Chicago Press, 1998) and given decisive architectural resonance by George Baird, *The Space of Appearances* (MIT Press, 1995). Compare, too, Kenneth Frampton's "The Status of Man and the Status of His Objects: A Reading of *The Human Condition*," in Melvyn A. Hill, ed., *Hannah Arendt: The Recovery of the Public World* (St. Martin's, 1979), 101–30. A short unpublished conference paper by Ronald Beiner was instrumental in my appreciation of the importance of architecture in Arendt's thought.

The idea of public space as the rational public sphere is defended throughout Habermas's later work but classically in the two-volume (in English) magnum opus, *The Theory of Communicative Action* (trans. Thomas McCarthy; Beacon, 1984 and 1987). John Rawls's distinct but cognate position is found in *A Theory of Justice* (Belknap, 1971), with important revisions and extensions in *Political Liberalism* (Columbia University Press, 1993). The two thinkers addressed each other directly in a celebrated exchange of the 1990s, beginning with Habermas. "Reconciliation through the Public Use of Reason: Remarks on John Rawls's Political Liberalism," *Journal of Philosophy* 92:3 (March 1995), to which Rawls offered his "Reply to Habermas," likewise *Journal of Philosophy* 92:3 (March 1995); reprinted in the later (1996 and 2005) editions of Rawls's *Political Liberalism,* 372–435. Compare also Christopher McMahon, "Why There Is No Issue between Habermas and Rawls," *Journal of Philosophy* 99:3 (March 2002), 111–29.

The critic seeing only nullity in this "new liberalism" is John Gray, in "Against the New Liberalism: Rawls, Dworkin and the Emptying of Political Life," *Times Literary Supplement,* 3 July 1992, 13. This is not the place to rehearse the so-called liberalism/communitarianism debate of the 1990s, but see my *A Civil Tongue: Justice, Dialogue, and the Politics of Pluralism* (Penn State University Press, 1995) for one kind of overview of the controversy, with references. In that work I read Habermas's communicative action theory against the pure rationality position found in the early Rawls.

Albrecht Wellmer's critique of utopian perspectives in architecture is "Architecture and Territory," in *Endgames: The Irreconcilable Nature of Modernity* (trans. David Midgley; MIT Press, 1998). Sociologist Nathan Glazer offers an architectural layman's informed assessment of modernism declension from reform project to stylistic tic in the essay collection *From a Cause to a Style: Modernist Architecture's Encounter with the American City* (Princeton University Press, 2007). Martin Filler, in *Makers of Modern Architecture* (NYRB, 2007), offers a more subtle but no less challenging summary of modern architecture, running from Louis Sullivan to Santiago Calatrava. I consider the two books in a comparative essay, "Modernism à la Mode," in *Harper's Magazine*, November 2007, 83–88. Adolf Loos's remark about the persistent and shared nature of architecture can be found, along with much else, in Franz Glück, ed., *Samtliche Schriften* (Brenner Verlag,

1962), 314 and following. Gottfried Benn's remark about modernism is quoted by Susan Ray in her study *Beyond Nihilism: Gottfried Benn's Postmodernist Poetics* (Peter Lang, 2003). Roland Barthes's pregnant and, to me, highly influential essay on the Eiffel Tower has been much reprinted; I rely on the translation offered in Neal Leach's excellent anthology of writing on the built environment, *Rethinking Architecture: A Reader in Cultural Theory* (Routledge, 1997), 172–81. A more complete discussion is found in Kingwell, *Nearest Thing to Heaven*.

4. The City of Tomorrow

Concrete Reveries

The best book on the peculiar juxtapositions of architecture in Shanghai is Tsung-Yi Michelle Huang, *Walking between Slums and Skyscrapers: Illusions of Open Space in Hong Kong, Tokyo and Shanghai* (Hong Kong University Press, 2004). See also the gorgeous book by Peter G. Rowe, of Harvard's Graduate School of Design, titled *Shanghai: Architecture and Urbanism for Modern China* (Prestel, 2004). *Shanghai Architecture & Design,* by Martin Nicholas Kunz, Christian Datz and Christof Kullmann (Te Neues, 2005), is also useful, as is Alejandro Bahamon's image-centered (and confusingly similar in title) *Architecture & Design Shanghai* (daab, 2005).

J.G. Ballard's *Empire of the Sun* (Simon and Schuster, 1984) succeeds in conveying the sense of pre-postmodern Shanghai, especially the contrast between the Bund and the various concessions of the city. The excellent 1987 Steven Spielberg film adaptation, starring John Malkovich and Christian Bale, gave the novel new visibility. See also Kazuo Ishiguro, *When We Were Orphans* (Random House, 2000). In *Shanghai and the Edges of Empire* (University of Minnesota Press, 2006), Meng Yue brings postmodern and hybridity theory usefully to bear on the new economic and political conditions of the city as it enters the twenty-first century. Trotsky's remarks about skyscrapers are quoted in Peter Conrad, *Modern Times, Modern Places.*

Three books of images of modern China convey the utter novelty of its twenty-first century version of hypercapitalism: *Burtynsky—China*

(Inextenso, 2005), which includes an essay of mine and others by curator Marc Mayer and journalist Ted C. Fishman; see also Burtynsky's *Manufactured Landscapes: The Photographs of Edward Burtynsky* (Yale University Press, 2003), which includes some works from the Three Rivers Dam project and other mega-undertakings of the new China. Greg Girard adds a new level of complexity with his luminous images of old and new Shanghai, especially buildings in the moment of condemnation or demolition, in *Phantom Shanghai* (Magenta Foundation, 2007). Many books, most of them of the quickie variety, claim to analyze the challenges of modernized China. Fishman's *China, Inc.: How the Rise of the Next Superpower Challenges America and the World* (Scribner, 2005) is one of the earliest and best.

5. Consciousness and the City

Aldo Rossi, working with his own version of a structuralist architectural theory indebted in part to Barthes, discusses monumentality in his provocative book *Architecture of the City* (MIT Press, 1982).

J.M. Coetzee offers a provocative account of embodiment, pain, rights and meaning in *Elizabeth Costello: Eight Lessons* (Viking, 2003), a novel structured as a series of addresses and lectures either delivered or attended by the fictional aging novelist, Elizabeth. Coetzee generated substantial controversy by delivering one of these, a stern and uncompromising argument about animal rights, apparently in propria persona, to an audience at Princeton University. Elaine Scarry makes her own provocative claims in *The Body in Pain: The Making and Unmaking of the World* (Oxford University Press, 1985). Condillac's thoughts about the animate statue are part of Dominique Laporte's funny and probing book *History of Shit* [*Histoire de la merde*] (trans. Nadia Benabid and Rodolphe el-Khoury; MIT Press, 2000; orig. pub. 1978); further reference is made to this book in Chapter 8.

The quotation from Thackeray is discussed in Terry Eagleton's survey of contemporary treatments of the human body in relation to thought, "I Am, Therefore I Think: The Plight of the Body in Modern

Thought," in *Harper's Magazine,* March 2004. This essay includes a riposte to Smith and Richardson on sentimentalism. Likewise in Joanna Bourke, "Sentimental Education," *Harper's Magazine,* May 2007, 89–93, which faults Lynn Hunt's *Inventing Human Rights: A History* (Norton, 2007) for imagining sentiment to be a reliable foundation, against power, for moral claims. For more, see Smith, *The Theory of Moral Sentiments* (Cambridge University Press, 2002; orig. pub. 1759), and many of the moralistic epistolary novels of Richardson, especially *Pamela: Or, Virtue Rewarded* (1740) and *Sir Charles Grandison* (1754), which were widely read for their sense of interiority and influenced, among others, Diderot and Rousseau on the Continent in thinking about the rights of others.

Freud's discussion of the smell of waste and its relation to the upright posture is extended by Erwin Straus in "The Upright Posture," in *Phenomenological Psychology: The Selected Papers of Erwin W. Straus* (trans. Erling Eng; Basic Books, 1966), which among other things links the rise of the body to the next movement, *peripateia.* See, on the latter point, Rebecca Solnit's remarkable book *Wanderlust: A History of Walking* (Viking, 2000), which renders a concrete phenomenology of walking that links Aristotle to the *flâneur* and jaywalker, with stops along the way at Rousseau, Jane Austen, Hazlitt, Dickens, Thomas Hardy, Oliver Wendell Holmes and numerous others. Will Self's long meditative rambles through various cities, studded with harsh judgments on most of them, are collected in *Psychogeography: Disentangling the Modern Conundrum of Psyche and Place* (Bloomsbury, 2007), illustrated by Ralph Steadman. The upright posture is equally notable, or more so, in its failure. I consider the act of falling, and getting badly hurt, in an essay called "On the Ausable," *Queen's Quarterly* 114:2 (Summer 2007), 169–86; it includes references to Freud, Straus and J. H. van den Berg, whose work on the phenomenology of everyday experience is cited below.

Insights on tools and posture naturally belong to Heidegger's analysis of equipmentality in *Being and Time* [*Sein und Zeit*] (trans. John Macquarrie and Edward Robinson; Harper and Row, 1962; orig. pub. 1921). Equipment, Heidegger notes, is never simply available in isolation, clear though it appears that a hammer, say, is just waiting there ready to hand, waiting to be used. This readiness to hand implies a whole world of use of which the hammer is a part: the nail poised to be grasped and placed, the planks (or what have you) lying in anticipation of being joined, the structure whose forms gathers them together, and so on. Here, as so often, Heidegger extends the teleological tendency of Aristotelian metaphysics in pursuit of the fundamental ontology that equipment at once conceals and reveals.

For more on posture, tool-making and comprehension, see Belinda Barnet, "Technical Machines and Evolution," *CTHEORY*, 16 March 2004 (www.ctheory.net); Jacques Ellul, *The Technological Society* (trans. John Wilkinson; Vintage, 1964); and Adrian Mackenzie, *Transductions: Bodies and Machines at Speed* (Continuum, 2002). These analyses naturally open up into posthuman and cyborg investigation of the sort pioneered by Donna Haraway in "A Cyborg Manifesto: Science, Technology, and Socialist-Feminism in the Late Twentieth Century," originally published in *Socialist Review* 15:2 (1985) and later included in her collection *Simians, Cyborgs, and Women: The Reinvention of Nature* (Routledge, 1991), 149–81. The cyborg brings technology inside the body so that the threshold between body and machine is first crossed, then blurred and eventually eliminated. Another sort of analysis is offered by Michel Foucault in Luther H. Martin, Huck Gutman and Patrick H. Hutton, eds., *Technologies of the Self: A Seminar with Michel Foucault* (University of Massachusetts Press, 1988), which illuminates the link between explicit body-machining (in the form of cosmetic surgery, say) and self-machining (in the form of psychotherapy, institutional disciplines or even style).

Gilbert Ryle provides deft unravelings of traditional philosophical problems, including familiar paradoxes from Zeno, in *Dilemmas: The Tarner Lectures 1953* (Cambridge University Press, 1969). The same dexterous application of logic is evident in his justly famous dismantling of orthodox Cartesianism via the notion of category mistake, in *The Concept of Mind* (Hutchinson, 1949). In brief, the argument notes that categories operate at different ranges, or levels of abstraction, and confusing these can lead to absurdities. Suppose I am shown the various buildings of a university, and I respond by saying, These are all very well, but which one is the university itself? (A more elegant version, accredited to A.J. Ayer: "She came in a taxi and left in a rage." Was it a four-door rage?) Thus, working backwards from the notion of matter as substance, Descartes argues that mind is likewise a substance, only of a wholly different kind. The difference then generates the mind-body problem. But what if it makes no sense to speak of mind as substance in the first place?

While much has been made of the cogency, or otherwise, of the category mistake, perhaps a more devastating, and yet simpler, critique is available on the question of localizability: When we ask, Where is the mind?, the Cartesian can have no answer, and yet, mindedness is experienced strongly as embodiment, in self and other. This argument links Ryle with Ayer and Wittgenstein, among others. See Wittgenstein, *Philosophical Investigations*, and Ayer, *Language, Truth, and Logic* (Gollancz, 1936); further discussion of this point is offered in Chapter 7. The canonical text of the standard view is of course René Descartes, *Meditations on First Philosophy* (trans. John Cottingham; Cambridge University Press, 1996; orig. pub. 1641); this edition includes a wise essay by the late Bernard Williams on the self-reflexive character of Descartes's text—an interpretation that considerably lessens the force of anti-Cartesian critique.

An elegant summary of this issue from a somewhat unlikely source: "The best books are … merely reflections of events, they do not express an 'inner reality.' B.F. Skinner, the behaviourist, is right to attack the idea that human behaviour is caused by 'indwelling agents'—the postulate so brilliantly demolished by Gilbert Ryle in *The Concept of Mind* and by such latter-day proponents of oriental philosophy such as Alan Watts, who says, 'I do not *have* a body. I am a body.' The prime cause of confusion in the artistic and/or intellectual world today lies in the failure to accept the erosion of the ancient duality of mind and matter, soul and body, ego and carcass, inner life and outer life" (*The Diaries of Kenneth Tynan*, 75; 21 October 1971 entry). The implied link to Skinner is apt: Ryle labeled his anti-Cartesian position "logical behaviorism." Note, too, that Skinner's attack on the model of indwelling agents is a version of the *homunculus regress* problem first mooted in Plato's dialogue *Theaetetus*: If perception involves perceiver "inside" my head—an homunculus or "little man"—what about the perceiver inside his head; and the one inside *his*; and so on?

William James's essay "Does 'Consciousness' Exist?" (1904) is a classic
of its kind, showing both the virtues (casual brilliance, almost poetic
expression) and the vices (imprecision, ambivalence) of its author.
It is included in his collection *Pragmatism: A Name for an Old Way
of Thinking* (1907). For an illuminating discussion, see Robert
D. Richardson, *William James: In the Maelstrom of American Modernism*
(Houghton Mifflin, 2006). Denis Donoghue's review of this book, "The
Pragmatic American," *Harper's Magazine,* January 2007, 88–94, is also
useful. A minor but significant coincidence: In his review, Donoghue
cites and discusses Jill M. Kress's book *The Figure of Consciousness*
(Routledge, 2002), which examines James's and Edith Wharton's ideas
of knowledge by a study of metaphor. Aptly enough for present purposes, the first line of that book runs this way: "In the Introduction to
her first book, *The Decoration of Houses* (1897), Edith Wharton stipulates two distinct ways to decorate a home: 'by a superficial application
of ornament' independent of the structure of the building, or 'by
means of those architectural features which are part of the organism of
every house, inside as well as out.'"

Well, exactly. But consider, too, a discussion of Emily Dickinson's
home in Amherst, Massachusetts, by Diana Fuss ("Interior Chambers:
The Emily Dickinson Homestead," in *differences: A Journal of Feminist
Cultural Studies* 10:3, 1–46). Fuss argues that Dickinson, that master of
interiority, saw private spaces also as public ones. Then, in 1855, the
family installed freestanding Franklin stoves in several rooms: "The
improved heating arrangements dramatically reconfigured social relations within the home, decentralizing the family and creating new
zones of privacy. More than any other revolution of the social interior,
the Franklin stove made it possible for individual members *within* the
family to seek privacy *from* the family." Compare, on this point,
Foucault's insights about the hearth, discussed in Chapter 7.

Lately better known as an ardent Darwinian apologist and opponent of
religious belief, Daniel Dennett has philosophy of mind that is distinguished by counterintuitive conclusions and vivid narratives urging
readers toward them. See, in particular, *Consciousness Explained* (Little,
Brown, 1991) and *Kinds of Minds* (Weidenfeld and Nicolson, 1996).
John McDowell is an altogether less accessible thinker. His complex
views are best approached by way of *Mind and World* (Harvard

University Press, 1996) and *Mind, Value, and Reality* (Harvard University Press, 1998). I cite these thinkers here not to denigrate them but rather as leading examples of an approach to consciousness whose conclusions, however powerful, are conditioned by scientistic premises that go largely unexamined.

If abstract models of consciousness fail to capture the embodied experience of living, how much more baffling is an eliminativist user-illusion or meme-nest theory of consciousness? Such a view suggests that your sense of self is just a residue of the brain's complexity. There is no you, only the deceptive feeling generated by a complex organism's functioning, plus various bits of evolutionarily competitive ideation, struggling for survival over time. Relevant here is the argument set out by the journalist Tor Nørretranders in *The User Illusion: Cutting Consciousness Down to Size* (Viking, 1998), which suggests, on the basis of some cobbled findings of thermodynamics and neuroscience, that the sense of self is like the graphic user interface (that is, the GUI or "desktop") that mediates between a computer and its interaction partners. Meme theory is somewhat more persuasive, though it, too, is ultimately corrosive of self. Coinage of the term *meme*—a bit of cultural information, as a gene is a bit of genetic information, subject to transmission or replication from host to host—is credited to Richard Dawkins in *The Selfish Gene* (Oxford University Press, 1976), where the discussion is brief and conjectural. It has since become neither. See, for example, J.M. Balkin's *Cultural Software: A Theory of Ideology* (Yale University Press, 1999), which uses the basic meme framework to investigate the transmission of social beliefs. I discuss this book, among others, in "Viral Culture," *Harper's Magazine*, April 1999, 83–91; reprinted in Kingwell, *Practical Judgments*, 194–211.

I will not attempt to list, let alone assess, the vast literature on rational choice models in economic and social theory, but two works are worth mentioning: Joseph Heath, in *Communicative Action and Rational Choice* (MIT Press, 2001), brings the game theory, rational choice and collection action literature into contact with Habermasian communicative action theory in a novel way, showing the limitations of the "pure" rationality model under complex (i.e., more than dyadic) conditions. Likewise, in the recent bestseller by Steven Levitt, *Freakonomics: A Rogue Economist Explores the Hidden Side of*

Everything (Morrow, 2005), readers are shown, often comically, how people fail over and over to act in the fashion theoretically dictated by reason. (What makes Levitt "rogue" is presumably his willingness to acknowledge this as a fact that cannot be modeled via further theoretical refinements.)

Thorstein Veblen's classic of early sociology is *The Theory of the Leisure Class* (Penguin, 1979; orig. pub. 1908), which contains the definitive account of positional goods among other, more familiar, insights regarding conspicuous consumption and the reduction of aesthetics to economics. The more recent companion volume, equally indispensable, is John Kenneth Galbraith, *The Affluent Society* (Houghton Mifflin, 1984; orig. pub. 1958), which argues the now familiar point that consumption itself is the product of late-model economies. The book is heavily influenced by Veblen and includes a neat ironic point about his book: "No one has really read very much if he hasn't read *The Theory of the Leisure Class* at least once," Galbraith asserts. But because of Veblen's precise-perverse use of language, at once condemning and morally neutral, it must be read carefully and slowly. "The book yields its meaning, and therewith its full enjoyment, only to those who too have leisure," Galbraith adds, which is to say, nowadays, mostly university professors.

The curmudgeonly character Leonard appears in Iris Murdoch's early work *An Accidental Man* (Vintage, 2003). Eric Hoffer's remark about the desire for praise is from his notebooks, discussed and quoted by Tom Bethell in "Sparks: Eric Hoffer and the Art of the Notebook," *Harper's Magazine*, July 2005, 73–77.

Circulatory models of the city are explored with great finesse by Richard Sennett in *Flesh and Stone: The Body and the City in Western Civilization* (Norton, 1994), from which I have learned a great deal and borrowed some details here; see also Sennett's superb earlier work *The Fall of Public Man* (Cambridge University Press, 1977). Jürgen Habermas addresses the circulation point in a rare work on architecture, "Modern and Postmodern Architecture," in John Forester, ed., *Critical Theory and Public Life* (MIT Press, 1985), 258–83. Compare, on the issue of lines of flight and routes of desire in the city, especially the surveilled city, Deleuze and Guattari, *A Thousand Plateaus* and, for an architectural version of some *deleuzoguattarian* ideas, Neil Denari, *Gyroscopic Horizons* (Princeton Architectural, 1999). These latter works are often cited in influence by contemporary architects, including Diller + Scofidio and Zaha Hadid, who won the prestigious Pritzker Prize in 2004 (the first woman to do so).

Rem Koolhaas's essay on "Junkspace" first appeared in *October* 100 (Spring 2002), 175–90, and has since been widely reproduced, including in Koolhaas, ed., *Content* (Taschen, 2004), pp. 162–71. That volume also contains a celebration of the architect's controversial CCTV building design in Beijing, "Dissecting the Iconic Exosymbiont: The CCTV Headquarters, Beijing, as Built Organism," (490–91). Theodor Adorno's arresting insights about functionalism and the misguided idea of baseline analysis are found in "Functionalism Today," *Oppositions* 17 (Summer 1979), 31–41. See also Denis Hollier, *Against Architecture: The Writings of Georges Bataille* (MIT Press, 1989). The alarming quotations concerning how evangelical Americans view the city of New York were reported be Jeff Sharlet in "Soldiers of Christ: Inside America's Most Powerful Megachurch," *Harper's Magazine*, May 2005, 41–54.

6. The Thought of Limits

Edmond Jabès's pregnant remark about the center being the threshold is quoted by Derrida in *Writing and Difference* (trans. Alan Bass; Routledge, 2001). Threshold is a central preoccupation of Derridean deconstruction since it constantly engages with the limits of the signifier/signified nexus, indeed the origin of language as a limit event, an event horizon. See especially the essays in *Margins of Philosophy* (trans. Alan Bass; University of Chicago Press, 1982) and the fine, if dense, discussion by John Llewelyn, in *Derrida on the Threshold of Sense*, which includes full references for Derrida's early work (i.e., to about 1985). Further elaboration and analysis can be found in Drucilla Cornell, *The Philosophy of the Limit* (Routledge, 1992).

Don DeLillo's novels need no introduction here, but *White Noise* (Viking, 1985) and *Cosmopolis* (Scribner, 2003) offer handy bookends to a central part of his concern with simulacral culture. The latter is a flawed tour de force of inaction: The movement of the book is one man's crosstown quest for a haircut, conducted in a Manhattan limousine.

I rely once more here on Heidegger's celebrated distinction between *Zuhandenheit* and *Vorhandenheit*, revealed in the totality of our immersion in equipmentality, as developed in *Being and Time*. The insights on dwelling are deployed in later, post-*Kehre* work, especially "Building Dwelling Thinking" and "... poetically man dwells ...," both included in the essay collection *Poetry, Language, Thought* (trans. Albert Hofstadter; Harper and Row, 1975). It is worthwhile here to compare a recent study by Adam Sharr, *Heidegger's Hut* (MIT Press, 2006), which offers the first comprehensive architectural reading of the famous (some would say notorious) small house in the Black Forest where Heidegger spent much of his later life, composing and thinking. My review of Sharr's book, titled "A philosopher's view," appeared in *Wilson Quarterly*, January 2007. A powerful extension of Heideggerian (and other) insights on building is offered by Karsten Harries in his volume *The Ethical Function of Architecture* (MIT Press, 1997).

I draw here again from Le Corbusier, *Towards a New Architecture,* on the issues of plan, geometry and order. Margaret Visser's *Beyond Fate* (Anansi, 2002) is a brilliant analysis of the relations among fate, choice and spatiality. It includes the discussion of Oedipus on the road to Colonnus—which discussion initially put me in mind of the subtle interpretation of Antigone and the city walls advanced by Gillian Rose in her sad and wonderful book *Mourning Becomes the Law: Philosophy and Representation* (Cambridge University Press, 1996). The remarks from Umberto Eco on the necessity of narrative closure for tragedy were offered to me in an interview, a partial transcript of which was published as "Umberto Eco: On the Nature of Truth and the Truth about Language," *The Globe and Mail,* 24 October 1998, D9. Slavoj Žižek's *Looking Awry: An Introduction to Jacques Lacan through Popular Culture* (MIT Press, 1991) contains many arresting insights about narrative, suspicion, detection and meaning. I pursue some of them in "Who Is the Suspect?" *Alphabet City 10: Suspect* (MIT Press, 2006), 33–57.

The quotation from Derrida on Hegel, Heidegger and metaphysics is from *The Truth in Painting* [*Vérité en peinture*] (trans. Geoff Bennington and Ian McLeod; University of Chicago Press, 1987). C.L.R. James's meditation on cricket and life is from *Beyond a Boundary* (Fontana, 1963); I consider some of the political implications of James's Marxism and cricket in "Keeping a Straight Bat: Cricket, Civility and Postcolonialism," in *C.L.R. James: His Intellectual Legacies* (University of Massachusetts Press, 1995), 359–87; reprinted in *Practical Judgments*, 116–52.

Ernst Cassirer, in *Kant's Life and Thought* (Yale University Press, 1981), discusses the centrality of limits for the project of critical philosophy. See also Immanuel Kant, *Critique of Pure Reason* [*Kritik der reinen Vernunft*] (trans. Paul Guyer and Allen Wood; Cambridge University Press, 1998; orig. pub. 1781). The preface to this work, the First Critique, contains the canonical summary of Kant's position on episte-mology: "Human reason has this peculiar fate that in one species of its knowledge it is burdened by questions which, as prescribed by the very nature of reason itself, it is not able to ignore, but which, as transcend-ing all its powers, it is also not able to answer." Gotcha!

Wittgenstein offers a different diagnosis of cognitive limits, and philos-ophy's chances, in *Tractatus Logico-Philosophicus* (trans. D.F. Pears and B.F. McGuinness; Routledge and Kegan Paul, 1961). The remark I have quoted here is from section 5.61. This work was, famously, repudiated by the later Wittgenstein, who regarded its picture of the language-world relation to be overly programmatic, if not straightforwardly in error.

Claude Lévi-Strauss delivers the definitive statement of structuralist anthropology in *The Raw and the Cooked* [*Cru et le cuit*] (trans. John and Doreen Weightman; University of Chicago Press, 1983), analyzing the necessity of thresholds in all cultural meaning, especially around basic functions such as eating, sex and defecation. For more on the natural and cultural origins of the disgust response—including analy-sis of why eating garbage is wrong and how disgust establishes social position—see, among others, William Miller, *The Anatomy of Disgust* (Harvard University Press, 1997), and Mary Douglas, *Purity and Danger* (Routledge and Kegan Paul, 1966). But the foreign object is not always rejected, even if disgusting. Hans-Georg Gadamer introduces the notion of the xenocyst as a trigger to possible fusion of horizons, hence understanding, in the magisterial central text of modern hermeneutics, *Truth and Method* [*Wahrheit und Methode*] (trans. Garrett Barden and John Cumming; Crossroad, 1988).

Garrison Keillor sings the praises of the inside-outside in "O the Porch," included in *We Are Still Married* (Penguin, 1990). Ian Frazier offers a similarly lyrical celebration of the mudroom—the place where boots, fishing waders, old jackets and other gear are respectively donned and shed—in "The Great Indoors," in *The Fish's Eye: Essays about Angling and the Outdoors* (Picador, 2002), 134–40. I am grateful to Robert Gibbs for the insight about the *unheimlich* quality of houses without vestibules. Frazier makes the same point without the scholarly trappings: "Houses that don't have catchall closets or rooms in which inhabitants can dump outdoor stuff always seem sinister to me. You see these houses more and more in movies nowadays, usually with Michael Douglas living in them, plotting hard-to-follow financial crimes" (139).

I first learned about *eruvim*, in particular the massive one in Manhattan, from Theodore Ross, "String Theory: Building a 4,000-acre house in Manhattan," *Harper's Magazine*, December 2006, 44–45. See also Yosef Gavriel Bachhofer, *The Contemporary Eruv: Eruvim in Modern Metropolitan Areas* (Booksurge, 2006), which provides both Talmudic interpretation of the *eruv* and do-it-yourself guidelines for how to establish the threshold using tollbooths, bridges, light standards and utility boxes.

Gaston Bachelard, in *The Poetics of Space* (Beacon, 1994), develops the classic position on the phenomenology of houses. See also Yi-Fu Tuan, *Space and Place,* and Richard Sennett, in "Plate Glass," cited earlier, for insights about windows and other transparent limits. Allan Hepburn makes some neat moves in his essay on cars and their windowed insides in "Driving: Fifteen Lessons in Destiny and Despair," *Journal X* 3:1 (Fall 1998), 34–48. Slavoj Žižek likewise remarks on the inside-outside phenomenology of the car in his essay "From Reality to the Real," in *Looking Awry*:

From the outside, the car looks small; as we crawl into it, we are sometimes seized by claustrophobia, but once we are inside, the car suddenly appears larger and we feel quite comfortable. The price paid for this comfort is the loss of any continuity between "inside" and "outside." To those sitting inside a car, outside reality appears slightly distant, the other side of a barrier or screen materialized by the glass. We perceive external reality, the world outside the car, as "another reality," another mode of reality, not immediately continuous with the reality inside the car. (15)

Immanuel Kant distinguishes interest and disinterest, beauty and decoration, and advances the central idea of beauty as purposiveness without purpose in *Critique of Judgment* [*Kritik der Urteilskraft*], of which there are many translations; I rely on that of J.H. Bernard (Haffner, 1951; orig. pub. 1790). A previous run at some of the issues raised in this chapter can be found in the essays "Sportspace," *Descant* 24:2 (Summer 1993), 61–70, and "Playing in the Digital Garden: Getting Inside by Going Outside," *Descant* 30:2 (Summer 1999), 123–40. Both are reprinted in my collection *Marginalia: A Cultural Reader* (Penguin, 1999), 154–64 and 31–41, respectively. See also "Tables, Chairs, and Other Machines for Thinking," *Queen's Quarterly*, Summer 2001, 169–87, and reprinted in *Practical Judgments*, 229–47. I tell a more detailed version of the burglary story in "Who Is the Suspect?"

7. The Limits of Thought

The Norwegian-born designer Thor Hansen significantly influenced graphic, textile and interior aesthetics in Canada during the 1960s in a manner similar to that of William Morris and his patterns in England earlier in the century. See Rachel Gotlieb, ed., *Thor Hansen: Crafting a Canadian Style* (Textile Museum of Canada, 2005) for a discussion, including this quotation. Michel Foucault reflects on hearths and thresholds and the lack of any fundament in "Space, Power, and Knowledge," in *The Cultural Studies Reader*, Simon During, ed.

(Routledge, 1993), 161–69. Jacques Derrida's insight about the minuscule hiatus or gap between representation and represented is advanced in *Memoirs of the Blind* [*Memoirs d'aveugle*] (trans. Pascale-Anne Brault and Michael Naas; University of Chicago Press, 1993; orig. pub. 1990). I am grateful to Len Lawlor for insight on this point.

There is no more influential recent text on mapmaking and realism than Simon Blackburn, *Essays in Quasi-Realism* (Oxford University Press, 1993). Note, as an example of the problem, the detail-obsessed mercenary played by Robert De Niro in the 1998 John Frankenheimer film *Ronin*: "The map, the map. The map is not territory." But compare Jean Baudrillard, on the reverse influence of hyper-reality in maps: "The territory no longer precedes the map, nor survives it. Henceforth, it is the map that precedes the territory—precession of simulacra—it is the map that engenders the territory." (*Simulacra and Simulation*, [University of Michigan Press, 1995], p. 97.) Reality is subverted, and deserted, by abstract renderings: this is what Baudrillard means by "the desert of the real"—a line famously quoted by the Laurence Fishburn character Morpheus in *The Matrix* (1999). The joke version of the insight has cartoon characters ascending in a hot-air balloon, marvelling that the landscape below them actually bears place names and cartographical boundaries.

Slavoj Žižek plays around with knowns and unknowns of empire in "What Rumsfeld Doesn't Know That He Knows about Abu Ghraib," *In These Times* 28:15. See also Harry Frankfurt, *On Bullshit* (Princeton University Press, 2005), a huge international bestseller that was a repurposed version of a journal article Frankfurt published many years earlier, included in his collection *The Importance of What We Care About: Philosophical Essays* (Cambridge University Press, 1988). Compare, on this important issue, Laura Penny, *Your Call Is Important to Us: The Truth about Bullshit* (Crown, 2005). See, too, Jonathan Lear's perceptive and critical review of Frankfurt, "Whatever," *The New Republic*, 21 March 2005. In Lear's view, Frankfurt ignores the most significant contemporary version of bullshit, which is the bullshit artist—someone who does not mask his bullshitting and so, in effect, invites us to be guilty parties to it even as we absolve the bullshitter of guilt:

Bibliographic Essay

In this way the bullshit artist raises a host of ethical problems that do not arise at the level of ordinary bullshit. For bullshit artistry demands our complicity. It is, in its own way, a demonstration of power. The bullshit artist in effect says, "This is bullshit, but you will accept it anyway. You may accept it as bullshit, but you will honor it anyway." In this respect, the bullshit artist is a knight of decadence. Frankfurt ignores this example; indeed, his analysis of bullshit rules it out as impossible. And in this way he fails to confront the most interesting—and influential—style of bullshit in our time.

There is another crucial limitation in the basic argument. Though Frankfurt alludes to the issue, there is no sustained analysis in any of these of the associations between shit and bullshit in reference to the city's sewage mechanisms, the *cordon sanitaire* of thought, and so on; see Chapter 8 for more on this issue.

Norbert Elias's *The Civilizing Process* [*Über den Prozess der Zivilisation*] (trans. Edmund Jephcott; Urizen, 1978; orig. pub. 1939) is a key text in understanding the evolution of modern manners as both function of, and establishing condition for, the domestic interior, especially in its bourgeois form of the single-family dwelling. I draw again on Margaret Visser's Massey Lectures here, published as *Beyond Fate,* but Visser's earlier work is perhaps even more relevant to the issue of the table as a negotiated space, especially *Much Depends on Dinner* (McClelland and Stewart, 1986).

Hegel's dialectic of master and slave (or lordship and bondage) is found in *Phenomenology of Spirit* (trans. A.V. Miller; Oxford University Press, 1977). For an extension of Ryle's position, discussed above, see Antonio Damasio, *Descartes' Error: Emotion, Reason, and the Human Brain* (Avon, 1994). Compare, likewise, the dismissive account offered by John Searle in *Mind: A Brief Introduction* (Oxford University Press, 2004). Some lively and inventive phenomenological meditations on scale, distance, perception and objects are offered by J.H. van den Berg in his *Things: Four Metabletic Reflections* (Duquesne University Press, 1970). "All things are themselves perceived things," he writes. "Perception belongs to things as something that is inalienable to them." Thus:

Concrete Reveries

In order for the length of a road to remain constant ... the hiker should then be neither well-rested nor exhausted, neither happy nor sad, neither hungry nor satiated, neither lonely nor with others. But there is no such person. Hence our conclusion is that the road has a constant length only if no one travels it. But such a road is meaningless; there is no such road. If no one travels the road, then that road does not exist.

Alfred Schutz's manifold insights about selfhood and social phenomena are ably communicated in his *The Structures of the Life-World* (trans. Richard M. Zaner and H. Tristram Engelhardt Jr.; Northwestern University Press, 1973). In his *Getting Back into Place,* Edward Casey extends the phenomenological analysis to the idea of place as a lived structure. There are naturally many editions and translations of Aristotle; I have relied here on *Physics* (trans. P. Wicksteed and E.M. Cornford; Heinemann, 1929), 208b, 28.

Imaginary deathbed psychodrama, as a phrase to describe philosophy, was coined, I believe, by Owen Flanagan, who used it during a radio interview he and I did as part of a conference on "The Pursuit of Happiness" at the Center for Philosophical Education, Santa Barbara City College, April 2003. I have since used it frequently, though perhaps not always memorably: One of my former students wrote to me recently and referred to the wisdom of defining philosophy as "imaginary psycho deathbed trauma"—not quite the same thing, one might have thought. (Some later students, thanking me for a talk on Derrida, gave me a T-shirt that reads "Philosophy: Dramatic Death by Imaginary Bed.")

John Berger speaks of paradise in his *Selected Essays* (Bloomsbury, 2001), while the baseball-park version thereof is beautifully articulated by A. Bartlett Giamatti in *Take Time for Paradise: Americans and Their Games* (Summit, 1989), which situates baseball in the narrative structure of romantic epics. It is a minor but dreary irony that this warm fan of the game, appointed commissioner of Major League Baseball from his position as a literature professor at Yale, should die soon after, brought down in part by the ongoing pressure of the Pete Rose betting-on-baseball scandal.

8. The Imaginary City

G.M.A. Grube's lucid translation of Plato's *Republic,* my favorite, was first published by Hackett in 1974. Jacques Derrida's influential late essay about law is "The Force of Law: The Mystical Foundation of Authority," in Drucilla Cornel, ed., *Deconstruction and the Possibility of Justice* (Routledge, 1992), 3–67. See also his *Rogues: Two Essays on Reason* (Stanford University Press, 2005), which begins to thematize, and dismantle, the prospect of future global democracy. Fredric Jameson's analysis of consumption is canonical; see his *Postmodernism, or, The Cultural Logic of Late Capitalism* (Duke University Press, 1991). Also, for a shift in focus nevertheless centrally relevant to the present book, see his recent volume *Archaeologies of the Future: The Desire Called Utopia and Other Science Fictions* (Verso, 2005), which reads certain speculative fictions as constant deferrals, and renewals, of the desire for justice.

There is a rich literature on the tropes of purity and defilement, but I will cite here only the key sources: Douglas, *Purity and Danger*; Paul Ricoeur, in *The Symbolism of Evil* (trans. Emerson Buchanan; Beacon, 1969), quotation in the text is at p. 37; and, for an overview, see also Richard Rorty, "Feminism, Ideology, and Deconstruction: A Pragmatist View," *Hypatia* 8:2 (Spring 1993). See, too, Jacques Derrida, "Plato's Pharmacy," in *Dissemination* (trans. Barbara Johnson; University of Chicago Press, 1981; orig. pub. 1968 in *Tel Quel*); quotations in the text are from p. 133 and p. 143, respectively. I am indebted to Bronwyn Singleton for insight on these issues.

Paul Virilio, in *City of Panic,* offers a keen diagnosis of failed security projects and the generalization of urban fear. It is worth noting here that "panic," now used typically as a noun, was originally an adjective, from Pan, the sub-deity of music, drunkenness and disorder. For an extended meditation on the project of hygienic control in the modern urban, see Dominique Laporte, *History of Shit.* Among other insights, Laporte notes how the underground sewage system is a kind of subconscious echo of the circulatory economies of the "legitimate" surface, the movement of bodies, goods and money along the streets and shopfronts (nowadays, also phone lines and swipe systems) of the city.

Georg Simmel's essay on metropolitan consciousness is cited earlier; see also Henrik Reeh, *Ornaments of the Metropolis: Siegfried Kracauer and Modern Urban Culture* (trans. John Irons; MIT Press, 2006), which discusses Kracauer's underappreciated writings on urban play, especially the way subjective consciousness can reappropriate urban life in the idea of "ornament"—a category that is, in the Kantian orthodoxy, disdained.

Louis Althusser's theory of interpellation draws on insights from Marx and Freud and can be classed with other "suspicious" interpreters of the social scene, such as Roland Barthes, Michel Foucault, Jacques Derrida and Julia Kristeva. (It may be considered ironic that theoretical suspicion issues, here, in a theory of the social revolving around implied state suspicion of the subject.) See Althusser, *Reading Capital* [*Lire le Capital*] (Verso, 1979) and *Essays on Ideology* (Verso, 1984). A standard criticism of the view is that it destroys agency and, hence, responsibility, even as it reveals the structures of state power. In this sense, as E.P. Thompson argues in *The Poverty of Theory* (Merlin, 1978), the view becomes itself ideological: "We can see the emergence of Althusserianism as a manifestation of a general police action within ideology, as the attempt to reconstruct Stalinism at the level of theory." Such purely theoretical Marxism, he added, revealed an author "who has only a casual acquaintance with historical practice."

Ernst Bloch's *Heritage of Our Times* [*Erbschaft dieser Zeit*] (trans. Neville and Stephen Plaice; University of California Press, 1991; orig. pub. 1935) is a critical analysis of the German political culture under the Weimar Republic. Bloch's writings on hope are relevant to the later stages of this chapter. See especially *The Principle of Hope* [*Prinzip Hoffnung*] (trans. Neville Plaice, Stephen Plaice and Paul Knight; MIT Press, 1995), and *The Spirit of Utopia* [*Geist der Utopie*] (trans. Anthony Nassar; Stanford University Press, 2000). Utopian architecture and the utopian impulse more generally are made vivid in Ruth Eaton's superb *Ideal Cities: Utopianism and the (Un)Built Environment* (Thames and Hudson, 2001), which includes illustrations of everything from ancient Babel-tower conceptions to contemporary and even science-fictional design for house-high-rises and radiant cities.

For a graceful application of Althusser's ideas to the genre of espionage fiction—a natural but neglected marriage—see Allan Hepburn, *Intrigue: Espionage and Culture* (Yale University Press, 2005), especially ch. 11. The mentioned case of 411/911 confusion—once a joke in an episode of *The Simpsons,* involving father Homer's lame attempt to sound cool at a U2 concert—is real. The incident occurred in October 2006 in Vancouver. For details, see Unnati Gandhi, "Couple Suing RCMP Officers over 911 Hang-up Aftermath," *Globe and Mail,* 5 April 2007, A2. Perhaps inevitably, the story prompted at least one response congratulating the Mounties on their thoroughness, suggesting they countersue.

Play is playfully analyzed by Bernard Suits in *The Grasshopper: Games, Life, and Utopia* (Broadview Press, 1978). I thank my former student Gwendolyn Bradford for bringing this work to my attention by way of her excellent article "Kudos for Ludus: Game Playing and Value Theory," published in *Noesis* 6 (2003). Mikhail Bahktin discusses the threshold-crossing of the carnivalesque in *Problems of Dostoevsky's Poetics* (trans. Caryl Emerson; University of Minnesota Press, 1984). See also Derrida, "Structure, Sign, and Play in the Discourse of the Human Sciences," in Jacques Derrida, *Writing and Difference* (trans. Alan Bass; Routledge, 2001), 278–94, which advances typically brilliant insights about center and margin, serious and playful, and the notion of *interdiction* that normatively sets off one from the other.

See Slavoj Žižek, *Looking Awry,* 12, for the formulation about desire and its "cause."

The Don DeLillo character who posts death as the limit-effect and underwriter of meaning is in *White Noise.* For more on iterability, see Derrida, *Limited Inc.* (Northwestern University Press, 1988), for his notorious engagement with the hygienic speech-act theory of John Searle as defended in *Speech Acts* (Cambridge University Press, 1969). Searle, claiming an inheritance of the project from J.L. Austin as set out in *How to Do Things with Words* (Harvard University Press, 1962), engages in an extended exercise of containment, trying by the methods of analytical philosophy to eliminate the lacunae and slippages in Austin's original taxonomy of performative utterances. The attempt reveals its deeper truth in its failure, and Austin's own ironic awareness is, as so often, lost in Anglo-American translation. A good overview of this triadic engagement is found in Simon Glendinning, "Inheriting 'Philosophy': The Case of Austin and Derrida Revisited," *Ratio* 13:4 (2000): 307–31. Christopher Ricks alertly chronicles the untidy literary tropes and tics that run through Austin's prose in "Austin's Swink," *University of Toronto Quarterly* 61:3 (1992): 297–315.

A discussion of the deconstruction of democratic politics within the concept of universality may be found in Judith Butler, *Excitable Speech* (Routledge, 1997), which attempts with limited success to amalgamate Derrida's insights about iterability with Althusser's concept of interpellation. Althusser's extended autobiography/self-defense is, appositely for present purposes, *The Future Lasts Forever* [*L'avenir dure longtemps*] (trans. Richard Veasey; Chatto and Windus, 1993; orig. pub. 1992). This memoir is compelling, not least for its gruesome details of a tortured personal life, including his mental unbalance and resulting murder of his wife, Hélène. (Althusser was judged not guilty by reason of insanity.)

Althusser also confessed to being "a trickster and a deceiver" who sometimes fabricated quotations and discussed works he had not read, relying on intuition to work out the "general drift or direction" of books by noting what thinkers they were opposed to. "In fact, my philosophical knowledge of texts was rather limited," Althusser admitted. He "knew a little Spinoza, nothing about Aristotle, the Sophists and the Stoics, quite a lot about Plato and Pascal, nothing about Kant, a bit about Hegel, and finally a few passages of Marx." Althusser here merely anticipates the argument made by psychoanalyst and literary critic Pierre Bayard in the bestseller *Comment parler des livres que l'on n'a pas lus?* [*How to Talk about Books You Haven't Read*] (Les Éditions de Minuit, 2007). It also has to be said that Althusser's honest catalog might well characterize any number of accredited philosophy professors, especially those working in the aggressively ahistorical analytic mode.

John Berger's *Ways of Seeing* (Penguin, 1972) contains the provocative notion that glamour is reflected envy. Walter Benjamin's more nuanced, and far more extensive, engagement with nostalgia is featured throughout his works, both in lovely exercises in it, especially *A Berlin Childhood* (Harvard University Press, 2006)—and in deconstructions of it—for example, in *The Arcades Project*. Benjamin, who for better or worse gave the world of cultural theory the notion of aesthetic aura in "The Work of Art in an Age of Mechanical Reproduction," in *Illuminations* (trans. Harry Zohn; Schocken, 1968; orig. pub. 1934)—a staple of analysis for Berger and many others—nowhere isolates the insight about positionality that is at the heart of Berger's too-brief discussion.

Here there is a useful joining of Benjamin's cultural awareness with the sometimes overbearing reductionism of Thorstein Veblen in *The Theory of the Leisure Class* (Houghton Mifflin, 1973; orig. pub. 1899). For Veblen, aesthetic judgments always, and usually swiftly, reveal—subject is "judgments" themselves as claims of status. Without going so far, we can accept the power of reading many "qualities" or "essence" as, in fact, claims of position. But even Veblen did not see what we can now observe everywhere: Positional goods do not even need to be goods in the sense of *material* bearers of status; position can be established by reciprocal proxy, that is, by *being judged enviable* or *being thought cool*.

Photo Credits

Pages vi–vii: Courtesy http://www.flickr.com/photos/yakobusan/280627593/in/set-72157594228910721/.

Pages 2–3, page 15: Courtesy http://www.flickr.com/photos/wordcat/266452605.

Page 7: Courtesy http://www.flickr.com/photos/eiriknewth/238685912/.

Page 10: Courtesy http://www.henry-davis.com/MAPS/EMwebpages/205FF.html.

Page 15 and pages 2–3: Courtesy http://www.flickr.com/photos/wordcat/266452605/.

Page 17: Courtesy http://commons.wikimedia.org/wiki/Image:Phalanstère01.jPage.

Page 21: Courtesy http://www.flickr.com/photos/98318718@N00/268608224/.

Pages 26–27: Courtesy http://www.flickr.com/photos/paulobar/2301345591.

Page 29: Courtesy Jon Morrice.

Page 31: Courtesy http://commons.wikimedia.org/wiki/Image:1847_Lower_Manhattan_map.jPage.

Page 32: Courtesy http://www.flickr.com/photos/absolutwade/129006908/in/photostream/.

Page 33: From the author's collection.

Page 37: Courtesy http://www.flickr.com/photos/lisaliang/62935109/.

Page 39: Courtesy Anthony Cortese, http://www.flickr.com/photos/snowdog101/90209404/in/pool-grandcentralterminal/.

Page 43: Courtesy Mo Riza, http://www.flickr.com/photos/moriza/149187332/.

Page 47: Courtesy http://commons.wikimedia.org/wiki/Image:Tall_buildings_1896.jPage.

Page 51: Courtesy http://commons.wikimedia.org/wiki/Image:Chrysler_building_du_bas.jPage.

Page 53: Courtesy http://commons.wikimedia.org/wiki/Image:Chrysler_Building_Midtown_Manhattan_New_York_City_1932.jPage.

Pages 58–59: Courtesy http://www.volker-goebel.de/GrafikenLaDefense3/036.jPage.

Page 62 : Courtesy Anthony Cortese, http://www.flickr.com/photos/snow-dog101/90679518/in/pool-grandcentralterminal/.

Page 65: Courtesy Milton Glaser.

Pages 66–67, page 74: Courtesy Adrian G. Sierra, www.oidem.com.

Page 69: Courtesy http://commons.wikimedia.org/wiki/Image:Lyon_-_Opera_1.jPage.

Page 70: Courtesy http://commons.wikimedia.org/wiki/ Image:Shanghai-Pudong-Skyline.jPage.

Page 72: Courtesy http://www.flickr.com/photos/gordieryan/1249448710/.

Page 77: Courtesy http://www.flickr.com/photos/davemorris/2305645/.

Page 79: Courtesy http://www.flickr.com/photos/foshie/450551176/.

Page 82: Courtesy Museum of Architecture Moscow, www.muar.ru.

Page 84: Courtesy http://commons.wikimedia.org/wiki/Image:Deserted_Speakers%27_Corner_-_Singapore_%28gabbe%29.jPage.

Page 86: Courtesy http://www.flickr.com/photos/nicpersinger/1388015159/in/set-72157602024409056/.

Page 88: Courtesy http://www.nlm.nih.gov/exhibition/historicalanatomies/gamelin_home.html.

Page 90: Courtesy christopherpeterson.com.

Page 91: Courtesy http://www.flickr.com/photos/deks/185651243/.

Page 92: Courtesy Rafal Dittwald.

Acknowledgments

Many people contributed to this book over its years of mutation and slow growth. I thank in particular Paul Slovak in New York and Diane Turbide in Toronto for allowing me the time to let ideas change shape and gather new focus. My literary agent Emma Parry is without peer, and has shown faith in this book over many hurdles.

Jonathan Webb was instrumental in helping the manuscript find a form, and offered many useful requests for clarification. Copy editor Judy Phillips did likewise. Tracy Bordian ably oversaw the book's interior design and production. Mary Newberry compiled a thorough index. The haunting cover image by Geoffrey James offers its own kind of concrete reverie.

Among other editors I am especially grateful to Roger Hodge and Jennifer Szalai of *Harper's Magazine,* Boris Castel of *Queen's Quarterly,* and William Saunders of *Harvard Design Magazine* for providing space to work out some of these thoughts in earlier versions. Other parts of the book were previously published in *PhaenEx, FORM, Wascana Review, Saturday Night* and the *National Post.* I thank the respective editors for their generous interest; publication details can be found in the Bibliographic Essay.

Thoughts on public places come naturally to public lectures. I have benefited from tolerant audiences at the following places and events, sometimes more than once, since 2002: the IDEA conference (Sydney); Words and Ideas Festival (Perth); the Shifting Ground conference of the Canadian Society of Landscape Architects (Vancouver); Tulane University School of Architecture (New Orleans); Harbourfront Centre (Toronto); City of Toronto "Higher Learning" Symposium; University of Toronto Faculty of Architecture; the Institute for Contemporary Culture at the Royal Ontario Museum; the Ontario College of Art & Design; Concordia University (Montreal); University of Regina; University of Calgary; University of Windsor; Nova Scotia College of Art & Design (Halifax); Berlin-Toronto Mayors' Symposium; Royal Architecture Institute of Canada; Radboud University (Nijmegen) and London Metropolitan University.

I extend particular thanks to colleagues at Baruch College, City University of New York, where I delivered the 2002 Marx Wartofsky

Memorial Lecture; and especially to those at my current intellectual home, Trinity College, University of Toronto, who offered me the chance to play around with, and within, the 2002 Larkin-Stuart Lectures.

Among particular colleagues I thank Ronald Beiner, whose thoughts on Hannah Arendt and architecture were a useful prod; Frank Cunningham for his ground-breaking ideas on grue and green cities; Patrick Turmel for discussion on cities and justice; and Harry Stevens for the invitation to Sydney that focused my preoccupation with thresholds. Graham Owen, George Baird, An Te Liu, Mary Lou Lobsinger, Bruce Kuwabara, Michael Taylor and Drummond Hassan are all architects from whom I have learned a great deal. Lavinia Greenlaw, Charles Foran and James Lahey are friends whose work constantly illuminates my understanding of otherness.

The efforts of David Owen Morgan and Wendy Banks, my able research assistants and former students, are evident in the look of the finished work. Other students, from both philosophy and architecture, have offered penetrating comments in recent seminars on utopian design, public space, and Derridean philosophy. I thank them for being subjects, mostly willing, in these ongoing experiments in intellectual threshold-crossing.

Finally, some grateful acknowledgment of the places that matter to me, expressed as mere addresses but really crucibles of thought and identity: 8 Vermont Avenue; 269 West 4th Street; 14 Morton Street; 28 Salisbury Avenue; and Isaac Cady House, New Hampshire. For inviting me across the thresholds of the last two, and for countless other gifts, I thank Molly Montgomery.

Index

Benjamin, Walter, viii–ix, 6, 18, 28, 58, 75, 114
    Arcades Project, The, 18, 28
    hausmannization project, 223
Benn, Gottfried, 90
Berger, John, 213–14
Berlin
    getting lost in, 58
    Jewish Museum, 71
    Potsdamer Platz, 70, 115
Berlin Wall, 195
Bernini, Giovanni Lorenzo
    Éxtasis de Santa Teresa, 212
Bilbao Guggenheim, 71, *72,* 73
Bloch, Ernst, 224–25
Blount, Jr., Roy, 38, 41, 44
Blur Building (Switzerland), 73
body, 131–34. *See also* consciousness
books, 20, 22–24
boredom, *229,* 230
Borges, Jorge Luis, 190
boundaries. *See also* threshold/s
    in conceptual contrasts, 173
    of death, 229
    for exclusion, 202, *203*
    of food and contagion, 174–75
    horizons as, 180–81, 192–93, 206
    limits as drawn, 171–72, 195
    limits as drawn by us, 208–9, 211, 213
    limits of the political, 170
    positional, 198–200
    skin as, 209–11, *210*
Brazil, 16. *See also* South America
brick, 5, 9. *See also* materials
bridges, 89
Brixton, 49
Bronx, 44, 49
Brueghel the Elder, Pieter
    The Fight Between Carnival and Lent, 233
brushed-steel handrails, 76
brutalism, 5, 11
building costs, 5–6, 8
Bull Durham (film), 169–70
Bund Center (Shanghai), 98
bunker-style institutions, 5–6
Burberry, 116
Bush, Jr., George, 110

Bush, Sr., George, 109

C

Cameron, Julia Margaret
    Mariana in the Moated Grange, 229
Canary Wharf (London), 71
capitalism, 68, 91, 104
cardboard, 8. *See also* materials
carnival, 232–33, *233–34*
Casey, Edward, *91,* 151, 180, 206
Cassirer, Ernst, 171
Castells, Manuel, 76
CCTV building (Beijing), 90, 99
celebrations of concrete, 8
celebrity-architects, 80. *See also* architecture
cemeteries, 231
Central Park, 57
Chanel, 116
Chang, Juliet, 113–14
Charpentier, Jean-Marie, 107, 115
Chen Jianbang, 122
Chiang Kai-shek, 104–5
Chicago
    civic architecture of, 106
    grid of, 52
    as OHR, 149
    Sears Tower, 120
    Southside, 49
    Wrigley Field, 169
Chicago School
    homo economicus, 141
Childs, David, 71, 120–21
China, economy of, 108–10. *See also* Beijing; Shanghai
China Commercial Bank (Shanghai), 99
China Life building (Pudong), 98
Chinatown (New York City), 58
choice, 161–63, 165
Chomsky, Noam, 75
Christianity/Christians
    account of sin, 131, 134
    in conflict with cities, 150
Chrysler Building, *32,* 50, *51,* 55
circles, 165–71, *168*
    spirals, 172, *173*
    waterfall, *164*

Index

Index